THE CRISIS OF
RUSSIAN POPULISM

We feared [our father] worse than fire. Just his glance, cold and penetrating, was enough to make us tremble, to fill us with a feeling of moral terror. Any physical punishment from a kinder person would seem easier to bear than the silent retribution of his eyes.

Father was absent frequently and for long periods of time; he would be making his rounds in the state forest. When he was home no one was afraid: he had a rifle in his den and everyone was calm. But when he was away, what could we do? There were only women and children in the house. A dark elemental fear came over all of us, from the smallest to the biggest.

VERA FIGNER

Aleksandr Engel'gardt   Gleb Uspenskii
Nikolai Zlatovratskii

THE CRISIS OF
RUSSIAN POPULISM

BY

RICHARD WORTMAN

Assistant Professor of History, University of Chicago

CAMBRIDGE
AT THE UNIVERSITY PRESS
1967

Published by the Syndics of the Cambridge University Press
Bentley House, 200 Euston Road, London, N.W. 1
American Branch: 32 East 57th Street, New York, N.Y. 10022

Library of Congress Catalogue Card Number: 67-12849

Printed in Great Britain
at the University Printing House, Cambridge
(Brooke Crutchley, University Printer)

CONTENTS

To my parents

PREFACE

Russian populism has not been slighted by the historian. The tale of the revolutionary events of the 1870s has been told many times, often very well, in scholarly studies. Yet, after reading the literature on the subject, one comes away with a curious sense of dissatisfaction. Most of the authors narrate the familiar sequence of events, and present the familiar cast of characters performing their celebrated exploits. From their treatment, one gains little appreciation of the populists as human beings and little understanding of what impelled them to embark on their seemingly futile course. As a result, populism appears fantastic and unreal, something divorced from Russian life of the time and irrelevant in its context, while the populists themselves wear the guise either of madmen or of gods.

The reason for this is not hard to discern. Since the publication of Sergei Kravchinskii's *Underground Russia* in the 1880s, populism has been surrounded by the aura of myth, while its history has become the preserve of polemicists and *littérateurs*. In the early twentieth century, when historical opinion on the subject took shape, populism was viewed in the light of the turbulent struggle against the autocracy. Representatives of the various Marxist and Social Revolutionary factions tried to place themselves in the mainstream of the revolutionary tradition by discovering in the earlier movement the origins of their own particular point of view. They therefore emphasized such matters dear to their own hearts as political change and revolutionary organization. The historiography of the 1920s continued in this direction and in the thirties Stalin terminated investigation of the subject by denouncing the revolutionaries of the seventies as liberal and bourgeois. As a result, the contemporary student is removed from the events not only by the time that has elapsed but by the highly tendentious nature of most of the secondary materials that treat them.

In recent years populism has become the subject of more serious and critical examination. In the Soviet Union, it has regained its revolutionary mantle and has received increasing attention from scholars. The publication of a collection of documents and the increasingly frequent appearance of sensitive studies based on fresh primary research are signs of a renewed scholarly activity which in the future promises to be even more fruitful. In the west, Franco Venturi's *Roots of Revolution* has provided us with a learned survey of the subject that is both exhaustive in its research and perceptive in its analysis. His book gives an invaluable portrayal of the breadth and the complexity of the movement, and it has been indispensable to me in the preparation of the present study.

But these recent works, which focus primarily on the active revolutionary movement, do not consider the problem of the basic nature of the populist ethos. We have learned much about the events, organizations, and participants of the movement, but little about populists themselves. We are presented with the traditional ideological pattern, leading from Herzen and Chernyshevskii through Lavrov, Bakunin, and Tkachev, but we know little about the kind of mentality that these doctrines contributed to or reflected. Few *intelligenty* repeated one or another of the points of view; most created their own particular amalgam of ideas and attitudes and did so with an intensity and determination that so far have remained unexplained. We do not know what was primary and what secondary in the populist mentality, what a vital and deep concern and what merely a strategic consideration. As a result, even the basic question of whether there existed anything that we can speak of as a populist mentality has not been adequately answered.

This has been pointed out in an incisive critique by Richard Pipes, published recently in the *Slavic Review*.[1] Professor Pipes shows the limited original usage of the term 'populism' in the latter part of the 1870s. He points out that its common meaning, designating the whole of the movement of the seventies, and for some historians reaching back to the sixties and the fifties, was chiefly the invention of Marxist polemicists of the nineties, who used it to include all those who did not accept their own notions of social development. He thus questions whether the coherence of viewpoint imputed to the pre-Marxist revolutionary movement is not illusory and whether economic and social conceptions usually identified with populism, such as a belief in the peasantry and in the peasant commune, were not merely strategical concomitants of the political struggle, without

[1] Richard Pipes, 'Narodnichestvo: A Semantic Inquiry', *Slavic Review*, vol. xxiii, no. 3 (September 1964), pp. 441–58.

great importance in themselves. He characterizes populism as 'a political attitude, devoid of specific programmatic content'.

I believe that Professor Pipes has probed the chief weakness in the historiography of the subject, but I suspect that in speculating on alternative answers he has risked even greater misconceptions. For while he has shown that the facile use of the term *narodnichestvo* has obscured meaningful analysis of the mainsprings of revolutionary action in the seventies, he has fallen into the opposite fallacy and assumed that because the term was used disingenuously and sloppily, the phenomenon referred to did not exist. I can see few grounds for such a contention. It has become fashionable in the United States and Britain to discount ideology as an effective historical factor, and to stress in its place organizational and practical concerns, perhaps in reaction to earlier approaches that concentrated on intellectual trends to the exclusion of all others. But in the case of the *narodniki* I think there can be little doubt that the attitudes towards the peasantry were central to the radical conception of the world, and that the Marxists were not inventing a fictional opponent but distinguishing themselves from something very real indeed. The mass of articles, memoirs, and *belles-lettres* of the 1870s and early 1880s is powerful evidence to this effect. Scarcely an issue of the major radical journals goes by that is not filled with works on peasant life, most of them written with a passion and intensity that allow no gainsaying of the depth of the authors' convictions. Indeed, to deny the importance of the peasantry and the notion of agrarian socialism for the intelligentsia of the seventies, one would have to dismiss nearly everything written in Russia at the time and most memoirs on the period.

Professor Pipes is correct in pointing out the absence of specific programmatic content in the *narodnik* groups he discusses, and I believe he has done a service in attacking the notion that the intelligentsia of the seventies subscribed to a defined monolithic ideology. But this in no way indicates the absence of a common conception of the world among them. What united the movement was not a particular programme, or particular pronouncements by Herzen or Chernyshevskii, but shared attitudes and preconceptions—hopes, fears, longings, and hatreds that were merely given shape by one or the other ideological formulation. The unity of these decades was less an ideological than a psychological unity, a common emotional bond with the rural population that at times grew into an enamourment. Programme and ideology were used as instruments to strengthen and to protect this bond. Politics as an end in itself was unknown, and even as much of a Jacobin as Petr Tkachev invoked it for negative reasons—to forestall the incursion of capitalism and thus safeguard peasant society. The absorption with the peasantry became apparent at the end of the fifties. It persisted into the sixties, and dominated the intelligentsia's psychology during the seventies. The populism of the late seventies represents not merely a particular political strategy, but the culmination of a psychological dynamic at work since the beginning of the reform era. This argument will be elaborated in the first chapter.

The emotional moment of populism becomes most prominent at the time of its crisis, at the close of the seventies and the beginning of the eighties. The disintegration of the populist world view then threatens not only the premises of radical action, but the individual's conception of himself as well. It transpires that populism is not merely a rationale adopted to promote change, but an integral and essential part of the personality of those espousing it. It is in times of crisis that the individual's defences and the mask he presents to society fall away and reveal the vital workings of his psyche, and it is during the crisis of populism that the populist mind discloses itself. Those who underwent personal crises and recorded their painful soul-searchings and inner turmoil have left glimpses into the populist mind that are closed to scholars who limit themselves to programmatic and doctrinal statements or to memoirs written long after. It has been the purpose of this study to examine several of these figures and to add a personal and psychological dimension to the history of populism.

My approach has been to treat my subjects within the context of the period of crisis, focusing on the evolution of their thoughts and feelings. This, of course, has made it impossible to treat other aspects of their work and life. I have therefore concerned myself little with the intrinsic worth of the authors' works, though often the latter can stand on their own merits even apart from their social significance. Engel'gardt's beautiful descriptions of peasant life retained their popularity well into the twentieth century and can be read with pleasure and profit even today. Uspenskii, though not ranking among the immortals of nineteenth-century Russian literature, nonetheless is a writer of staggering intensity and power, who is widely read today in the Soviet Union and should be better known in the West. Daniel'son's and Vorontsov's economic theories possess an interest in their own right, as part of the development of economic thought in nineteenth-century Russia. But I have refrained from both extensive literary analysis of Uspenskii and extensive economic analysis of Daniel'son and Vorontsov.

This approach is justified, I think, by the fact that these writers all subordinated their particular endeavour to the more urgent social and personal impulses of the moment, and called agronomy, literature, and economics to the defence of their ideals. Though Vorontsov falls under the category of economist, and Zlatovratskii under the category of writer, Vorontsov disclaimed expertise in economics and Zlatovratskii disavowed literature as art, both dedicating themselves totally to the preservation of the populist ethos. Indeed much that was written by the one could have been written by the other. I have also devoted little attention to the provenance of ideas or to the shape they took before becoming the property of the populists. The ideas of these writers are of little interest in themselves; they are derivative and were usually borrowed whole, uncritically, with little concern for their original content or intent. Their interest lies in the way they expressed the powerful hopes and feelings they were meant to justify.

My approach to the sources has been governed by these considerations. Where the authors revised their works with the aim of making them more polished and consistent, I have turned to the earliest available versions, which display the initial doubts, confusion and vacillations. Thus I have used Vorontsov's and Zlatovratskii's articles in *Otechestvennye Zapiski* (*Annals of the Fatherland*), rather than the former's heavily edited *Sud'by kapitalizma v Rossii* (*The Fates of Capitalism in Russia*) and the latter's book version of *Ustoi* (*The Foundations*). In the case of Uspenskii all the variants are reproduced in the massive *Polnoe sobranie sochinenii*.

I would like to convey my appreciation and thanks to all those who have assisted me in the preparation of this book. Leopold Haimson first awakened my interest in populism and has been the ideal mentor, both demanding and generous, reading through all the various versions of the work and administering, when necessary, the proper doses of criticism and encouragement. Michael Cherniavsky's excellent comments on the original dissertation suggested new and fruitful paths to follow in the revisions. Michael Confino's astute challenges have been indispensable in working out my own point of view. S. S. Dmitriev, while faithful to a conception of the world and of history utterly different from my own, was an erudite and thoughtful adviser to my researches in the Soviet Union.

I owe an especial debt of gratitude to Eugene Vinogradoff, who read through the manuscript with extraordinary care and precision and offered sensitive and incisive suggestions on every aspect of the substance and writing; his extraordinary sense of style and organization was of immeasurable help to me in judging and revising my work. Other invaluable criticisms were provided by Robert Crummey, Phillip Pomper, and Reginald Zelnik. Mrs Mary Fisch, who typed the manuscript, is deserving of unending praise for her patience, sensitivity to the author's desires, and uncanny ability to read my handwriting.

To my wife Marlene, who in her own gentle way is among the most ruthless of critics, I cannot begin to express my gratitude here. I can only thank her for the long hours she spent reading and re-reading this work from the beginning of the task to the end, and for her unfailing understanding, which, more than anything else, made it possible for this book to be written.

I am most grateful for the grants I have received from the Ford Foundation, the Inter-University Committee on Travel Grants, the Social Science Research Committee, and the College of the University of Chicago. None of the aforementioned institutions is in any way responsible for the views expressed here, which are my own. Whatever shortcomings may be found in the pages of the book are also my own, while for its strengths I am most indebted to those who helped me.

R. W.

Chicago

June 1966

THE CITY AND THE COUNTRYSIDE

In the capitals there is noise,
Orators thunder in the boiling war of words,
But out there, in the depths of Russia,
Eternal silence reigns.

NEKRASOV

The Great Reforms of the 1860s struck at the moral foundations of Russian state and society. Alexander II's decision to
overhaul the nation's political and social institutions was an
implicit acknowledgement of the weakness and injustice of an
autocratic order long presented as the embodiment of strength
and right. What had been declared sacrosanct during the
oppressive reign of Nicholas now appeared fallible. The claims
to unquestioning obedience suddenly seemed founded on no
more than hollow formulas used to disguise incompetence and
abuse. The impulse to reform impeached the principles of
legitimacy that had allowed the tsar and his advisers to domi-
nate Russian life and opened the floodgates to the critical
tendencies they wished most to avoid.

To be sure the government endeavoured as best it could to
carry out the reforms in a conservative spirit and, as has been
frequently shown, preserved the old social relationships and
the old injustice more than it changed them. It remained
averse to adventurous new economic policies that would stimu-
late social flux, and, as before, stood adamantly opposed to any
pretension on the part of society to play a role in the decisions
of state. But if the reforms left the objective conditions of
Russian life fundamentally unchanged, they shattered the old
attitudes of the thinking public. Everything hallowed by tradition now had to be judged anew, in the scathing light of reason
and justice. Not only political institutions but the whole complex of established social relationships came into question. The
most sensitive and best educated members of society began to
re-evaluate their attitudes toward themselves, their families and
society at large. They perceived the marks of the old order on
everything—the deep scars of suspicion and fear left by the

dehumanizing tyranny of Nicholas's regime. Once tradition lost its aura of sanctity, the youth began to look upon the ways of the older generation with new eyes. To them, both past and present appeared tainted with injustice. Only the future held out hopes of dignity and virtue.

The time-honoured callings that had been followed by generations of Russian youth took on the stigma of the old regime. Rather than pursue their fathers' livelihood or heed conventional notions about rising in the world, the new generation began to rebel against the patriarchal order that surrounded them. Many refused to devote themselves to serving a system that seemed justified by no higher end than its own survival. Raising their voices in protest and self-affirmation, they assailed the landlords for their parasitism, the church for its ignorance and venality, the bureaucracy for its corruption and indifference to human needs. They created a spirit of criticism and opposition and introduced new and strident notes into the intellectual discourse of the time.

Like no previous generation in Russian history, the generations of the reform era entered maturity with a psychology of change. The unthinking submission to the dictates of tradition gave way to a total rejection of existing reality and of the conventional ethics that governed Russian life. The young intellectuals of the fifties and sixties yearned to transform themselves into new men with personalities suited to the society they envisioned and to purify themselves of the elements of the past they sensed within them. They sought the guidelines of the future in the social doctrines of the West and studied them assiduously for principles and values they could embrace.

The scene of their quest was St Petersburg. Large numbers of the most intense and dedicated youth gathered in the capital as the spirit of free thought spread across the empire. There they took part in a life of reason and intellect far removed from the humdrum world of the provinces. They met in circles to discuss the latest radical theories and the means to realize their ideals. They examined the principles of natural science, psychology, sociology and ethics for their bearing on the destinies of the individual and nation. St Petersburg, the symbol of the autocracy, endeared itself to all those yearning for a more just life. Although they were oppressed by its harsh climate and by the odious presence of the institutions of state, they could never stay away for long. Grigorii Eliseev, an influential radical publicist of the sixties and seventies, wrote:

Whatever you may say about Petersburg, in the end one must admit that for the time being it is the only city in Russia similar to a European city. Whoever finds provincial life suffocating 'for various independent reasons' [bureaucratic oppression]; whoever is stirred by vital thought demanding recognition, sympathy, encouragement and help; whoever is so unfortunate as to feel the clash and contradiction between ideal and reality without, however, being able to close his eyes to it; whoever is sickened by a monotonously tranquil and unchanging course of life, with the same unchanging faces, the same morons, boors, dodgers, wise men and jokers, etc.; he will find no harbour anywhere in Russia but Petersburg. Petersburg is the single asylum for all *the toiling and the downtrodden*.[1]

The word 'intelligentsia' originated in Petersburg during the 1860s to designate this group united by a common devotion to enlightenment and the cause of the ideal. It was part of the jargon called into existence by the pronounced neo-Hegelian cast of mind of this and subsequent generations of radical youth. 'Intelligentsia' expressed the faith that reason was unfolding ineluctably in history, leading men to more just social forms, and that the bearers of intellect would be the ones to perceive and promote the more rational and humane noumenal reality. It asserted their claim to supersede traditional authorities, who were wedded to the doomed phenomenal world, in charting Russia's future. Later the meaning of the word would seem ambiguous, and often to obscure the distinction between the educated and the politically advanced. But the generations of the fifties and the sixties knew of no such distinction. For them education was the conveyor of reason and the educated man was one who would inevitably appreciate the irrationality of existing conditions and the need for swift and profound changes.[2]

To take leave of the past, the radical youth had to sever their emotional attachments to class and family. This step liberated them and gave them the opportunity to shape their

[1] G. Eliseev, 'Proizvoditel'nye sily Rossii', *Otechestvennye Zapiski*, no. 176 (February 1868), p. 450.
[2] For a penetrating discussion of the term 'intelligentsia' see Martin Malia, 'What is the Intelligentsia?' in *Daedalus* (summer 1960), pp. 441–58.

own lives. But, at the same time, it cut them off from the strength of the adult world and deprived them of the confidence and inner certainty afforded by traditional forms of behaviour. They suddenly found themselves with no group to belong to, whose values they could share. The need for a strong class identification, bred in them during their childhood, could not be fulfilled once every class appeared implicated in the sinister dynamic of the social system. The feeling of affection for their parents also became suspect. In a diary entry of 1857, the twenty-one year old Nikolai Dobroliubov, soon to become Russia's foremost radical literary critic, wrote, 'The voice of one's blood ties has become scarcely audible. It is being drowned out by other, higher and more general interests...If intellectual and moral interests diverge, respect and love for one's kin weaken and can, in the end, disappear.'[1] But love for one's kin did not disappear. A conflict raged in the youths between new aspirations and old sympathies, splitting their personalities into irreconcilably warring halves. The father, tainted by his involvement with the old order, could no longer serve as a model of manhood, and the filial love he evoked had to be suppressed at all costs. The theme of fatherlessness runs through the writings of the period, from the novels of Turgenev and Dostoevskii to the memoirs of Dobroliubov, Figner, and Iakubovich, not to mention the works treated in subsequent chapters. In some cases, such as that of Dobroliubov, where the son regarded his father with enmity, the latter became a symbol of the oppressiveness and irrationality of the old order, and childhood rebellion, reinforced with the conviction of social righteousness, was acted out as a bitter and aggressive attack on all founts of authority.[2] Where affectionate relations prevailed between fathers and sons, as was certainly more often the case, the father came to be viewed as an emasculated victim of the old conditions, an object of both pity and embarrassment. In all circumstances the spirit of change eroded the bonds of sympathy and admiration that cement successive generations and left the youth without personal attachments or a heritage that could have meaning for them in their future.

[1] N. A. Dobroliubov, *Polnoe sobranie sochinenii* (Moscow, 1934–9), VI, 478.
[2] See the interesting if extreme interpretation of F. Weinstein, in *Nihilism and Death: A Study of the Life of N. A. Dobroliubov*, unpublished dissertation (University of California at Berkeley, 1962).

With the feeling of release, the young members of the intelligentsia experienced a loss of bearings, a confusion about their origins and nature that their enlightened view of the world could do little to alleviate. The writings of the first years of Alexander's reign tell of their futile groping for a new personality consonant with the demands of the new era. The novels of Turgenev described the plight of young nobles, heir to a genteel, effete way of life, who lacked the resolve and determination necessary to act as they longed to. In his critical articles, Dobroliubov, who came from the rural clergy, assailed the flaccid and hypocritical attitudes of the privileged class and called for 'new men', who were endowed with common sense and possessed the 'enterprising, decisive, persistent' character that would enable them to bring their ideas to fruition.[1] Dobroliubov, like many others, expected this type to appear among the *raznochintsy*, those, who like himself, had come from humble backgrounds and had abandoned the fixed callings of the past to participate in the intellectual life of the capital. But the problem of the *raznochintsy* proved no less stark. Lacking the cultural and intellectual breadth of the nobility, they had difficulty finding any qualities at all in themselves that did not derive from their disowned milieu. They had grown up with personalities suited to the stations that awaited them in life, and when they embarked on a totally new path, they felt an uneasy emptiness in themselves, an absence of firm values and emotions of their own. During the first surge of excitement, they revelled in the corporate spirit that reigned among the radical youth of the capital. They joined radical circles, self-help societies, and charitable organizations, and participated in the 'Sunday school' movement to teach workers to read and write. But as these associations dissolved, or lost their efficacy under growing government pressure, they found themselves without a role or purpose amidst a world unknown to them. They passed from one solution to the next, trying to find in each the certainty that would enable them to define their new characters. As each failed, they sank deeper into personal and ideological confusion.

Their dilemma was expressed in the words of Cherevanin, the autobiographical hero of N. S. Pomialovskii's novel *Molotov*. Cherevanin, like Pomialovskii the son of a rural cleric, foreswore his past and premised the meaning of his life on a successful

---

[1] Dobroliubov, II, 344–5.

break from the old ways. Those who remained bound by them, he declared, had no distinct existence of their own. 'Everything they have has been received by inheritance. Their virtues are not their own, their vices are not their own. Even their mind belongs to another. What are you, you honourable man? Where is your individuality, your talent—have you added a *grosh* to it?'[1] But Cherevanin could find nothing to replace his own lost heritage and sensed that his life had become devoid of all meaning and direction.

Where is my childhood? It has become the object of speculation, fantasy, general phrases and blind reminiscence. The whole makeup of body and soul, everything that comprises life, has fallen into oblivion. With time all events have lost the colour of detail and have become deprived of inner meaning. The chain of life has been broken into bits. Its springs and links have fallen apart. How am I to prove that I have even lived?[2]

The lives of the *raznochintsy* of the fifties and sixties bear a dual aspect. In their writings and deportment, there was an air of bluster and confident self-assertiveness characteristic of those defying the niceties of society. But underneath ran an undercurrent of weakness, an uncertainty about the meaning of their lives that in time gave rise to a mounting self-hatred, an urge for self-destruction that drove many of them to seek oblivion in dissipation and drink. The biographies of the leading *raznochintsy* writers of these years, such as Pomialovskii, Reshetnikov, Dobroliubov, Nikolai Uspenskii, are bitter tales of disappointment and anguish, which frequently end with early, self-inflicted death.

Reason alone could not answer the demands of feeling to fill the emotional void left by the broken attachments to family and class. The youth continued to crave a group they could cherish and emulate, an object in Russian life for their powerful but ungratified affections. Turgenev characterized their longing in the words of Elena, the heroine of *On the Eve*. 'How can one live without love?' she exclaimed, disillusioned in her family and friends. 'Yet there is no one to love.' They found this object in the Russian peasantry. They transferred their filial affections to the great masses of the Russian people, who, like themselves, had not been tainted by participation in the old

[1] N. G. Pomialovskii, *Polnoe sobranie sochinenii* (Moscow–Leningrad, 1935), I, 240.
[2] *Ibid.* I, 180.

order and had suffered as its victims. Elena finally discovered feelings in common with all the poor and suffering in Russia and bestowed her love upon them. The young *intelligenty* in the city, estranged from their homes and early environment, felt a strong bond and sense of identification with the people. They beheld the peasant as an ally, an *alter-ego* whose sentiments were akin to their own. The peasantry became the powerful force through which reason would be realized in Russia and the outmoded social order swept away. The identification with the peasant bolstered their feelings of self-esteem and made possible a meaningful role for them in Russian life. With the peasant as their beloved, they could find something to love in themselves; they united themselves with a source of strength and vitality that could imbue them with new confidence.

The *raznochintsy* in the capital sought spiritual companionship in the peasants and in the lower-class elements of the capital. Pomialovskii would disappear for weeks on end to consort with the poor and degraded who shared his forlorn sense of homelessness.[1] A. S. Reshetnikov, the orphaned son of a poor village deacon and postman, could feel warmth and friendship only toward the peasants, and his love for them sustained him through his brief and unhappy life. His writings are a powerful expression of the attraction that the radical youth of the reform era felt toward the peasantry. Looking into the lives of the most destitute and helpless inhabitants of the countryside, Reshetnikov could respond with sympathy for their plight and understanding of their aspirations, while the ordinary individual remained unmoved.

How many carts passed by them with people in warm furs! Those sitting in the carts not only failed to nod to them but didn't even look their way. They didn't know how much Pila and Sysoiko had endured. They didn't know that their whole life had been only privation, misery and bitter tears; that Pila and Sysoiko couldn't remain in their village; that they were sick of their native region and because of need were leaving to venture into the cold, going somewhere in search of a good place, where life would be better, where there would be plenty of bread and they would be free...[2]

The bond with the peasantry took form as an essential element of radical thought in the years preceding the

---

[1] Pomialovskii, *Polnoe sobranie sochinenii* (St Petersburg, 1889), 1, p. xlii.
[2] F. M. Reshetnikov, *Sochineniia* (Moscow, 1874), 1, 98.

promulgation of the emancipation. Though the members of the generation of the fifties strove for an objective, scientific view of the world and prided themselves on their ability to confront and acknowledge the unsightly features of Russian life, they soon felt the need for something to idealize and to embrace. Once the gentry and autocracy revealed their determination to pursue narrow class interests, the radical youth began to turn to the peasants as the only group in Russia likely to share their disaffection. They felt akin to the peasants by virtue of a common alienation from the existing order: a common pedigree of suffering more enduring and meaningful than class or blood ties. They believed that the peasants would feel impelled to join the intelligentsia in the transformation of self and society, and their hopes seemed to be borne out by the widespread unrest in the countryside in the years preceding and the months immediately following the emancipation.[1]

The ideological formulation of these attitudes was the work of the mentor of the new generation, a bookish *raznochinets* already entering his thirties, Nikolai Chernyshevskii. Chernyshevskii commanded wide learning and the kind of sharply defined and all-embracing world view that appealed to the youth. His 'anthropological principle', which he borrowed from European scientific thought of the time, reduced all human behaviour to simple general laws. The 'anthropological principle' denied body–soul duality and held that all men were composed of the same matter and responded in like manner to similar causes. Chernyshevskii could thus show that he and the intelligentsia possessed urges and thoughts in common with humanity in general. To understand the peasant, one had only to understand oneself.

So, I say, if you know [that all men inside are the same], then you don't have to worry about studying [the people] in order to know what they need and how it is possible to act upon them. Assume that they need what you need and you will not be mistaken. Assume that the same calculations and motivations act upon ordinary individuals among the people that act upon ordinary individuals in your sphere and that will be correct.[2]

[1] See Akademia Nauk SSSR. Inst. Istorii. Glavnoe Arkhivnoe Upravlenie. Tsentral'ny Gosudarstvenny Istoricheskii Arkiv SSSR v Leningrade, *Krest'ianskoe dvizhenie v Rossii v 1857–1861 (iiun) gg.; dokumenty* (Moscow, 1961), *passim*.

[2] N. G. Chernyshevskii, *Polnoe sobranie sochinenii* (Moscow, 1939–53), VII, 864.

Though most peasants, Chernyshevskii admitted, suffered from the same flaws and weaknesses as civilized men, there were also those who could rise above the ordinary and change the world around them—people 'of energetic mind and character, capable of thinking over a given situation, understanding a given conjuncture, becoming conscious of [their] needs, considering the means to their satisfaction, and under given circumstances, acting independently'.[1] With the analogical reasoning permitted by the 'anthropological principle',[2] Chernyshevskii conjured into existence a group of peasants whose position in the village was equivalent to that of the intelligentsia in educated society—the *intelligent*'s doubles, who cherished his ideals, his realistic outlook and his thirst for action. When conditions ripened, and the masses began to chafe under their burden, these conscious peasants would join the intelligentsia and lead in the destruction of the old order.

But the expectation of change stirred fear as well as hope. If not harnessed to their ideals, change could work to their disadvantage, and destroy the values they cherished and the grounds for a just social order. With their ambitions for the future went deep apprehensions about its true nature. They feared lest history be not the unfolding of justice on earth but the triumph of evil. They knew Russian reality to be inhabited by powerful and malevolent forces that they were unable to cope with. Reared in close familial surroundings, accustomed to the understanding and affection of parents, friends and servants, they had reacted with horror and loathing to their first glimpses of Russian life. The ethos of brute domination that governed the master's relations to his serfs, the teacher's to his pupils, the bureaucrat's to his subordinates, had frightened them. The cruelty, depravity and greed that confronted them everywhere had filled them with revulsion. Many had retreated into their families or into a life of reading and contemplation, but their feelings of fear never left them.

The belief in the peasantry gave them the strength to resist their fear. The peasants became their guardians of virtue and kindness against the evils of the alien civilization they dreaded. The peasants showed that not all mankind had been corrupted. Unspoiled by the vices of civilized life, the peasants, Nikolai Dobroliubov wrote, were still able to hearken to the voice of

[1] *Ibid.* VII, 887.

common sense issuing from nature. They maintained their faith
in human dignity, while educated society paid respect only to
the caprices of etiquette and propriety. 'There [among the
peasantry], there is more attentiveness to the worth of the
individual man, less indifference to what my neighbour is like,
and what I appear like to my neighbour.'[1]

Most of all, the members of the intelligentsia dreaded the
prospect of uncontrolled economic change and the behemoth
of modern industrialism, which, being unknown and distant,
assumed terrible proportions in their imaginations. They feared
the chaotic development that they envisioned blighting the
West and threatening to engulf Russia. Capitalism embodied
for them the callousness and egoism that had appalled them in
Russian life, and its spread promised to destroy everything they
held dear. Their succour was the peasant land commune, which
they hoped would serve as a bulwark, against capitalism. In
1857 Chernyshevskii described the commune as the 'sacred
and redeeming heritage bequeathed to us by our past life,
the poverty of which is atoned for by this one invaluable heritage'.[2] The communal organization, he showed, ensured land
to each member, and kept peasant economic life free from the
officious hand of the government. In this way it discouraged
the exploitation of the helpless by the rich and powerful and
forestalled the growth of a proletariat.[3] It was, in his words, an
'anti-toxin', which was 'extremely effective in preventing those
sufferings that we witness in the West'.[4]

Chernyshevskii and his followers, however, were not prone
to idealize the commune in its existing state; nor did it figure
as the central tenet of their doctrine. Rather, it was one article
of faith that made the prevalence of a virtuous peasant society
seem conceivable and even probable. They regarded it as an
institution that might enable social progress to follow the
pattern they envisaged and not that dictated by the vagaries
of a free economy. Though imperfect, it furnished a system of
relationships that could be developed into a just and rational
social organization. In an article of 1857, Chernyshevskii
provided ideological substantiation for these hopes. He elaborated the notion, first advanced by Alexander Herzen after the
revolution of 1848, that the commune was a possible embryo

---

[1] Dobroliubov, II, 270, 295–6.   [2] Chernyshevskii, IV, 341.
[3] *Ibid.* V, 615–18.   [4] *Ibid.* IV, 341.

of future socialist institutions. Using the logic of the dialectic, he showed that the highest stage, socialism, was merely a perfected form of the lowest, the commune, and that the middle stage, capitalism, was the antipode of both. In the West, the commune had been negated by its antithesis, private property or capitalism, which would, in turn, be superseded by socialism. Chernyshevskii argued that if the commune could be preserved until Europe reached the highest stage, then Russia could make use of the experience of more advanced nations and pass directly into socialism. The commune could be turned into a socialist institution and Russia would be spared the adversity of capitalism.[1]

But the events following the emancipation of the serfs in 1861 rapidly dispelled the hopes of achieving a common cause with the peasantry. The government's ruthless suppression of peasant unrest and the subsequent quiet in the countryside made it clear that the masses could not be counted on as active support for some time. The intelligentsia of the sixties, as a result, had to face the problem of social change alone. Its members had to place utmost reliance on themselves and suppress their longing to participate in Russian life. The keynote of the new decade was 'realism'. By mastering the truths of science, they hoped to emancipate themselves completely from the society around them. A host of 'new man' novels appeared, telling of individuals who endeavoured to embrace rational ethics and a rational way of life. The 'new men' had no truck with the past; they strove to remake themselves through education and self-denial, offsetting the absence of adult models with a single-minded pursuit of the ideal.

But the doctrines of self-improvement current in the sixties did not imply the renunciation of the goal of social transformation or of the hope of achieving a rapport with the peasantry. Rather than abandoned, these were relegated to the future. The *intelligent* declared his autonomy from all parts of Russian life only so that he could uplift himself morally and intellectually and reach the level where his intellectual claims would be strong enough to enable him to direct the course of future social development. He suppressed his longing for the peasants with the implicit hope of achieving a higher unity with them in the end. The most popular of the 'new man' novels, Cherny-

[1] *Ibid.* v, 357–92.

shevskii's *Chto delat?* (*What is to be Done?*) depicted a group of young people who had thrown over the tyranny of home and society to lead a life of 'enlightened self-interest'. They lived with whom they pleased, formed cooperatives, and studied science. Rakhmetov, the most advanced of them, had overcome his need for comfort and happiness, for all instinctual satisfaction, to dedicate himself exclusively to the cause of the new world. And only he, completely purged of the old habits, could recognize his own interest as being one with that of the people.

The most outspoken representative of the attitudes dominant in the sixties was Dmitrii Pisarev, a young nobleman, the son of an army officer. Reared in a household of women, Pisarev had grown up with no model of masculine conduct before him. His entry into maturity had been fraught with severe emotional strain from which he suffered a nervous breakdown in 1860, at the age of twenty.[1] After his recovery, he found his guide to life in science, and dismissed everything else unconditionally. 'There is only one evil in humanity and that is ignorance,' he declared. 'Against it there is only one medicine and that is science; but this medicine must be taken not in homeopathic doses but by the bucket and garbage-pail full.'[2] The answer to Russia's economic problems was to increase the supply of educated manpower by expanding the ranks of the intelligentsia. To trouble oneself with the spread of education to the masses was premature. 'The fate of the people is decided not in the people's schools but in the universities.'[3]

Pisarev took Bazarov, the hero of Turgenev's *Fathers and Sons*, as the model youth of the new scientific era. He admired Bazarov's lonely quest for truth, his denial of his own emotions and rejection of traditional values. Bazarov, Pisarev noted approvingly, stood alone 'on the cold heights of sober thought'; engrossed in his scientific pursuits, he welcomed his isolation from the society around him, including the peasantry. Bazarov felt little affection for his parents, but did not regret this, and remained on civil terms with them as long as they did not disturb his work. The youth who needed no father, in whom filial love was all but dead, was the ideal posed by Pisarev for the generation of the sixties.[4]

---

[1] A. Coquart, *Dmitri Pisarev et l'idéologie du nihilisme russe* (Paris, 1956), *passim*.
[2] D. I. Pisarev, *Sochineniia* (Moscow, 1955–6), III, 122.   [3] *Ibid.* III, 126.
[4] *Ibid* II, 30.

But Pisarev too denied emotion and affective ties only so that they could be sublimated and fulfilled in a purified, more exalted form. Now and then his ruthless verbiage faltered, revealing the deep longing for kinship masked behind the elaborate science metaphor that enabled him to comprehend the world. 'Science' or 'knowledge' (*nauka*) proved to mean not only the results of learned study and experimentation but also the peasant's understanding of when to sow and reap, where to plant, and what fertilizer to use. The peasant's skill was 'the embryo of science, the first attempts of man to grasp the secrets of living nature'.[1] The peasants were the only other group in Russia capable of achieving a scientific outlook; like Chernyshevskii, Pisarev saw them as the one social class in Russia that could attain the heights of consciousness. Despite appearances, he showed, the intelligentsia and peasantry were generically related, for both worked for others and were exploited. The members of the intelligentsia served science and humanity and, like the peasants, did not seek to enrich themselves at the expense of the rest of the population. Pisarev bestowed upon them the title 'thinking proletariat', thus gratifying his and the intelligentsia's desire to resign from educated society and join the wage-earners, the suffering population of the world. 'When you labour,' he asserted, 'your interests correspond with the interests of all other labouring men. You are a worker yourself. All workers are your friends. All exploiters are your natural enemies because they are the enemies of all humanity, including themselves.'[2]

Pisarev's reasoning served as a justification for study and self-improvement, pursuits dear to the *intelligent*'s heart but seemingly remote from the immediate interests of the peasantry. The generation of the sixties became the generation of scientism, whose members steeped themselves in knowledge of the natural world, hoping to find there the key to mastery over reality. They counterposed science to conservative prejudice and made scientific experimentation and discovery radical virtues. But the ultimate result of such attitudes was to divert the thought and energies of the radical youth from their social mission. The sixties saw a cooling of the old ardour. The few revolutionary groups that formed exerted little influence on the intelligentsia as a whole and proved weak and short-lived. Despite Pisarev's

---

[1] *Ibid.* III, 119–21. [2] *Ibid.* III, 16.

notion of a common purpose for peasantry and intelligentsia, the youth in the cities began to feel themselves alone in Russia and without the hopes of the previous decade. Radical circles dissolved or turned into dismal conclaves where the disappointed gave vent to their desolation in self-pity, or drowned it in drink.

At the close of the sixties, science appeared neither to be bringing the union with the peasants closer nor to be furthering social change. Those who had pursued their own scientific self-education had merely become isolated in their own narrow world and even further removed from the people. The youth coming to the capital were impatient with the maxims of the previous decade. They longed to abandon the posture of forbearance and embark on the transformation of reality. The recent experience of the West aroused their hopes. News from comrades studying abroad informed them of the growing strength and self-assertiveness of the European workers' movement. Not scientific enlightenment but the natural awakening of the masses seemed to presage the realization of reason on earth. The people began to appear not as passive participants but as active agents of social change. As the new conception of the people's role spread, it dispelled the despondency and torpor reigning in intelligentsia circles. The central questions became how to approach the people and how to bring their dormant energies to life.

The caution that marked earlier 'realistic' attitudes toward the peasantry now began to disappear. The longing for swift social change was given substance by invoking increasingly enhanced images of the peasantry and increasingly optimistic conceptions of their revolutionary feelings. The waiting on a favourable turn of events of the fifties, the painstaking introspection and asceticism of the sixties, gave way to a relaxation of the critical sense and a blurring of the distinction between wish and reality. Sensing their inability to act alone, the members of the intelligentsia made the peasantry the instrument to realize their hopes. They conceived of them as a revolutionary army of the discontented that was imbued or could be imbued with ideals similar to their own. In the fifties and sixties the *intelligent* had been the dominant figure in the relationship with the peasant, the one who could help and pity his less fortunate brother. Now that relationship was reversed. He respected the peasant as one who was more fit than himself to carry on the social struggle and to enter the future.

The new sense of oneness with the peasantry inspired them and created a spirit of solidarity as Pisarev's intellectualized solutions could not. It quieted the doubts of those unsure of their own worth and importance in the Russian setting. It gave them assurance that the virtues they treasured in themselves were valued in the outside world and would ultimately be embodied in social forms. The feeling of identity and comradeship with the peasant afforded each *intelligent* strength to triumph over his own flaws and shortcomings, the legacy of his past that still tormented him. The unresolved conflicts of youth, the anguished uncertainty about who he was and what role he had to play, vanished from consciousness once he believed his fate linked to that of the people. The feeling of kinship with the peasantry forged a bond between men of diverse backgrounds and dispositions, creating in them a common sense of belonging and a common conviction that they alone had the interests of the Russian people at heart. It was the syndrome of an era, uniting men in the service of a grandiose illusion.

The writings of the leading ideologists of the seventies fanned the hopes of an imminent *rapprochement* with the people. Petr Lavrov's *Istoricheskie pis'ma* (*Historical Letters*), the gospel of the radical youth of the early seventies, taught that the intelligentsia could not limit its task to self-education. The *intelligent*, Lavrov proclaimed, had to swell the ranks behind him and enlist the people in his cause; by improving himself alone, he fostered not general progress but merely his own advancement. The movement of progress required the education of the masses as well, the uplifting of the people to consciousness, so that they too could participate in a new, just and rational social order. The *intelligent* was to erase the gap between himself and the peasant by making the peasant similar to himself.[1]

By the beginning of 1874 Lavrov's writings had been surpassed in popularity by those of Mikhail Bakunin, who declared that even the preliminary work of educating the people was superfluous. The peasants, he preached, already nurtured a strong socialist spirit. 'It is not even necessary to delve deeply into the historical consciousness of the people to define the

[1] P. Lavrov, *Istoricheskie pis'ma* (St Petersburg, 1905), *passim*.

characteristics of the ideal.' The features of the present commune that Chernyshevskii had taken as mere rudimentary forms of more just social relationships became, for Bakunin, actual manifestations of peasant sympathy for the ideal. The commune's guarantee of equal use of land to all members, he asserted, indicated their basically socialistic instincts. Its state of quasi-autonomy from the administration enabled it to resist tsarist authority and to harbour potent oppositional sentiment.[1] To be sure, Bakunin qualified his statements with descriptions of the commune's negative attributes. He showed that the commune suffered from both intrinsic shortcomings—such as the patriarchal worship of authority—and extrinsic ones, such as the tax-collecting mechanism imposed by the state. But this did not mar the exhilarating optimism of his message. The egalitarian anti-governmental forces of the people would take the upper hand, overthrow the social order, and rid the commune of its patriarchal spirit and bureaucratic excrescences. The uprising would be led by strong dissident elements, particularly brigands (*razboiniki*) like Razin and Pugachev, 'Russia's first revolutionaries'.[2] Bakunin presented a picture of a countryside smouldering with discontent. The *intelligenty* had only to go to the people to ignite and channel their impassioned revolutionary instincts.

In such a situation, what can be done by our intellectual proletariat, our honourable, sincere Russian youth, devoted to socialism to the bitter end? They must, without doubt, go to the people, because now, everywhere, but especially in Russia, outside of the people, outside of the multi-million masses of the workers, there is neither life, nor a cause, nor a future.[3]

Bakunin merely expressed what the members of the intelligentsia wished to believe. He gave them assurance that the masses would reciprocate their sentiments and rally behind them in their cause. They began to feel that they were no longer alone in their desire for revolution. 'Our people are the natural allies of anyone who seriously and sincerely hates the present and longs for a better future,' a revolutionary proclamation of 1874 announced.[4] The radical literature of the early seventies reveals the striking degree to which the intelli-

[1] B. S. Itenberg (ed.), *Revoliutsionnoe narodnichestvo semidesiatykh godov XIX veka* (Moscow, 1964), I, 45.   [2] *Ibid.* I, 46–9.
[3] *Ibid.* I, 51.   [4] *Ibid.* I, 145.

gentsia credited the peasantry with its own thoughts. The stories of Nikolai Naumov described case after case of victimized and exploited peasants who united in defence of their own interests. Naumov's 'peasant heroes' spoke in words heartening to the intelligentsia. They gave vent to bitter attacks on the whole economic system, like the following remonstration with a cozening fish merchant in the story '*Iurovaia*'.

All you do is come and take what has already been made and then go off and by hook or by crook swindle and cheat everyone out of everything, and what the peasant does is to work day and night to store up what you come along and take. Yes, he who goes fishing freezes not only in his shoes but through his body and fingers. Yes, fish is good to eat, but try to catch it and find out how the peasant sweats and bleeds on the ice. So why should we bear this yoke for someone else's pockets when we have our own to worry about? We are fools, fools, but we are learning sense. We have plenty of other yokes too. The *muzhik* makes food and drink for all while he himself starves.[1]

As the members of the intelligentsia placed greater hopes in the peasantry, they yearned to escape their civilized character and achieve a new purified identity by uniting with the forces of the future they believed were stirring in the countryside. Responding to Bakunin's blanket indictment of civilization as the product of force and exploitation, they strove to enter into the guise of their increasingly assertive *alter ego* and to assimilate his characteristic traits. The revolutionary proclamation cited above declared science and the professions tools of the exploiting classes. The *intelligent* would not become a scholar or scientist when he knew very well that 'the applications of science are used only by the exploiting classes and for the greatest part to intensify the exploitation of the people'. Only as a manual worker could he honestly associate with the peasantry and earn their trust. The peasants would regard such a person as 'a *confrère* sharing with them the labour, the unhappiness and the grief of their routine, unattractive life'. Failing that, he could serve in humble positions, such as veterinarian, nurse, or petty clerk. The *intelligent* was to erase the gap between himself and the peasant by making himself more like the peasant.[2]

[1] N. Naumov, *Sobranie sochinenii* (St Petersburg, 1897), I, 318.
[2] Itenberg, *Revoliutsionnoe narodnichestvo...*, I, 147–51.

In the summer of 1874 the radical youth, inspired by the signs of success that they themselves had projected on reality, abandoned their academic pursuits to plunge, inexperienced and untutored, into the countryside. Their hopes of an enthusiastic welcome evaporated on first contact with the peasantry. The image of the peasant as incipient revolutionary corresponded little with the sullen country folk they met, who, seemingly resolute in their trust of autocracy, met them with distrust and hostility. Hopelessly vulnerable to arrest once they strayed outside the capital, they were herded into prison by the hundreds.

But the trauma of the 'going to the people' (*khozhdenie v narod*) only reinforced the prevailing notion of the peasant. The blow the *intelligent* sustained merely weakened his self-esteem and deepened his dependence on the peasants for assistance and consolation. Like a rejected lover, he only longed the more powerfully after his beloved when rebuffed, and cast the blame for his failures upon himself. The peasants' hostile stares seemed to convey reproach for his remoteness from rural life and his inability to grasp its essence. Their indifference to his exhortations seemed to attest to his own lack of socialist sentiment and spirit, which they had been quick to perceive. Humbled, he began to look upon the peasants with even greater respect and admiration. Radical literature began to treat peasant life as if it already embodied socialist principles—even before the revolution—and to ascribe the flaws that were present to external economic and political factors alien to the peasants' basic nature. The village appeared as a realm apart from the depraved egoism of the city. As the distance between peasant and *intelligent* loomed uncomfortably large, hopes of becoming like the peasant began to fade. Some continued to strive to remake themselves in the image of the peasant. But most achieved their feelings of identity with him by invoking their formidable powers of empathy. Remaining in the city, they lived vicariously in the experience of the people, making the intentions, aspirations, and fears they ascribed to them their own.

The new feeling of deference to the peasant was expressed in 1875 and 1876 by a young nobleman, Petr Chervinskii, in the pages of the newspaper *Nedelia* (*The Week*). Chervinskii emphasized the distinctiveness of Russian social development and the Russian peasantry. He argued that the peasants, by virtue of their attachment to the land and their freedom from egoistic interests, had attained a far higher moral level than urban dwellers, among them the intelligentsia, who lived in the midst of a capitalistic European civilization.[1] The intelligentsia's cold, anaemic, abstract love for humanity was feeble in comparison with the powerful, immediate impulses of the peasant. 'How pitiful the *intellectual* humanity and love for "man" is before the direct feeling of some downtrodden peasant woman!'[2] Even the peasant's most ignorant and seemingly objectionable behaviour concealed a moral concern which was fundamentally laudable.

The peculiar features of superstition, idol worship, and other related practices are crude and coarse in form and sometimes even scandalous. But at the same time a great feeling lies here in embryonic form—the urge to submit one's egoistic self to something broader and more elevated to which man has moral obligations and on occasion may wish to sacrifice his individuality. Most important of all is that this feeling is not intellectual like the ideological love for humanity with which it has much in common, but physiological, pervading body and soul; the common man will not be able to debate about it, and, indeed, doesn't know where it came from.[3]

Chervinskii adjured the intelligentsia to 'stop speaking the philosophy of Russian life in a foreign tongue', to help Russia pursue its national destiny by 'developing those everyday peculiar features that contain the guarantee (*zalog*) of a better future', to abandon the capital and live near the peasants in the countryside.[4]

Nikolai Mikhailovskii, the prominent young social theorist and literary critic of *Otechestvennye Zapiski* (*Annals of the Fatherland*), the most influential of the radical journals of the seventies, took issue with Chervinskii's strictures on the intelligentsia and his glorification of the peasantry. Mikhailovskii cautioned the *intelligent* against attempting to submerge himself and his civilized values in the backward, ignorant masses of the countryside. He acknowledged the injustices of Western society and held that if Russia followed the right path, it might be able

[1] See A. N. Pypin, 'Narodnichestvo', *Vestnik Evropy*, no. 19 (February 1884), pp. 711–14.

[2] Quoted in Koz'min, *Ot 'deviatnadtsatogo fevralia' k 'pervomu marta'* (Moscow, 1933), p. 176.

[3] Quoted in N. K. Mikhailovskii, *Polnoe sobranie sochinenii* (St Petersburg, 1907–13), III, 765–6.   [4] Quoted *ibid*. 762–4.

to avoid them and achieve a more rational and humane social order. But such prospects, he thought, were only inchoate. Existing conditions in Russia were primitive and the intelligentsia had to guide their development if they were to conform to the highest values of humanity and civilization. The commune had lost its primeval purity and suffered the destructive influence of the social and economic system. Centuries of bondage had left a deep imprint upon the peasant's morality: superstition and the subjugation of women were common aspects of peasant life; even human sacrifice had been practised occasionally. The ignorant peasantry could not be trusted to determine their own best interest, and the members of the intelligentsia dared not hearken to 'the voice of the countryside' as Chervinskii had bidden them: 'The voice of the countryside too often contradicts its own interests,' Mikhailovskii wrote, 'and the problem consists in sincerely and honourably recognizing the interests of the people as one's goal, while preserving in the countryside only what corresponds to those interests.'[1]

But Mikhailovskii's warning went unheeded in radical circles. 'We considered it slanderous to the peasant,' wrote Nikolai Rusanov, later one of his warmest admirers, 'for we believed that the "ideas" of the Russian village, for whose "interests" the best part of the intelligentsia had sacrificed itself, should, in the end, correspond with our own.'[2] It was this attitude that prevailed in the midst of the revolutionaries who worked to reconstitute the movement after the *débâcle* of 1874. Their leader Mark Natanson declared that the revolutionaries should aspire to be no more than humble assistants of the people in the imminent upheaval, for the peasants were already imbued with communal sentiment and an aversion to private property.[3] They proclaimed their admiration for the common people, the *narod*, by adopting the name '*narodniki*', which had previously been used only as a term of derision for fanatical Bakuninist elements.[4] A statement of principles dating from 1876 or 1877

[1] *Ibid.* 706–7, 777. For an account of Mikhailovskii's life and thought, see James Billington, *Mikhailovskii and Russian Populism* (Oxford, 1958).

[2] N. S. Rusanov, 'N. K. Mikhailovskii i obshchestvennaia zhizn' Rossii', *Golos Minuvshego*, no. 2 (February 1914), p. 18.

[3] L. Tikhomirov, *Vospominaniia L'va Tikhomirova* (Moscow–Leningrad, 1927), pp. 85–6.

[4] B. Koz'min, '"Narodniki" i "narodnichestvo"', *Voprosy literatury*, no. 1 (September 1957), pp. 116–19; Richard Pipes, 'Narodnichestvo: A Semantic Inquiry', *Slavic Review*, vol. xxiii, no. 3 (September 1964), pp. 441–58.

announced a more practical approach to agitation and an acceptance of more modest immediate goals. The people, they realized, could not be induced to rebel for abstract ideals which were beyond their comprehension. 'We are narrowing our demands to those actually attainable in the near future, i.e., *to the needs and desires of the people*, whatever they are at a given moment.' The overriding needs of the people were for land and freedom; these became the grounds for their agitation in the countryside, and the goals of their new organization, Land and Freedom (*Zemlia i Volia*).[1]

The initial version of Land and Freedom's programme, drafted in either 1876 or 1877, began with the admission that 'the realization of anarchic ideals in all their breadth at the present moment is impossible'. However, it went on to affirm that 'the basic character of the Russian people is socialistic to such an extent that if the desires and strivings of the people were realized at a given moment a firm foundation would be laid for further progress of the socialist cause in Russia'. In the peasant's thinking, it declared, 'every tiller of the land has the right to the amount he can cultivate *by his own labour*'.[2] By the time of the revision of the programme in 1878, the members had lost their original circumspection and the reservation about the feasibility of socialism was then eliminated. In neither version did the authors make mention of intrinsic defects in the commune; for the members of Land and Freedom, the commune preserved its democratic egalitarian nature, despite the inroads made by the state tax mechanism and the exploiting classes that subsisted by taking advantage of the peasants' poverty. Whereas the revolutionaries of the early seventies drew little distinction between the varieties of exploitation prevalent in Russia and in the West, the adherents of these programmes viewed reality in terms of a struggle between two systems, one pristine and native, the other alien and corrupt. The pressure

[1] S. N. Valk (ed.), *Arkhiv Zemli i Voli i Narodnoi Voli* (Moscow, 1930), p. 53; S. S. Volk (ed.), *Revoliutsionnoe narodnichestvo 70-kh godov XIX veka* (Moscow–Leningrad, 1965), II, 33–4. The dating of this document and the two versions of the programme has been placed in doubt by recent research in the Soviet Union, reflected in the treatment in Volk. See G. M. Lifshits, K. G. Liashchenko, 'Kak sozdavalas' programma vtoroi "Zemli i Voli"', *Voprosy Istorii*, XL, no. 9 (September 1965), pp. 36–50. This is an interesting and often ingenious analysis of the documents, though I find their criticism of Valk more persuasive than their own explanations.

[2] Valk, pp. 58–9; Volk, p. 27.

of the growing money economy was threatening to destroy the communal matrix of rural life. The revolution was urgent,

> because the development of capitalism and the greater and greater penetration of Russian life by the sundry poisons of bourgeois civilization (thanks to the protective influence and efforts of the Russian government) threaten the commune with destruction and a greater or lesser distortion of the people's world view [on political and economic problems].[1]

Making the revolutionary struggle entirely the work of the people, the revolutionaries limited themselves to organizing the nascent forces in the countryside. This task, the second programme recognized, required considerable patience and application. No longer was a brief visit to the countryside deemed sufficient for agitation. The revolutionary had 'to settle in one spot' (*sest' na odnom meste*) long enough to familiarize himself with the local population and the conditions of its life. Serving in posts such as *volost'* clerk, teacher, or nurse, he would seek to appear respectable and win the peasants' confidence. At first he would devote himself to peaceful activity, providing advice and assistance to the villagers. When grievances arose, he would encourage legal forms of protest. Only after the peasants had been fully disabused of their respect for their authorities would he urge them towards an insurrection (*bunt*). Through his links with comrades elsewhere, he would try to ensure that the unrest in his village contributed to the final goal of a national uprising (*vosstanie*). To unify the scattered insurrections the members of Land and Freedom declared it their intention to form 'a tight and well-formed organization of well-prepared revolutionaries, from both the intelligentsia and the workers, who agree to act in the spirit of our programme'.[2]

Relinquishing the role of combatant, the revolutionary assumed that of technician of revolution. The new identity was epitomized in the young leader of the St Petersburg Land and Freedom group, Aleksandr Dmitrievich Mikhailov. Mikhailov saw the revolutionaries as those 'standing above the masses, well equipped with ability and decisiveness', who 'hearken to the summons to organize and direct those burning with the

---

[1] Valk, p. 60; Volk, pp. 27, 30–1.
[2] Valk, pp. 60–1; O. Aptekman, *Obshchestvo Zemlia i Volia* (Petrograd, 1924), p. 139; Vera Figner, *Zapechatlenny trud* (Moscow, 1921), I, 87–8.

desire for struggle'.[1] After leaving home in 1875 at the age of twenty, Mikhailov could find the missing purpose and structure of his life only in the company of his fellow revolutionaries. He dedicated himself totally to welding them into a tight and disciplined organization, resistant to the whims and inconsistencies of the individual members, and shunned all emotional attachment himself. Expecting the same ascetic devotion from his comrades, he waged, in his words, 'the most stubborn struggle against the broad Russian nature'. He mercilessly imposed the rules of Bakunin's *Catechism of a Revolutionary* upon all those who fell under his tutelage, frowning upon the slightest indulgence of personal desires. At his instance the members of Land and Freedom adopted a strict code of conduct that demanded the individual's complete submission to the group, obliging each member to put his energies, means, talents, and even life exclusively at its disposal and to free himself of personal sympathies and antipathies. The leaders of the organization— the 'basic circle'—had to heed even more rigorous standards of conduct and to give up all personal property.[2]

In Land and Freedom the revolutionaries attempted to combine two identities: the humble assistant of the people, who went to the countryside to learn and direct, and the active conspirator, who lived for revolution and achieved gratification in action. The reconciliation of the two identities was possible, however, only if the people responded immediately, for only then could the submergence of one's personality be justified as a pre-condition to action. But the peasant village again proved an inhospitable environment for revolutionary activity. Scattered across a large expanse of the Volga region, the members of Land and Freedom saw their energies dissipated in peaceful efforts that never gained the expected revolutionary momentum. Resigned to a secondary role in the struggle, committed not to stir feelings of discontent that were not already present and demanding expression, they found themselves in the frustrating position of awaiting an insurrection which was to come of its own accord, but which showed no sign of occurring. Indeed, police reports recorded that the revolutionaries

---

[1] A. D. Mikhailov, *Narodovolets Aleksandr Dmitrievich Mikhailov* (Leningrad, 1925), p. 104.
[2] *Ibid.* p. 47; P. M. Plekhanova, 'Perifeiny kruzhok Zemli i Voli', *Gruppa Osvobozhdenie truda, Sbornik IV* (Moscow–Leningrad, 1926), pp. 91–2; Valk, p. 65.

of the central Volga region had engaged in no activity of a revolutionary nature, and that in some cases they seemed to have avoided all contact with the peasantry.[1] Under continual police surveillance, they were constantly endangered by the very individuals against whom they were uniting the peasants—the *kulak*, the local merchant, the tavern-keeper. One young revolutionary, N. I. Sergeev, finding the peasantry indifferent to 'ways of changing its bitter lot for the better', returned to the conspiratorial apartment in Saratov at the end of 1877 to discover it crowded with comrades who, like himself, had been disenchanted with their life among the peasantry.[2]

In fact, despite the currency of *narodnik* ideas, the countryside exerted little attraction on most of the youth of the capital. Nearly all of those who established settlements in the countryside came from the central circle of diehard revolutionaries who had been in the movement from the beginning of the seventies. Vera Figner writes that not a single recruit joined her group in the Saratov region in 1877 and 1878 though the area was well organized and therefore ideal for a novice.[3] Plekhanov's descriptions of ferment among the Don Cossacks evoked eager interest among the youth, but he could induce none of them to leave Petersburg to partake in revolutionary agitation.[4]

The revolutionary excitement of 1877 and 1878 was generated not by peasant unrest, but by the struggle with the autocracy taking place in the capital. In 1877, when the government mounted a series of trials to expose the revolutionaries to public disgrace, its show of justice backfired, bringing to light, instead, the inglorious cruelty and inefficiency of officialdom. In the most spectacular, 'the trial of the 193', the accused, apprehended at the time of 'the going to the people', used the court as a rostrum to proclaim their love of the people and to denounce the bureaucracy. The state's inept handling of the case, the sufferings of the revolutionaries—seventy-five of whom had died, committed suicide, or lost their sanity while awaiting the

---

[1] L. Deitch, *Za polveka* (2 vols.; Berlin, 1923), II, 247; A. I. Ivanchin–Pisarev, *Khozhdenie v narod* (Moscow–Leningrad, 1929), *passim*; V. I. Ginev, 'Revoliutsionnaia deiatel'nost' narodnikov 70-kh godov sredi krest'ian i rabochikh srednego povolzhia', *Istoricheskie Zapiski*, no. 74 (1963), p. 239.

[2] Ginev, p. 240.   [3] Figner, *Zapechatlenny trud*, I, 149.

[4] G. Plekhanov, 'Predislovie', A. Thun, *Istoriia revoliutsionnykh dvizhenii v Rossii* (Geneva, 1903), pp. xxx–xxxii.

trial in prison—won general sympathy for the accused and aroused both the anger and the courage of the revolutionary youth.[1] The latter began to abandon their posture of restraint and to answer government provocation with direct attacks on tsarist officials. The day after the close of 'the trial of the 193', Vera Zasulich shot and wounded Trepov, the Governor of St Petersburg, for his brutal treatment of imprisoned revolutionaries; her trial, which concluded in her acquittal, also became a revolutionary *cause célèbre*. In February, Valerian Osinskii, a leader of the southern group, attempted unsuccessfully to kill Kotliarevskii, the vice-prosecutor of the Kiev tribunal. In August, Sergei Kravchinskii of the Petersburg Land and Freedom group shot and killed the chief of gendarmes, Mezentsov.[2] The accelerating tempo of terror caught the imagination of the youth. The leading terrorists in the organization, Vera Figner wrote, 'created a propaganda of action, gave the impetus, pointed to a concrete goal and the way to attain it. They inspired the youth with an example, stirred them from their immobility, and incited them to battle—to heroic feats of daring and of courage.'[3]

In the capital the members of Land and Freedom found the oppositional spirit they had anticipated in the countryside. The discontent among students and workers provided them with opportunities for participation in demonstrations and strikes.[4] The pages of *Nachalo* (*The Beginning*) and *Zemlia i Volia* (*Land and Freedom*), the first illegal newspapers to be printed in Russia, described strikes, demonstrations, murders, arrests, attempted escapes from prison, and inveighed against the abuses of the tsarist police, while mention of life and agitation in the countryside was scant. 'The threads linking the interests of the capital and provinces are breaking more and more with each additional step,' wrote V. Sopelkin, deploring the abandonment of the countryside. 'Things have gone so far that the active participants in one and the other place have completely ceased to understand and sympathize with each other.'[5]

But while St Petersburg had become the scene of the

---

[1] S. M. Kravchinskii (Stepniak), *Podpol'naia Rossia* (St Petersburg, 1905), pp. 28–9.
[2] Franco Venturi, *Roots of Revolution* (London, 1960), pp. 587–612.
[3] Figner, *Zapechatlenny trud*, I, 149.
[4] V. A. Tvardovskaia, 'Krizis Zemli i Voli v kontse 70-kh godov', *Istoriia S.S.S.R.* (1959), no. 4, pp. 62–4; Valk, *Arkhiv 'Zemli i Voli' i 'Narodnoi Voli'*, pp. 197–9.　　　　　　　　[5] Valk, p. 321.

revolutionary movement, the idealized view of country life and the revolutionary potentialities of the peasantry maintained its sway. Terrorism was regarded as merely a means of self-protection that would frighten the state into ceasing its persecution of the revolutionaries, and permit the agitational work to proceed freely in the countryside. Kravchinskii wrote in justification of his murder of Mezentsov, 'Outlawed by the Russian government, deprived of all the guarantees that are provided by a social bond on the basis of the higher right of every individual to self-defence, we must take upon ourselves the defence of our human rights like a person or a group living in a wild primitive country.'[1]

While the news columns of the revolutionary newspapers related the urban struggle, the programmatic sections continued to stress agrarian ideals and to urge the youth to the countryside. In the lead article of the first number of *Zemlia i Volia*, dated October 1878, Kravchinskii proclaimed the primacy of the people in the revolution: 'The revolution is the work of the masses of the people. They are prepared by history. The revolutionary can rectify nothing. He is only history's instrument.'[2] Kravchinskii preferred to leave agitation among the factory workers, important though it was, 'in the shadow'. Terrorism was a form of defence, he warned, and not the revolutionaries' central concern. 'Against a class only a class can rise; only the people themselves can destroy the system...the chief mass of our forces must work in the milieu of the people.'[3] Kravchinskii saw the cause of the revolutionaries' failures in their distance from the people; they had to discard their civilized characteristics and become 'men of the people' (*narodnye liudi*). He summoned them to 'tear from socialism its German clothing' and to 'garb it in a peasant's *sermiaga* [caftan]'. 'Steep yourself in the great sea of the people,' he exclaimed. 'Throw open your eyes and your ears.'[4]

Among the non-revolutionary progressive intelligentsia the contradiction between thought and action was no less acute. For them as well, their identification with the peasantry and the commune represented the sole guarantee of their participation

---

[1] Kravchinskii, *Smert' za smert'* (*Ubiistvo Mezentsova*) (Petersburg, 1920), p. 13.
[2] Iakovlev, V. Ia. (B. Bazilevskii) (ed.), *Revoliutsionnaia zhurnalistika semidesia-tykh godov* (Paris, 1905), p. 120.
[3] *Ibid.* p. 124.   [4] *Ibid.* pp. 129–30, 120.

in the evolution towards a just life in Russia and their self-fulfilment as progressive individuals. The chorus of support for the commune and the insistence on the rural nature of Russian society were unanimous in the liberal and radical legal press of these years; one seeks in vain for assertions that the commune was retarding economic progress or was inherently unjust in its distribution of land. The only benefactors of the destruction of the commune were thought to be the exploiting classes and the state; and the few eccentric conservatives, like Boris Chicherin, who favoured its demise were viewed as spokesmen for those dubious interests. Yet the influx of hopeful young *intelligenty* from countryside to city continued unabated. Sergei Krivenko wrote of these years:

Poets enticed the *intelligent* with the spaciousness of the steppe and the silence of sleepy forests; moralists with the absence of vanity and sin. Economists moved him with the need to introduce technical innovations into rural life; teachers, knowledge; jurists, jurisprudence. Meanwhile, the cultured individual continued to flee the countryside, and with such haste that the decade 1870–1880 will probably be called 'the exodus from the countryside'.[1]

Locked in their urban habitat, the intelligentsia gazed out wistfully at the pristine peasant world that constituted the source of their hopes. Devoid of outlet, their longing sublimated itself in a craving for knowledge, an insatiable thirst for facts, figures, personal accounts, anything that would give them a clue to the mysteries of rural life. Study of the peasant became the new means of establishing rapport with him. If long residence in the countryside was difficult and unrewarding, if the peasants appeared remote and aloof; competent, educated individuals could still make forays into the countryside and make contact with village life by investigating it. Then they would return to the cities to put their experience in writing, for a large and eager audience awaited such material. Men devoted themselves without stint to amassing knowledge that they hoped would confirm the ideals for which they lived. Books on peasant life began to issue from the publishers in large numbers; articles on the subject filled the radical and liberal organs of the legal press. Scholars abandoned their narrow pursuits to study the peasants, or, as was more common, remodelled their

S. N. Krivenko, *Na rasput'i* (Moscow, 1901), p. 99.

disciplines into instruments for analysing them. Authorities of all kinds began to write about the countryside: ethnographers, historians, philologists, and archaeologists all felt the powerful impulse to study the economic and social conditions of the people.[1]

The most staggering and influential of all the considerable investigatory achievement of this period was the creation of a body of exhaustive statistical materials by a new class of *zemstvo* statisticians. Disturbed by the absence of reliable facts about the people and by the necessarily subjective nature of the intelligentsia's opinions about them, a group of young men, many of whom had been connected with the radical circles of the early seventies, began to look to statistics as the sole means of answering the puzzling questions of peasant life. In the simplicity and seeming objectivity of figures, they hoped to find a signal clarification of rural conditions and a key to future change and reform. 'Statistics is the cause of the future. It will heal all Russia's economic sores and raise the national economy to its necessary level, and open brilliant perspectives of national productivity,' Semen Vasiukov ironically, but not inaccurately, characterized their mentality.[2] Their extensive hopes for this discipline impelled them to spare neither health nor their own personal lives in producing meticulous and thorough studies, often of prodigious scope. One of the most successful of their number was Petr Chervinskii, who left publicistics in 1876 to take the post of chief statistician of the Chernigov provincial *zemstvo*. He directed the compilation and publication of a masterly fifteen-volume study, which served as a model for all later studies of small provinces.[3]

In 1875 a twenty-seven year old *raznochinets*, Vasilii Orlov, embarked upon what was to become the most spectacular and momentous of all these investigations—a statistical survey of Moscow province. Appointed head of the statistical committee of the Moscow provincial *zemstvo*, Orlov chose to include all aspects of the economic life of the province in his survey. Sceptical of the opinions of the local intelligentsia, he under-

---

[1] Pypin, no. 19 (January 1884), pp. 152–3; no. 19 (February 1884), pp. 310–11.

[2] S. I. Vasiukov, 'Bylye dni i gody', *Istoricheskii Vestnik*, no. 113 (July 1908), p. 107.

[3] Aptekman, 'Zachatki kul'turnogo narodnichestva v 70–kh godakh (Kruzhok studentov Zemledel'cheskogo Instituta),' *Istoriko-revoliutsionny sbornik No. 1* (Leningrad 1924), p. 26; 'Chervinskii, P.P.', *Entsiklopedicheskii slovar' Brokgauz-Efron*, LXXVI, 530.

took to gather all the necessary information with the help of only a coterie of trusted young assistants. In each district under investigation, they visited every factory, estate and peasant commune. They interviewed as many heads of peasant households as possible, taking detailed notes of their economic resources and needs. The massive results were published in nine volumes over a period of nine years, at the end of which, in 1885, Orlov succumbed to a stroke. His masterpiece, *Formy krestianskogo zemlevladeniia v moskovskoi gubernii* (*Forms of Peasant Land Tenure in Moscow Province*), published in 1879, summarized materials assembled in visits to 5,500 settlements, in each of which 150 questions had been posed of the inhabitants. Aside from his own work, Orlov did his best to fulfil the requests that flowed in from other *zemstva* anxious to solicit his assistance in mounting their own investigations. Under his guidance, statistical bureaux began functioning in many other provinces, staffed by indefatigable men of inexorable curiosity, like himself.[1]

Studies of the rural commune represented the largest category of specialized works on rural life. The commune had long been the subject of learned discourse and debate in educated society, but only now were its actual economic and juridical features examined in detail. The seminal work in this respect was *Obshchinnoe zemlevladenie* (*Communal Land Tenure*), the doctoral dissertation of Aleksandr Posnikov, published in 1876–7. Endeavouring to dispute the supposed technological superiority of private landholding, Posnikov showed with copious documentation that improvements in England and Germany had not, as was commonly thought, been introduced by owners, but by long-term lessees or the state. The fact that the members of the commune did not possess title to their land could not, then, in itself discourage them from making improvements, and if they were guaranteed the use of their plots for a reasonable period they would be expected to show as much initiative as the English lessee. Communal land tenure, moreover, with its 'collective spirit', would permit large-scale undertakings, like the drying of bogs, which were beyond the capabilities of private owners.[2] Other studies supported Posnikov's position

---

[1] Isaac A. Hourwich, *The Economics of the Russian Village* (New York, 1892), pp. 12–17; V. P. Vorontsov (V.V.), 'Nekrolog — V. I. Orlov', *Vestnik Evropy*, no. 20 (November 1885), *passim*; 'V. I. Orlov', *Russkii biograficheskii slovar*, XII, 342–3.   [2] A. Posnikov, *Obshchinnoe zemlevladenie* (Odessa, 1878), *passim*.

by exposing the ruinous effects of private landholding within the empire, thereby absolving the commune of responsibility for the peasants' wretched economic state. Lev Kotelianskii's *'Ocherki podvornoi Rossii'* ('Studies of Private Land Ownership in Russia') documented the misery and social disintegration in the Ukraine, where communal traditions were weak and in some regions absent. Describing the increasing inequality and class stratification, it disclosed the swift and inevitable growth of a landless proletariat. As the population increased, plots were fragmented into strips too small to support rational agricultural practices, and the owners were left helpless and impoverished.[1]

If they had adopted the system of communal land tenure, then land and income would be distributed equally among all. The inevitable and sizable deficit would necessarily be covered by outside earnings. Of course, even then, peasant agriculture would not flourish: the shortage of land and cattle, the absence of meadows would affect it extremely unfavourably. But we still would not be made witness to such pathological signs as yearly ploughing of land without fallow and the abandonment of the land in areas where agriculture is the only available occupation. The exhaustion of the soil, also, would not have reached the serious extent that local proprietors tell of.[2]

Individuals and organizations launched investigations to explore the nature of communal life in Russia and to highlight its positive features. Posnikov appended a plan for the study of the commune to the second volume of his *Obshchinnoe zemlevladenie*, published in 1877. In 1878 the noted ethnographer, Petr Efimenko, published a well received project in the journal *Slovo* (*The Word*), which served as a model for a part of a questionnaire that members of Land and Freedom were supposed to complete. Independent studies were begun by such eminent scholars as F. L. Barykov, E. I. Iakushkin, and V. Trirogov, and Vasilii Orlov began his examination of communal institutions in Moscow province. In 1877 both the Imperial Geographic Society and the Imperial Free Economic Society announced that they were contemplating major surveys of communal life; shortly thereafter the two agreed to collaborate.[3] The sudden urge to collect data on the commune

---

[1] L. Kotelianskii, 'Ocherki podvornoi Rossii', *Otechestvennye Zapiski*, no. 240 (September 1878), p. 48.   [2] *Ibid.* p. 49.
[3] A. N. Pypin, *Istoriia russkoi etnografii* (St Petersburg, 1891), II, 334 n.

was explained in the provisional programme of the Imperial Geographic Society by the need to base opinion on concrete truth. Conceptions of rural life, it stated,

> are founded on insufficient materials of a precise nature, or a few facts, assembled unsystematically and poorly related to the aggregate of rural conditions; or they are founded on conceptions and theories borrowed from the economic teachings of Western Europe, applied, without critical verification, to situations in our life that are in essence distinct from those in the West.[1]

The authors of the programme took no pains to conceal their confidence that the facts collected would substantiate their *narodnik* belief. The opening lines announced the premises of their investigations. 'Russia presents basic differences from Western European states, which developed under conditions of Roman Law and Feudalism.' The two chief differences were 'the preponderance of state and public peasant landholding over individual' and the 'preponderance in peasant landholding of the communal form or *mir*'.[2]

The countryside that awaited the *intelligent*'s scrutiny at the end of the seventies was the scene of widespread social breakdown and impoverishment. The economic change and the spread of a money economy, which had begun long before the emancipation, now accelerated, and the peasant, deprived of his master's tutelage, found himself at the mercy of forces beyond his control and comprehension. With serfdom abolished, the cohesive element in agricultural production disappeared and the immemorial ways of tilling the land, particularly the three-field system, lost their support in the social structure and began to pass out of existence. In many areas the peasants desperately farmed their land to exhaustion, forcing out of it what they could, and famines began to assume a greater magnitude and to last longer than ever before. In the chaotic struggle for survival that ensued, old ways of thought and old institutions afforded little assistance or comfort. The ideals and aspirations in which the intelligentsia saw so vital and creative a force, proved no more than hollow formulas used to disguise inhumanity no less sordid and deplorable than that which appeared in the cities. The large peasant family, taken by many as a model of human

---

[1] Imperatorskoe Geograficheskoe Obshchestvo, 'Opyt programmy izsledovaniia pozemel'noi obshchiny', *Otechestvennye Zapiski*, no. 239 (August 1878), p. 332.

[2] *Ibid.* p. 331.

co-habitation and co-operation, lost some of its hold on the population and in many areas began to break up. The peasant commune, though maintained by state fiat, also felt the new pressures. Equality of the members became even more of a fiction than it had been before, and communal institutions turned into weapons that the strong could use to victimize the weak. The intelligentsia and peasantry of the seventies had in common not an allegiance to a particular set of ideals, or a particular way of life, but a similar feeling of confusion and disorientation—a common loss of the values of the past and doubt as to what the future would bring.

The powerful absorption of the Russian intelligentsia with the peasantry in the second half of the 1870s was the culmination of a psychological dynamic at work since the first intimations of reform broke the accustomed placidity of Russian life. It was the expression of a state of mind with roots deep in the social and political malaise of the period. The allure the peasants held is thus not to be explained merely by the strategic service they could render the intelligentsia at a particular moment or by the particular institutions they possessed that were amenable to the intelligentsia's designs. For the individual cut off from the tight bonds of Russian society and family, the alliance with the peasant had far more than mere political significance. It was a psychological necessity that gave him the emotional strength to assert his independence of his rejected childhood self. It afforded him a mature identity he could respect and enabled him to conquer the anxiety and doubt attendant upon his renunciation of his old attitudes, feelings, and character traits. It blotted out the consciousness of the enormous gulf in his personality between what he was and what he wished to be.

When the image of the peasant fell into doubt, it was this consciousness that returned to torment the *intelligent*. The investigation of the countryside at the close of the seventies and beginning of the eighties disclosed a bewildering world which sometimes won the intelligentsia's admiration and sometimes did not, but which, in either case, corresponded little with the generally held notions of rural life. Those who made a serious effort to study and describe the peasantry found little of what they had expected and met with unanticipated difficulties in trying to establish rapport with them. The illusion of a con-

genial reality, which had comforted the *intelligent* in his isolation
and helplessness, then began to dissolve. The props of his mature
identity fell away and in many cases there ensued a recurrence
of the repressed fears of his early life and a desperate reversion
to childhood and adolescent defences that could preserve his
essential self-respect. The crisis of the movement became the
crisis of its members as the failure of the general outlook destroyed the bases of the individual's faith in himself. Each
began to drift away from the mainstream of populist feelings
and to isolate himself in a search for personal consolation.

The three figures treated in the subsequent chapters,
Aleksandr Nikolaevich Engel'gardt, Gleb Ivanovich Uspenskii,
and Nikolai Nikolaevich Zlatovratskii, were the first to depict
and to analyse peasant life with the preconceptions and sentiments that had grown up during the sixties and the seventies.
Writing primarily in *Otechestvennye Zapiski*, they described the
countryside in rich detail and bared the extent and the nature
of the economic and social change that the members of the
intelligentsia had previously only dimly appreciated. The effect
of their revelations on their contemporaries' conception of the
peasantry was deep and far-reaching. What they wrote shattered
the simple faith of the era and made it clear that the countryside was a realm of untold complexity, whole areas of which
were unknown or incomprehensible to the intelligentsia. Never
again could reality be regarded with as little heed to fact.
Their findings and their reactions provided objective grounds
for discussions of the problem of the peasantry and abundant
materials for later radical treatment of the countryside.

Their writings, however, did not merely present a picture of
rural life of the time. They also described the implications of
what had been discovered for the authors themselves and
revealed the inner turmoil that each experienced. Engel'gardt,
Uspenskii, and Zlatovratskii were not thinkers, whose ideas
exerted an important influence on contemporaries and pos-
terity. It is their experience and not their thought that merits
interest. Like most members of the intelligentsia, they were
men who lived by ideas conceived by others, and their stark
personal histories give insights into the populist mind which are
present in few other documents of the period. Each of them
grew up wedded to the ethos of change, and each, in his own
way and for his own reasons, sought in the peasantry what was

lacking in himself and in civilized society. All three found the stability of their lives threatened when they encountered a reality that did not reflect their ideals. Engel'gardt's writings give only a bare outline of his crisis, but both Uspenskii's and Zlatovratskii's describe vividly the reliving of their early conflicts and the resort to defences used in childhood and adolescence. Each struggled to restore his psychological equilibrium by reconciling reality with his ideal. In doing so each followed his own personal byway and sought a solution that answered his particular emotional needs.

Engel'gardt, a nobleman, teacher, and scientist, was not a radical and never espoused the *narodnik* cause. But his social ideals and hopes of self-fulfilment gave rise to an involvement with the peasantry no less impassioned than that of the *narodniki*, and made his experience on his estate pertinent for the intelligentsia as a whole. Uspenskii and Zlatovratskii were both *raznochintsy* writers whose fathers had left the rural clergy to take minor posts in the bureaucracy. But if their social origins were alike, their psychologies, and consequently their conceptions of the peasantry, differed strikingly. All three depicted their experience with unflinching honesty. However modest their literary gifts, they were guilty of neither reticence nor deceit in portraying their personal feelings and the blows that their ideals were sustaining from a hostile reality. Their candour illuminates the agony of the breakdown of an ideology.

ALEKSANDR NIKOLAEVICH ENGEL'GARDT AND THE ARTIFICIAL RECONCILIATION

A sad fate befell A. N. Engel'gardt's chemistry library, however. After his exile, the library lay in boxes for several years. Then my mother brought it to her apartment, and set the books out on the shelves along all the walls. On the very morning that she intended to insure it, a fire broke out underneath our apartment. Various means were used to extinguish it, and smoke filled the top floor. We just managed to escape with a few valuables when the firemen appeared, enthusiastically poured water over the books, and turned everything into *kasha*. But there was no danger at all and the books didn't even burn. There was just a great deal of smoke. However that may be, the library perished and only a few pitiful remnants remain.

There is some evil force in Russian life that conscientiously destroys all that is good and one way or another ruins the fruit of labour and talent.

NIKOLAI ALEKSANDROVICH ENGEL'GARDT

In the May 1872 issue of *Otechestvennye Zapiski* there appeared a letter entitled 'From the Countryside' ('*Iz derevni*'), by the distinguished Russian agronomist and erstwhile rector of the St Petersburg Agricultural Institute, Aleksandr Nikolaevich Engel'gardt. Its vivid tableaux of estate and village life immediately caught the attention of the intelligentsia.

Everyone noticed it. Some agreed with it, others didn't, but everyone read it. It excited everyone, as used to happen with a work above the common run. We awaited the next 'Letter from the Countryside', but it did not appear until the next year. From this time on for eleven years, in one of the last issues of *Otechestvennye Zapiski* for the year, a 'Letter from the Countryside' usually appeared and with it the reading of the issue customarily began.[1]

Engel'gardt's 'letters' told of his striving for a new, honourable identity, purified of the traits of the Russian nobleman and estate owner. The countryside in his depiction was not merely a set of economic and social relationships; it was the

---

[1] N. Engel'gardt, 'Davnye epizody', *Istoricheskii Vestnik*, no. 124 (April 1911), p. 57 n.

scene of his struggle to define himself, and the life he described came alive with human emotion and meaning. He groped for a new ethical way to live and new humane attitudes, and the crops he raised, the peasants he met, the organization of his estate, all became integrally involved in the drama of his personal quest.

Engel'gardt's quest had begun in the 1850s, when, as a youth, he rejected the example of his father, a conscientious Smolensk landlord, and came to Petersburg to pursue the study of science. His successes as a chemist and agronomist were swift and formidable, but science signified far more to him than laboratory research and learned articles. In the fifties and sixties it held out hopes of personal liberation to the youth, and Engel'gardt saw in it a new, higher calling that would enable him to escape from his gentry heritage and to participate in the transformation of Russian life.[1] Science, he believed, could help him and other young intellectuals sever their links with the past and join the forces of the future awakening in the peasantry. The faith in science and the peasantry endowed him with a powerful sense of mission and convinced him of his role in Russian life. Previously, scientists had been outcasts with no function in society, he wrote in 1863, men who 'withered like plants in a hothouse, without bearing fruit', turning into functionaries or landlords. But now they could find allies in the peasants, who, freed from bondage, were also seeking the new world. 'Our young people have been attending to the needs of society', he wrote, 'and have discovered a way out of their plight: that is the spreading of science to the masses.'[2]

Engel'gardt actively promoted the cause of scientific enlightenment. In addition to writing popular articles on agronomy, he helped to found the first Russian chemistry journal and the first Russian public chemistry laboratory.[3] In 1863, when he returned to Smolensk province for the first time in

---

[1] 'Aleksandr Nikolaevich Engel'gardt', *Russkii biograficheskii slovar'*, XXI, 241–2; N. Engel'gardt, 'Aleksandr Nikolaevich Engel'gardt i Batishchevskoe delo', in Aleksandr Nikolaevich Engelgardt, *Iz derevni: 12 pisem* (St Petersburg, 1897), pp. 3–4; N. Engel'gardt, 'Davnye epizody', *Istoricheskii Vestnik*, no. 119 (February 1910), pp. 540–1.

[2] A. N. Engel'gardt, 'Liebig v russkom perevode', *Sankt-Peterburgskie Vedomosti*, no. 272 (6 December 1863), p. 1105.

[3] N. Engel'gardt, 'Aleksandr Nikolaevich Engel'gardt i Batishchevskoe delo', pp. 3–4; *Russkii biograficheskii slovar'*, XXI, 242.

fifteen years, his published impressions revealed his trust in the power of science to remedy the ills bequeathed by the old system. He saw the landlords' estates in ruin. Their homes were dilapidated, their fields desolate, their orchards neglected. Deprived of the free labour resources of serfdom, he explained, they had proved incapable of operating their estates.[1] The peasants, meanwhile, seemed to be using their knowledge and capital to good effect. They were working hard clearing over-grown areas. 'In a few years,' he predicted, 'peasant plots will be all field and meadow.'[2] Signs of peasant prosperity struck him everywhere. No longer were they concealing their wealth. They built better homes, 'not huts with holes instead of chim-neys, not huts without ovens, but clean, bright huts'. They ate better bread, wore better boots, and fitted their horses with better harness.[3] The intelligentsia, Engel'gardt believed, should help the peasants to continue to improve their lives and methods of farming. He hoped that the educated would go to the country-side 'to work the now desolate land, and use their experience to show the peasants the means there are at hand to raise the productivity of the land and make its cultivation easier'. He envisioned the time when 'in place of barren fields you will see rich farms run by men conversant with the science of agri-culture'.[4]

Engel'gardt evoked a congenial peasant life which he con-trasted with the stale, effete atmosphere of the capital. In Peters-burg, he wrote, 'they argue, they scream, they are carried away to the skies and there is no sense in any of it'. In the com-mune he discerned 'an absence of formalism', 'an order in debates', 'a swiftness of decision', 'a complete absence of vanity and pride'.[5] The youth could find their calling and deliverance in the countryside.

In Petersburg, young people are living in poverty; day and night they sit over proofs, articles, papers, and all simply to subsist—to breathe vile air and eat rotten provisions. Meanwhile people are needed in the countryside and there are none. Teachers, doctors, midwives, estate managers, female supervisors, agronomists, trades-men are needed.

Whoever can live in an *izba* and be satisfied with one or two simple

---

[1] A. N. Engel'gardt, *Iz derevni: 12 pisem* (St Petersburg, 1897), pp. 657–8.
[2] *Ibid.* p. 657.   [3] *Ibid.* pp. 656, 659.
[4] *Ibid.* pp. 660, 663.   [5] *Ibid.* p. 672.

foods; whoever doesn't need a servant, coachman, theatres or operas needs little money in the countryside. But things to do! How many things there are to do there![1]

But like most members of the intelligentsia of the sixties, Engel'gardt did not allow his affinity for the peasant to distract him from his scientific pursuits, or the ordinary course of his life. His researches on mineral fertilizers won him new prestige and he succeeded to the chair of chemistry at St Petersburg Agricultural Institute and then to the position of rector. He attended the theatre and opera, rode in a carriage, wore fashionable and expensive clothing, and dined at elegant restaurants.[2] The cost of such pleasures, coupled with the maintenance of a wife and two children, exceeded his yearly salary of 3,000 rubles. He drew what he could from his large, unproductive estate of Batishchevo, but this was insufficient and he sank ever deeper into debt.[3]

By the beginning of the seventies, Engel'gardt had begun to become uneasy with the life he had created for himself in the capital. He found himself surrounded by the civilized comforts he had hoped to transcend. Successful as his researches and teaching were, they had brought a new humanity and a new society no closer. The news of famines in the countryside, particularly in his native Smolensk province in 1867–8, sobered him to the true condition of rural life and dispelled his simple faith in progress. His sense of mission seemed unfulfilled, and he seemed, despite his efforts, to be living the proper and superficial life of an educated nobleman.

In 1870 the tranquillity of Engel'gardt's life was suddenly shattered. As rector, he had imprudently condoned and even attended student meetings, thus provoking the suspicions of the authorities. Though it is unlikely that he was guilty of indiscretions, the government, frightened by the political ferment of the time, was wary of any leniency in high places. An informer's report, accusing him of 'trying to instill the ideas of socialism and revolution in the students' led to his arrest and imprisonment. After several months of confinement, he was convicted of spreading 'immoral and democratic ideas' and banished

[1] A. N. Engel'gardt, *Iz derevni: 12 pisem* (St Petersburg, 1897), p. 691.
[2] A. N. Engel'gardt, *Iz derevni: 12 pisem* (Moscow, 1956), p. 135.
[3] Engel'gardt Archive, Pushkinskii Dom, Leningrad, 577/46, p. 1.

from Petersburg and all other university cities, a sentence destined to remain in force for over twenty years.[1]

Engel'gardt's exile came not as a misfortune but as a welcome opportunity to escape the burden of civilized life and to meet the natural stratum of Russian reality. He refused invitations to live on the estates of wealthy friends and relatives where he could have continued his scientific researches. Instead, he went in pursuit of his past—to the very estate of Batishchevo which had fed his extravagance.[2] There, at the age of 39, he hoped to take leave of his old self.

On a raw January day in 1871, seen off by his wife and children, who were remaining in Petersburg, and a few friends and relatives, he boarded the train for Smolensk. Clad warmly in a heavy German suit, a fur coat and cap, a scarf. and tall felt boots, he sat in the unheated, lower-class car. As the train pulled away, he found that no matter how tightly he bundled himself, the thirty-degree-below-zero cold pierced through. When he breathed, the air cut his throat and his body quivered with fever. Finally, unable to endure it any longer, he paid the difference and moved into the first-class car.[3] But there psychological suffering replaced the physical. He had failed his first test, and the bleak northern countryside passing by the windows of the train began to appear alien and forbidding.

You look through the window of the car at where you are supposed to live and work and all you see is snow, snow, and more snow. Everything was covered with snow, frozen, and had there been no smoke arising from the huts covered with snow that flashed by the window then you would think you were crossing an uninhabited tundra. I looked at the little huts and I wondered how people lived in them, how I was to live, what I was to do, how I was to farm, if from the first day I already felt that I lacked the strength to bear the dreadful cold. This thought was so bitter that I fell into a depression and felt that the energy with which I had left Petersburg was abandoning me.[4]

An even more disturbing sight, however, confronted him when he reached Batishchevo. His patrimonial estate lay in ruin. His prodigality and indifference to real life were embodied

---

[1] P. Nechuiatov, *Aleksandr Nikolaevich Engel'gardt* (Smolensk, 1957), p. 33; N. Engel'gardt, 'Davnye epizody', *Istoricheskii Vestnik*, no. 119 (February 1910), pp. 535–9.

[2] A. N. Engel'gardt, *Iz derevni: 12 pisem* (Moscow, 1956), p. 137.

[3] *Ibid.* pp. 137–9.   [4] *Ibid.* p. 138.

before him in a scene of utter waste and desolation. Buildings were in shambles, fertile fields overgrown. Only one third of the land that had been farmed before emancipation was in use. The rest was covered with brush, as were the 400 *desiatiny* that had never been cultivated. More than five sixths of the estate was 'neglected, abandoned, sown with arborial seed, overgrown with birchwood'. The meadows were producing only one third of their former yield of hay, and this was of such low quality that, although the cattle ate sufficient quantities, they had become weak and emaciated and produced inadequate dung for fertilizer.[1] The inventory was also in wretched condition. The sheds were without roofs and doors. There were no troughs, and the straw and chaff lay scattered carelessly on the ground. Nowhere on the estate could a plough be found. The ponds dug by his father for irrigation had dried up and were also overgrown with brush.[2] The destruction he had wrought was terrible for him to behold and his labours for the cause of science seemed frivolous and nugatory. The nature of rural reality appeared unrelated to civilized learning.

In Petersburg, I was at the very source of agronomy in Russia: I, myself a professor of chemistry, was continually in the society of professors and agronomists who were studying all the fine points of foreign agronomical science. I read agronomical journals which compiled the very latest investigations of famous agronomists abroad. I attended the meetings of learned agronomical societies where the finest problems of agronomy were debated; where it was argued whether we should raise the Alkhaus or Dutch varieties of cattle; where we discoursed on what kind of ploughs must be used to cultivate our land and what kind of machines to reap our grain; we held forth on superphosphate and nitrate fertilizers... I myself sinned in elaborating on similar problems... And suddenly I find myself in the country in, so to say, the essence of the agricultural problem. And what do I see?[3]

The landscape of ruin stretched across the entire province. Riding through the countryside, he saw that the cultivated area had shrunk since 1863, that much less feed was being produced, and that the number of cattle had fallen off sharply.

[1] A. N. Engel'gardt, *O khoziastve v severnoi Rossii i primenenii v nem fosforitov* (St Petersburg, 1888), pp. i–iii; A. N. Engel'gardt, 'Iz istorii moego khoziastva', *Otechestvennye Zapiski*, no. 224 (January 1876), p. 99.

[2] A. N. Engel'gardt, 'Iz istorii moego khoziaistva', no. 224, pp. 88, 95–6.

[3] *Ibid.* pp, 87–8.

Riding through the district and seeing the ubiquitous desolation and destruction, one might think there had been a war, the invasion of an enemy, had it not been evident that the destruction was not violent but gradual, that everything was going to destruction of its own accord, vanishing from starvation. Under serfdom we succeeded in accomplishing nothing in regard to agriculture, and so from serfdom little has remained.[1]

The prosperity among the peasants that he had observed in 1863 had vanished without trace, and the local population was suffering in helpless poverty. Left without a source of employment by the nobles' flight to the city, many were forced to abandon the land.

The landlords do not run their estates. They forsake them and won't live on them. What is left for the peasant to do? There is no work near home. He can only leave his plot and go for work to the city, where the landlords have flocked to enter state service, and this the peasants have done.[2]

Engel'gardt witnessed the peasants' life during their most trying period of the year, the winter, the time when the members of 'society' were enjoying their most active social season. Having sold much of their grain in the fall to pay their debts, the peasants now watched their supplies dwindle. The price of bread was high, and few, in any case, had money. Many wandered through the countryside begging handouts. The summer of 1870 had been one of crop failure, and Engel'gardt was confronted with stark and disquieting scenes of hunger.

This year not only children, women, old people, lads and lasses went out begging, but many heads of households themselves. There is nothing to eat at home—do you understand that? Today, they ate the last loaf, from which pieces were being given to beggars. They ate it and set forth into the world. There is no bread. There is no work. Everyone would be glad to work, if only for bread, but there is no work.[3]

In the spring a fresh crop would rise, but, Engel'gardt knew, this would not help the peasants to improve their condition. They would squander their money at the mill for vodka, and after the exactions of the tax collector little would remain. Since work was difficulty to find and pay was low, the peasants were

[1] A. N. Engel'gardt, *Iz derevni: 12 pisem* (Moscow, 1956), p. 112.
[2] *Ibid.* pp. 40–1.   [3] *Ibid.* p. 31.

inevitably compelled to sell their animals, which deprived them of manure and hastened the exhaustion of their land. 'A poor harvest is bad, a good harvest is also bad,' Engel'gardt concluded.[1]

Engel'gardt watched his herdsman Petr, who, besides caring for his own plot, looked after Engel'gardt's cattle day and night, yet barely secured subsistence. He knew that most of the other peasants were living in even worse conditions than Petr and would have gladly stepped into his position.[2] Confronted with scenes of genuine human suffering, Engel'gardt felt the hollowness and hypocrisy of his statements of humanity. Tormented by the consciousness of his own complicity in the impoverishment of the peasantry, he comprehended the vicious deception that had shielded him from his guilt.

It seems that 'obrok' is true income, the same as any salary. But it seems this way only in Petersburg. There, in Petersburg, when you have finished working the month, whether poorly or well, you go off to the treasury and receive your payment. Where this money comes from, how it got into the treasury, you don't know, and it is serenely stashed away in your pocket, particularly since you believe that you merited it, that you earned it. Here it is not that way at all. Take, if you please, your 'obrok' from a person who eats chaff bread (pushnoi khleb) and takes his morsel of pure rye bread into the house for the children... And remember that you can no longer delude yourself by thinking that you merited, that you earned this money.[3]

The peasants' suffering, in Engel'gardt's eyes, was merely a symptom of the general malady of the gentry character. The landlord could prosper only when the peasants were at his mercy. He stood to gain when the price of the grain the peasants bought from him rose and when the wages he paid them fell. 'Every landlord, every steward will tell you that if the peasants were not impoverished, he could not continue farming.' Engel'gardt concluded that he could not help the peasants until he had extirpated all traces of his gentry heritage and learned to farm without exploitation. He vowed to build an estate that would benefit the peasants rather than prey upon them. This would show them the advantages of scientific methods and would yield high wages to those who worked it. He envisioned it as a prototype for similar endeavours across Russia and himself as a model for a class of men who, fortified with knowledge

---

[1] Ibid. pp. 99–100.   [2] Ibid. pp. 25–26.   [3] Ibid. p. 24.

and skill, would cultivate the land not for profit but to improve Russian agriculture.[1] When Mikhail Saltykov-Shchedrin invited him to write for *Otechestvennye Zapiski* in March 1871, Engel'gardt seized the opportunity to publicize his experience and win adherents for his new kind of agriculture.

His letters told of his attempts to overthrow his gentry parasitism and begin a life of devotion to the task of agricultural improvement. Striving to reduce personal expenses and increase his investment in the estate, he divested himself of his extravagant genteel tastes. He renounced the comforts of civilization and tried to imitate the peasants' simple way of life. He kept no cook or coachman, making do with only two helpers, his peasant supervisor (*starosta*), Ivan, and the latter's wife, Avdot'ia, who cared for the house and the animals. He let his hair grow long, discarded his Petersburg clothes and dressed in simple attire: a bright red flannel shirt, peasant pantaloons (*shariovary*), and in winter a peasant sheepskin (*polushubok*). He ate a coarse diet of *shchi*, *kasha*, and bread. Meat and milk were served only on rare occasions.[2]

He learned to rely for guidance in running his estate on the peasants' advice and on his own common sense. He quickly abjured books on agriculture, which, he concluded, displayed 'a complete absence of practical knowledge, an oxen flabbiness, as if they were written by castrates'.[3] The peasants, unencumbered by learning and cerebration, provided him with much useful assistance. He listened attentively to the suggestions of Ivan and Avdot'ia and watched them at work. 'I could teach Avdot'ia nothing about the farm, dairy farming, watering the calves, etc., and I must confess that I have learned much more from her than I have from books.'[4] He spent his evenings presiding over them, like a dean before his *kafedra*, as they recited reports on their daily activity. Avdot'ia would tell the amount of milk produced and describe the health of the cattle. Ivan would discuss the operations of the estate and the plans for the coming day and would relate the rumours current in the village. The talks were long and occupied the empty evening hours.[5]

In addition to practical understanding, Engel'gardt dis-

[1] *Ibid.* pp. 112–13, 136.
[2] N. A. Engel'gardt, 'Batishchevskoe delo', *Knizhki Nedeli*, no. 18 (April 1895), p. 11; A. P. Mertvago, *Ne po tornomu puti* (St Petersburg, 1900), pp. 23–4.
[3] A. N. Engel'gardt, *Iz derevni: 12 pisem* (Moscow, 1956), pp. 88–9.
[4] *Ibid.* p. 22.　　　　　　　　　[5] *Ibid.* p. 35.

cerned in the peasants a high moral sense that had evolved in the healthy rural surroundings. Drunkenness in its degenerate forms was much rarer among the peasantry than among the urban population. 'Such drunkards as we meet among factory workers, house-servants, retired soldiers, clerks, *chinovniki* and landlords, who go to drink and dissipate to the last degree, are rarely found among peasants, people at work in the open air.'[1] Although the privileged classes were convinced of the peasants' dishonesty, Engel'gardt had heard of no incident of peasant theft, and all who owed him money paid their debts promptly. The peasants were naturally industrious and if they did not work hard it was due to the indifferent attitude of their absentee employer. Often they did such work as flax-pounding and road-mending without pay, just 'for honour'. In contrast Petersburg functionaries worked from two until five in the afternoon and during these hours did all they could to shirk their obligations.[2]

Despite the natural infertility of the Smolensk land, Engel'-gardt's self-denial and application of rational techniques yielded results. By selling part of his forest, he acquired the means to purchase better cattle and high-quality feed. He cleared over-grown areas and planted flax, rye, and soil-replenishing grasses on them in a complex fifteen-crop rotation.[3] After his first year of farming, the yield of rye and oats doubled, and of flax quin-tupled. Wheat, which had not previously been raised at Batish-chevo, was harvested in large quantities.[4] Moreover, he was elated to see that the neighbouring peasantry were renting overgrown lands, clearing them, and planting rye and flax in imitation of his method. Their results were excellent, and many who had previously been destitute began to prosper. Only the landlords were ignoring his innovations; they were 'sitting and admiring their birch trees'.[5]

But the successes of Engel'gardt's system won little approval from the members of the intelligentsia in the capital. In their eyes, his practice of farming with hired labour was exploitation, whether it produced poor or good results. His successes, indeed, were taken by them as proof of the severity of his exploitative practices. D. A. Klements, writing in the April 1878 number

[1] *Ibid.* p. 42.   [2] *Ibid.* pp. 119, 59–67.
[3] A. N. Engel'gardt, *O khoziastve v severnoi Rossii...*, pp. iii–iv.
[4] A. N. Engel'gardt, *Iz derevni: 12 pisem* (Moscow, 1956), p. 136.
[5] *Ibid.* p. 195.

of the journal *Slovo* (*The Word*), pointed out the dependence of Engel'gardt's estate on exploitable peasant labour and asserted that his successes could only occur where the peasant was in need and would accept niggardly wages. 'To act like Engel'-gardt', he wrote, 'intelligence, knowledge, character are necessary, but chiefly one must make one's goal the acquisition of bourgeois profit.'[1] A month later Iosef Kablits (Iuzov), writing in the newspaper *Nedelia* (*The Week*), claimed that Engel'gardt had achieved his brilliant results 'with the aid of science and of *batrak labour*' [*batrak*: a landless farm worker]. He denounced Engel'gardt for forsaking his obligation to work for the welfare of the people and accused him of not attending to the dictates of his conscience.[2] The following year, Petre Tkachev, in *Delo* (*The Cause*), characterized Engel'gardt derisively as 'our famous "farmer" exploiting labour power by the most modern and rational methods'.[3]

The hostile reaction shattered Engel'gardt's rationale. The amelioration of the peasants' condition would merely deprive him of a source of labour, he realized; like all gentry estates, his was dependent upon the poverty of those who worked it. His gentry ancestry lay like a curse on all his acts, forcing him, against his will, to prey upon the peasantry. In 1871 the peasants searching for morsels of bread appeared to be victims of defective agricultural techniques and faulty management; by 1878 the social system of which he was a part seemed to be at fault. His confidence faltered, and, watching his peasants toil, he was again afflicted with pangs of guilt.

It was a joy to look upon the luxuriant clover growing in the fields of Batishchevo, but the joy was poisoned when I saw the peasant obliged to cut the clover for money he would receive in the winter when he had no bread. I admired the fat cows that gave me a pail of milk apiece. But, at the same time, it was painful for me to think of the bitter fate of the milk-maid milking the cow...It is very painful to live by exploitation, when in your exploitation you come into direct contact with the exploited, when every day and every hour you must do violence to yourself.[4]

[1] D. A. Klements (Toporin), 'Iz russkoi zhurnal'noi letopisi', *Slovo*, no. 1 (April 1878), part 2, p. 138.

[2] I. Kablits (Iuzov), 'Publitsisty Otechestvennykh Zapisok', *Nedelia*, no. 13 (May 1878), p. 600.

[3] P. Tkachev (Nikitin), 'Muzhik v salonakh sovremennoi belletristiki', *Delo*, no. 13 (August 1879), part II, p. 1.

[4] N. Engel'gardt, 'Aleksandr Nikolaevich Engel'gardt...', p. 51.

All of his strictures on the gentry character, Engel'gardt now understood, applied to himself; all of his projects could be viewed as schemes for self-enrichment. Unknowingly, he had re-enacted the role of his rejected father, having lived by the parasitism he had vowed to exterminate. He could find nothing in himself but the mark of his malignant heritage. With the loss of faith in his own ability to transform himself and society, Engel'gardt searched for the redeeming elements of Russian life in the peasantry. In their communal production and in their collectivistic family life, Engel'gardt sought the justice and fraternity lacking in his own past. His identification with them turned into total absorption. Like the *narodniki* in the city, he sacrificed his self and tried to live in the experience of the people.

But Engel'gardt's own experience had belied the idealized view of the peasant. Since his arrival in the countryside, he had ruefully watched as the peasants deserted their communal traditions and followed the path of individualism and exploitation. In 1873 he commented that the peasant's desire to live and work apart from his comrades was one of the chief reasons for his poverty. In a village of fourteen households, fourteen ovens were heated and fourteen wives prepared food. 'What an enormous waste of labour, food, materials, etc.!'[1] He saw peasant *artel'* cultivation—work performed in common, with the product often shared equally by the participants—vanishing from the countryside; *artel'* practices appeared to be surviving only in non-agricultural pursuits: crafts, ditch-digging, carriage. In 1874 the commune that had previously mowed his hay in common, with equal distribution of wages, insisted that his fields be divided into hundreds of tiny strips to be worked individually. Despite the obvious inefficiency of this arrangement, Engel'gardt could not induce the members to return to the old procedure. Meanwhile, the strong workers were enriching themselves at the expense of the weak, thus destroying the primitive equality of the commune.

Before, when the neighbouring village cut my hay together, in an *artel'*, all the peasants had enough hay for the winter. Those who had few horses even sold part...But now some have a large quantity of hay, while others have little or none. And if there is no hay there are no horses, and if there are no horses then there is no grain.

[1] A. N. Engel'gardt, *Iz derevni: 12 pisem* (Moscow, 1956), p. 116.

Some are becoming rich, while others, less conscientious and less skilled, are becoming impoverished and are abandoning their land to become agricultural labourers (*batraki*), for whom there is always work, and who are always ready to do another's bidding.[1]

Engel'gardt dwelt nostalgically on the large peasant household. Where such relationships survived, several generations lived together harmoniously, cultivating their large, undivided plot in common without hired labour. The patriarch safeguarded and enforced this benign family tradition with a stern but just authority. 'The more efficient, the more despotic the elder, the stronger morally, the more respected by the commune, the more efficient and prosperous is the household.' But he realized that this institution, too, was passing out of existence. With the elder's death the young peasants were seizing portions of the joint holding and establishing themselves as private proprietors. Large plots were being divided into small, highly inefficient strips, leaving the owners with inadequate equipment and few animals. Many soon found it impossible to maintain their homesteads and abandoned the land to join the swelling class of proletarians.[2]

Engel'gardt longed for a state of innocence to which he could feel spiritually akin and which would endow him with a sense of his own purity and justice. If such a state was but a bygone memory, then his work would come to nothing and he would never be free of the stain of his past. But Engel'gardt refused to accept the breakdown of traditional peasant institutions fatalistically. A scientist by training and temperament, he nurtured a faith in the power of the educated mind to shape the world on a more rational model. If the peasantry was following a course he abhorred and abandoning their communal traditions, then he, by demonstration and example, would teach them the error of their ways. He would reconcile the real and the ideal by artificially creating the ideal. He resolved to build communes which would reveal the great potentialities of collective labour to the peasants and show them how they had gone astray. Disappointed in the peasantry, he chose to create the epitome of his ideal humanity out of young members of the intelligentsia eager to remould themselves as new men. Under his tutelage they would turn themselves into 'educated peasants', a new human type combining the virtues of both groups. In them—his

[1] *Ibid.* p. 188.　　　　[2] *Ibid.* pp. 266–70.

children—he now sought his liberation and his immortality. 'When I die everything will go to pieces, if my children don't go over to a *new form* of agriculture, if they don't become *farmers* themselves, if they are unable to form a *village of intelligenty*, working on the *artel'* principle.'[1] It was with this in mind that Engel'gardt founded his famous 'practical academy' at Batishchevo to train the youth in rural life. At the end of 1878 he urged them to come to him to learn the skills that would transform them into true peasants.

You must develop in yourselves such qualities that you will be able to get along without the peasant. You must acquire peasant legs, arms, eyes and ears. You must develop yourself so that a peasant proprietor will agree to hire you as a *batrak* [landless labourer] and pay you the same wages as he pays a peasant *batrak*.[2]

Having learned to support himself by his own labour, the *intelligent* then could pursue his special talent on the side. He could live close to the peasants and better their lot. 'There must be *peasant mechanics, peasant engineers, peasant architects*, i.e., intelligent men able to work for the peasant.' 'The *intelligent* must not reduce the peasant to bondage, but must serve him; he must not alienate him, but must live with him, with one life and one thought.'[3] But most important, some would master the communal qualities of the peasant. Such *intelligenty*, working together harmoniously, could present the peasant with a glimpse of a perfected collectivistic life. They could emulate peasants and become superior peasants, so that the peasants could emulate them.

How much good could be done by intelligent people who wish to work at farming, settle in villages and form such *arteli* among themselves! Having learned to work, and without this nothing will come of it, they could form *arteli* for the renting of estates, and what a splendid example these *artel'* farms of civilized people would be for the peasants![4]

Engel'gardt entertained no hopes or intentions of undergoing this transformation himself. He felt himself too old, too wedded to his gentry way of life to take on the arduous existence of a manual worker. 'He would not, himself, work behind the

---

[1] *Ibid.* p. 313.   [2] *Ibid.* p. 307.
[3] N. A. Engel'gardt, 'Batishchevskoe delo' (April 1895), pp. 22–4.
[4] A. N. Engel'gardt, *Iz derevni: 12 pisem* (Moscow, 1956), p. 307.

plough,' his son Nikolai wrote. 'He continued as before to be the lord (*barin*).'[1] But he saw himself not as the *barin*, but as the patriarch, the father of the new era wielding authority in the name of a new kind of common life. Like the family elder, he would impose the discipline necessary to curb the individual appetites of the members and instil the selflessness and toughness necessary to cope with the onerous work and to live in harmonious cooperation. He promised prospective students in his academy a hard, bleak apprenticeship, with few moments of relief or pleasure, a regimen calculated to discourage all but the most zealous aspirants. They were to toil along with the farm workers, under the direction of the peasant *starosta*, executing whatever tasks they were assigned. Specialization was forbidden: all students were to learn to discharge all farm tasks, thus freeing themselves forever from reliance upon outside, hired labour. They were to live with the peasant workers in a common hut, sleep on hard benches, and address each other only with first names and in the familiar form *ty*, as was the practice among the peasants. They were to eat peasant food: rye bread, *shchi* or *borshch*, *kasha*, milk products (usually only cottage cheese) only in July, tea only on Sundays and holidays, and no beef during the summer. They would work without pay until they had acquired rudimentary farm skills and then would receive only token wages. When they had attained the peasant's competence, they would be paid the full peasant wage.[2] Engel'gardt warned prospective students that he would tolerate no *balovstvo*—indulgence, frivolity, fooling around—and his definition of *balovstvo* was a broad one. 'Tell your friends,' he wrote, 'that I consider the drinking of tea and milk an indulgence (*balovstvo*), and that I find this kind of indulgence disgusting. Tell them that I myself live more than modestly.'[3] But he believed that the ordinary member of the intelligentsia could meet his demands.

I am convinced—experience has convinced me—that with a sincere desire to become an agricultural worker, with unstinting work any healthy, strong, agile, half-way intelligent person from the intelligentsia can acquire the qualities of an average worker in two years.

[1] N. Engel'gardt, 'Bukovskii intelligentny poselok', *Novoe slovo*, no. 1 (April 1895), 2, p. 23.
[2] N. Engel'gardt, 'Aleksandr Nikolaevich Engel'gardt...', pp. 21–2.
[3] Mertvago, pp. 53–5.

If he is especially attentive he can even learn to get along without the peasant, that is, he will have the ability to make himself an axe-handle or rake, to attach a scythe or *sokha*, to take care of the cattle, break in the horses, even build himself a hut.[1]

Many youths, eager to learn about the countryside and to be near the peasantry, responded to Engel'gardt's invitation. The *narodnik* ideas of Natanson and Land and Freedom had impressed them with their incomprehension of the countryside, and physical labour seemed one way of overcoming the gap separating them from the peasantry. Several groups of Land and Freedom had worked with peasants in Rostov and Khar'kov provinces in 1876; but, before they had established themselves among the local population, fear of the police had forced them to disperse.[2] Engel'gardt's 'academy' offered a unique opportunity to be schooled in rural life for those who yearned to live among the peasants but had been estranged from them by their upbringing. Semen Vasiukov, a young *raznochinets* who had participated in the Chaikovtsy circles of the early seventies, felt this attraction and left the stale atmosphere of the Moscow intelligentsia for the refreshment of physical work and peasant society. He wrote:

Here is a real life, a difficult life, perhaps, but in it there is such freshness, such a powerful tranquillity that it was worth trying and finally, on the spot, deciding your relationship to the peasant. Yes, to be at work with him, and share all the conditions of his life. I am young with broad shoulders and plenty of strength. Won't I be able to take it?[3]

Also drawn to Batishchevo was Pelagea Metelitsyna, the daughter of an Odessa merchant, a member of Land and Freedom and a participant in the Kazan Square demonstration of 1876. Metelitsyna came to work with the peasants and to learn to live without exploiting them. 'You can become an independent farmer', she wrote, 'only when you yourself can do everything that is done on a farm.'[4] Others, like Dubov, a

---

[1] A. N. Engel'gardt, *Iz derevni: 12 pisem* (Moscow, 1956), pp. 307–8.

[2] M. P. Popov, 'Iz moego revoliutsionnogo proshlogo', *Byloe*, no. 1 (May 1905), pp. 278–80.

[3] S. I. Vasiukov, 'Bylye dni i gody', *Istoricheskii vestnik*, no. 113 (August 1908), pp. 469–70.

[4] 'Pelagea Metelitsyna', *Deiateli revoliutsionnovo dvizheniia v Rossii* (Moscow, 1927–34), ii, 919; P. Metelitsyna, 'God v batrachkakh', *Otechestvennye Zapiski*, no. 252 (September 1880), pp. 71–2.

student at St Petersburg University, sought creative work at Batishchevo 'so as not to become the fifth spoke on the wheel'.[1]

The majority of those who came were quickly discouraged and left, often with bitter recriminations.[2] Those who remained, seventy-nine in all, usually did so only for the duration of the summer and harvest season, and returned to the city for the winter. Their introduction to farm work was gradual, but, even for the most successful, the first weeks were painful. They were given simple tasks, called 'warm water', usually consisting of pulling up brush in overgrown areas. They then were graduated to more challenging work such as sowing, ploughing, and milking. The difficulty of labour that they had previously taken for granted crushed their egos. The simplest chores stymied them and sent them reeling from fatigue. But even more exasperating than the physical hardship was the chagrin they felt before the amused peasants, who were baffled by their desire to do physical work and called them, ironically, 'thin-legged ones' (*tonkonogie*). Metelitsyna, who remained for two years and became one of Engel'gardt's ablest students, wrote of her first attempt to milk a cow:

I grabbed the udder and squeezed with all my might, but no milk came, not a drop. Everything within me began to rage, my hands raged too, and the sweat rolled down my face in drops. My head began to spin. 'You're not squeezing strong enough,' the milkmaids around me yelled.[3]

Of his first time behind a plough, Dubov wrote, 'After the second turn around I became terribly tired and lost patience. I did not expect such a trial, and then there was the consciousness that I was simply spoiling the ploughing and someone else would have to do it over. I felt angry and ashamed.'[4]

Their civilized stomachs quaked at the rude peasant food. 'I took a few spoonfuls of the Smolensk *shchi*,' one young *intelligent* wrote, ' and immediately felt full. This is not to say that the *shchi* was revolting. It was simply not pleasant to the taste.' 'Our innards are clearly different,' he concluded, ' and must undergo long training before they can be made to obey'.[5]

---

[1] Dubov, 'Leto sredi sel'skikh rabot', *Otechestvennye Zapiski*, no. 239 (July 1878), p. 5.
[2] Vasiukov, no. 113, p. 477.
[3] Metelitsyna, 'God v batrachkakh', p. 73.
[4] Dubov, p. 20.   [5] Mertvago, p. 28.

Metelitsyna, despite an otherwise ascetic nature, recorded even stronger reactions to the Batishchevo soup.

> They served *shchi*. I didn't know how to go at it. It was very fatty. You couldn't cut through the fat. I made an attempt to get something out from underneath, but it tasted bad and lacked flavour. After the third spoonful, I preferred to eat only bread.[1]

The *intelligenty* also found the peasants' company little to their liking. Despite the few attempts they made to strike up acquaintanceships, the barriers between the two groups remained insuperable. Rather than live with the peasant 'in one life and one thought', they mingled only with their own kind except during work. The peasants resented the presence of the youth, who seemed to threaten them with competition for the available jobs. A peasant girl told Metelitsyna, 'If you become a milk-maid, then the lord will pay you wages. And in your place would have been one of our women.'[2] Engel'gardt resigned himself to the incompatibility between the intelligentsia and peasants and justified the arrangements at Batishchevo as merely a temporary expedient until the *intelligenty* went out to form their own villages.

> It is completely understandable that uniting on one farm workers from the peasantry and the intelligentsia in the same material conditions would be feasible only as a temporary measure. Such a combination is inconvenient and disadvantageous for an operational farm, and is uncomfortable for the *intelligent*, who is accustomed to other conditions of life.[3]

But Engel'gardt was pleased by the performance of most of the youth. Maintaining his professorial bearing, he graded each of his students according to ability to toil. Of the seventy-nine who lasted, fourteen received grades of poor, fifty-one of satisfactory, and fourteen were awarded special certificates vouching that they could work as well as peasants.[4] In 1879 he felt prepared to embark on the creation of the first of the independent *arteli* that he had envisioned. Izot Sychugov, the twenty-five year old son of a rural priest, was the first to accept the challenge. A participant of the 'going to the people' move-

---

[1] Metelitsyna, 'God v batrachkakh,' p. 74.   [2] *Ibid.* p. 77.
[3] N. Engel'gardt, 'Aleksandr Nikolaevich Engel'gardt...', p. 52.
[4] A. I. Faresov, *Semidesiatniki* (St Petersburg, 1905), p. 28; N. Engel'gardt, 'Aleksandr Nikolaevich Engel'gardt...' pp. 23–4.

ment, Sychugov had been arrested in 1874. After his release, he had felt the urge to learn about the peasants and live close to them, and in 1877 he arrived at Batishchevo, where he distinguished himself as a superior worker and received a certificate.[1] Upon leaving, he was offered a lucrative position as an estate manager, but Engel'gardt strongly recommended that he refuse it. 'It would be difficult to think of anything more vile,' he wrote. 'First the dependence on another person; second the obligation to exploit not only the land but labour as well... To use your abilities, your mind and knowledge to exploit people for the good of some merchant—only the devil knows what this is.'[2] Sychugov took Engel'gardt's advice and embarked upon the formation of an *artel'*. He interested another young *intelligent*, Semen (surname unknown), in the project. Semen had not worked at Batishchevo, but he seemed enthusiastic and struck Sychugov as 'good, honourable, and humane'. Together they purchased land in Ufimskaia province and, with Semen's brothers and sisters, set up the *artel'* 'Red Hill'. Being the most experienced of the group, Sychugov assumed the position of head (*bol'shak*) and directed the colony's activities. Their first efforts met with unexpected success. The crops were excellent and during the harvest season all the members worked and cooperated well. But after the exaltation of gathering the grain cooled, the inhabitants of 'Red Hill' found it difficult to live together. Semen resented Sychugov's authority. Sychugov found Semen lazy, incompetent, indifferent to agricultural work, and unfit to engage in a communal undertaking. Having made the deed out in his own name, Semen simply expelled Sychugov, who was left penniless and had to support himself by delivering beer. An observer, who visited 'Red Hill' a few months after its downfall, wrote:

Everything is black and filthy, uncombed, unwashed, and coarse. Everything is in far worse condition than in the homes of respectable peasants...On the faces and in the surroundings there is not a sign of intelligence; on everything are visible signs of apathy towards the world around them and towards each other—vulgar, apathetic attitudes.[3]

[1] 'Izot Sychugov', *Deiateli revoliutsionnogo dvizheniia v Rossii*, II, 1660; Engel'gardt archive, 24/A3.
[2] N. Engel'gardt, 'Aleksandr Nikolaevich Engel'gardt...', p. 28.
[3] *Ibid.* pp. 31–5; N. Engel'gardt, 'Batishchevskoe delo', (May 1895), pp. 144–7; Faresov, pp. 18–20.

Engel'gardt was disappointed but not surprised at the colony's fate: Semen and his family had not been inured to the hardships of rural life at Batishchevo. He wrote to Sychugov:

What happened was bound to happen sooner or later, and the sooner the better in such a case: what can you expect if people are indifferent to farming and take a careless attitude towards it; when they show a reluctance to work? Perhaps there was even dissatisfaction with their situation as peasants. These people started out, not from love of work, but probably from various illusions they nurtured. They probably thought that they had simply to settle on the land and lemons would fly into their mouths.[1]

Determined that so talented a disciple should not be lost to the cause, Engel'gardt sent out another of his crack workers, a young *intelligent* of noble extraction named Viktor Veselovskii, to find Sychugov and form a settlement composed exclusively of Batishchevo students, people 'of one school, who can understand each other with monosyllables'.[2] In his advice, Engel'gardt once again employed the ingenious mirror work of his rationalization and bade them take the model of the very class they were endeavouring to reform. He warned Viktor that only by acquiring the humility of the peasant could they succeed in living and working together. They would have to be individuals who 'can be on simple terms with the *artel*'; and for this one must be simple. (Do you understand the meaning of this word?)'[3] Pointing to the peasants as models of sincerity and personal flexibility, he impressed on the prospective participants the need for self-effacement and subordination of their egoistic personal needs to the demands of the group. They had to become 'simple, humane, tranquil, not proud, not self-loving. (Self-loving, according to the peasant, is what we call egoistic.)' Often men who seemed humane actually lacked the true communal qualities, and only the peasants, with their superior capacities of personal judgement, could perceive this. 'They are all angry, as the peasants say. They aren't simple. They don't accept the peasants as they are but want them to be as they want.'[4]

[1] N. Engel'gardt, 'Batishchevskoe delo' (May 1895), p. 148.
[2] *Ibid.* no. 18 (June 1895), p. 80; 'Viktor Veselovskii', *Deiateli revoliutsionnogo dvizheniia v Rossii*, II, 188.
[3] N. Engel'gardt, 'Aleksandr Nikolaevich Engel'gardt...', p. 36.
[4] *Ibid.* pp. 36, 38.

Veselovskii found Sychugov in a saloon and together with Aleksei, another Batishchevo graduate, they planned to form a new *artel'*. Their first attempt, however, was a dismal failure, for they purchased land that was unsuited to any kind of cultivation. Undaunted, they prepared to begin again. 'All eyes are turned on Viktor and you,' Engel'gardt wrote to Sychugov. 'All are waiting to see how you will set yourselves up on the land, how you will bring the ideals of Batischevo to fruition.' Veselovskii was chosen head. A talented organizer, commanding the respect of both Sychugov and Aleksei, he directed the new *artel'* skilfully and all went well at the beginning. The members worked and lived together harmoniously and the first crops appeared to be excellent. Veselovskii enthusiastically wrote to Engel'gardt, 'We still aren't completely set up, but everything seems to be going well. I am speaking not in terms of agriculture, but of our moral life.' But at the end of the summer Veselovskii caught a serious cold while bathing. Exhausted by the exertion of running the *artel'*, he became seriously ill and died. With the absence of the leader, the driving force of the *artel'* disappeared and the members went their separate ways.[1]

The collapse of the second *artel'* dealt Engel'gardt's hopes a severe blow. He concluded that the intelligentsia could rise to the moral level necessary to submerge their egoistic instincts only with great difficulty. It seemed that a higher authority was still needed to prevent individual differences from infringing upon the solidarity of the whole and to enforce the harmony that would serve as a model for social progress. Engel'gardt began to believe that it would be necessary to exert control over the fledgling colonies until their members learned to live together, just as his firm hand had exacted sacrifices at Batishchevo. When the second colony had encountered its initial difficulties, he urged its members to return to Batishchevo in the event of a failure, and start anew under his guidance.[2] With its break-up he began to entertain the hope of forming a new *artel'* in the grounds of his estate, where his supervision could keep the animosity, greed, and laziness in tow. A group of eight or ten *intelligenty* would begin to farm the land, first with the aid of *batrak* labour, and then, when they had attracted a full complement of members, on their own. He imagined

[1] *Ibid.* pp. 43–7; N. Engel'gardt, 'Batishchevskoe delo' (May 1895), pp. 83–5.
[2] Faresov, p. 22.

Batishchevo as an *artel'* centre for all of Russia, where the youth would flock to learn how to work and to study agriculture. He dreamt of an actual agricultural institute with a large library and chemical laboratories.[1]

When an opportunity to realize these notions arose one day, Engel'gardt enthusiastically embraced it. A retired army officer, whose name comes down to us simply as 'the captain', approached him with an offer to form and help finance an *artel'*. The two gathered around them a group of interested young people, and Engel'gardt presented the plans he had recently settled upon: the participants were to begin at Batishchevo, working with the assistance of hired labour. But they indignantly rejected his proposals and vowed that they would neither live by exploiting labour nor submit to his authority.[2]

Nonetheless, Engel'gardt gave his full support, both moral and financial, to the undertaking. He assisted in the purchase of a plot of land at Bukovo near Batishchevo. He drafted the colony's rules, which forbade the division of labour, obliged the members to partake in all activities, and to live and eat together. He had no authority over the colony, nor even a voice in its affairs, but he visited it often, following its life and rejoicing in its successes.

All my sympathy was with Bukovo. From its founding, I ceased completely to take any interest in my own estate and gave myself completely to Bukovo. Helping Bukovo materially as much as I could, I also gave myself spiritually. The interests of the Bukovo farm were more important to me than the interests of my own estate. I lived Bukovo.[3]

The captain, who paid most of Bukovo's expenses, became its titular head, but since he knew little about agriculture and was too old to perform much work, the real leadership was preempted by a young native of Smolensk, Ivan. A good worker and an experienced farmer, Ivan was, however, overbearing and tyrannical. At the beginning, when his views and the captain's coincided, there was little friction and the *artel'* functioned smoothly. The crops were good the first summer. Although the colony did not cover costs, the members made up their losses by taking outside jobs and borrowing money

---

[1] N. Engel'gardt, 'Aleksandr Nikolaevich Engel'gardt...', pp. 52–3.
[2] *Ibid*. p. 53.　　　　　　　[3] *Ibid*. p. 53.

from Engel'gardt. In addition to their farm work, they taught peasant children how to read and write and opened a school in the neighbouring village.[1] The second year the number of members grew, and, 'singing from morning till night', they raised even larger crops than in their first attempt. They still suffered losses, but Engel'gardt was elated by the fact that the crop they had raised was larger than the local peasants', and he did not begrudge the money he was asked to donate.[2]

But, like the other colonies, Bukovo was plagued by dissension. The members, Engel'gardt observed, were unwilling to sacrifice any of their personal freedom on entering the *artel'*, and thought that membership freed them from all constraint.[3] The principle that they had to work so as not to exploit others was the sole precept that enjoyed the homage of all members. When it was broken, centrifugal tendencies again prevailed and the *artel'* began to disintegrate. The trouble began in the second year when the wives of the married members found themselves too ill to continue the heavy farm labour and in rapid succession hired housekeepers and gave up threshing and caring for the animals. A feud over the wives' responsibilities broke out between the married men, led by the captain, and the bachelors, led by Ivan. Ivan insisted that all the members adhere strictly to communal principles, which meant that every member had to work. The captain argued that the *artel'* should operate like the Russian peasant commune, in which land, and thereby work, was alloted according to the number of male members in each household. While the captain was spending the winter in Petersburg, Ivan recruited new members, all sympathetic to his views, and with their support adopted a set of draconic rules unacceptable to the married members. The latter promptly withdrew, leaving Ivan to rule unrestrained, and he soon turned into an unmitigated despot. The remaining members, thereupon, left one by one, and by 1884 Ivan was operating Bukovo alone, with the aid of hired peasant labour.[4]

The failure of Bukovo broke Engel'gardt's hopes. Again the intelligentsia had proved unable to rise above their petty

[1] Mertvago, pp. 177–81.
[2] N. Engel'gardt, 'Bukovskii intelligentny poselok', (April 1895), part 2, p. 22; Faresov, p. 66.
[3] N. Engel'gardt, 'Bukovskii intelligentny poselok', (April 1895) p. 22.
[4] *Ibid.* pp. 24–5; Mertvago, pp. 180–5; Faresov, pp. 23–6.

shortcomings to create a model of the harmonious life. He wrote of Bukovo:

Each was going to conduct the farming in his own way, in the sense that I, they would say, am my own boss. I am the director, everything is run by me. The further course showed this to be exactly the way it was. People were too petty and had not matured to the level where they could accomplish such a great task.[1]

'Perhaps a new contingent will appear,' he wrote sheepishly, but a new contingent did not appear, and the downfall of Bukovo brought an end to his faith in the capacity of the intelligentsia to uplift the people and redirect the course of Russian social development. Reality had proved unyielding to his attempt to reconcile it with the ideal, and gradually instead he reconciled himself with reality. He took solace from the advances the peasants had made. In 1880, after the failure of the second colony, he was encouraged by the successes of the neighbouring peasant proprietors who were applying his techniques. By using their wages to rent more land, and by planting crops in Engel'gardt's rotation, many had freed themselves completely from the need to work for others and were devoting all their time to their own plots. They were beginning to understand the advantages of fertilizers and high-quality seed. Their unquestionable advances, coupled with the clumsy failures of the intelligentsia, began to temper Engel'gardt's misgivings about peasant individualism. Egoism appeared to be a natural, integral component of the peasant mentality; every peasant was at heart a *kulak*. He wrote at the end of 1880:

The ideals of the *kulak* reign among the peasantry; every peasant is proud to be the pike who gobbles up the carp. Every peasant, if circumstances permit, will, in the most exemplary fashion, exploit every other. Whether his object is a peasant or a noble, he will squeeze the blood out of him to exploit his need.[2]

Engel'gardt now drew a distinction between peasant egoism and the egoism of the privileged and moneyed classes. Notwithstanding their spirit of acquisitiveness, the peasants maintained a sense of deep human sympathy, and this was why the *intelligent* found it so difficult to live with them. 'Look how humanely [the peasant] treats the baby, the idiot, the madman, the

---

[1] N. Engel'gardt, 'Aleksandr Nikolaevich Engel'gardt...', p. 53.
[2] A. N. Engel'gardt, *Iz derevni: 12 pisem* (Moscow, 1956), p. 398.

heathen, the prisoner, the beggar, any unfortunate person.'
Only in the case of 'the real *kulaks*' did the peasants' desire for
gain stem from avarice.

Every peasant is, in certain cases, a *kulak*, an exploiter, but while he
is a peasant on the land, while he toils, works, takes care of the land
himself, he is still not a real *kulak*, he doesn't think only of grabbing
things for himself, doesn't think how good it would be if all were
poor, in need, and he doesn't act in this way. Of course he takes
advantage of others' need and forces them to work for him, but
he doesn't base his welfare on that need, but on his own labour.[1]

Having thus rationalized peasant individualism, Engel'gardt
could comfort himself with the certainty that scientific, essentially non-exploitative agriculture was flourishing in Russia.
But his own experience and the experience of his pupils led
inescapably to the conclusion that his gentry heritage was
immutable; feeling in all his actions the legacy of his forebears,
he could no longer continue farming. As in the fifties, he
retreated from gentry life into the serene and orderly world
of science. After his eleventh letter, published in 1882, he ceased
writing about Batishchevo. In 1884 he announced that he
would accept no more students and advised applicants to join
other settlements of intelligentsia in the region. A few months
later he turned the management of the estate over to his
daughter and joined a geodetic survey of Smolensk province.
His correspondence from this trip deals exclusively with
chemistry and agronomy. When he returned to Batishchevo,
he engrossed himself in experimentation with phosphate
fertilizers.[2]

The youths at Batishchevo remained unconsoled by the technical advances of the peasants. The world would not yield to
their desire to live and have others live without preying on the
poor and helpless. Their successive failures, revealing their
personal inadequacies, had proved the everlastingness of their
civilized traits and crushed their hopes of kinship with the
peasantry. Some tried to purge themselves of their shortcomings
through ascetic religion. In the early eighties, copies of Tolstoy's
Confession, *The Discussions* of St John Chrysostom, and collec-
tions of evangelical texts began to circulate on the estate.
Debates centred less on social and economic issues and more
on the mysteries of religion. After leaving Batishchevo, many

[1] *Ibid.* p. 398.   [2] Mertvago, pp. 186–9; Faresov, p. 71.

drifted to Tolstoyan colonies where they strove to attain personal purity, simplicity, and modesty rather than to transform the outside world.[1]

The intelligentsia in the city, likewise, remained unconvinced by Engel'gardt's final resolution of his problem. In their eyes he had chosen efficiency over justice, thus betraying the image of the peasant that underlay all their hopes. 'He likes and respects only the enterprising peasant (*khoziaistvenny muzhik*) like Khor from Turgenev's *Sportsman's Sketches*, and, like Turgenev's Khor, he is prepared to snicker at and pick on the spiritual (*dushevny*) peasant,' the literary critic Mikhail Proto-popov wrote in the Journal *Delo* in 1882. Protopopov refused to accept Engel'gardt's distinction between the enterprising peasant and the 'real *kulak*'. Though the enterprising peasant toiled himself, he employed another to obtain a profit, 'a profit that is immoral and unjust because it is received in the form of an increment to the value of personal farm labour'.[2] If one could not farm without exploitation, Protopopov thought, then one should not farm at all. 'It is better and worthier to be a good man', he concluded, 'than a good farmer.'[3]

Engel'gardt, of course, also felt it was better to be a good man than a good farmer, which is why he gave up farming and banished the social problems of the countryside from his mind to return to science. But this escape was closed to most *intelligenty*, for, in the populist frame of reference, science was not accepted as a permissible alternative to the pure life existing beyond the bounds of civilization. To them the trends that Engel'gardt found at work in the countryside bespoke in-admissible truths about the Russian peasantry, and the fate of his experiment merely confirmed their distrust of external, intellectual agencies in directing social development. Their trust was in reality and if reality belied their trust, then catas-trophe was in the offing. The dire implications of a collapse of faith for one incapable of abandoning his conception of the peasantry were revealed in the life of Gleb Uspenskii, which unfolded without artifice or pretension in the pages of *Otechestvennye Zapiski*.

[1] N. Engel'gardt, 'Davnye epizody', *Istoricheskii vestnik*, no. 124 (June 1911), p. 845; Faresov, pp. 29–30.
[2] M. Protopopov, 'Khoziaistvennaia delovitost'', *Delo*, no. 16 (September 1882), part II, pp. 5–6, 14.   [3] *Ibid*. p. 18.

3

GLEB IVANOVICH USPENSKII
AND THE IMPOSSIBLE
RECONCILIATION

His speech is confused and feverish, like raving; it is furious and not always intelligible. But in his words one can discern something that is fine, and when he speaks you can recognize in him both a madman and an individual. It is hard to convey his insane talk on paper. He speaks of the baseness of mankind, of violence treading upon truth, of the wonderful life which in time will exist on earth, of the bars on the window which remind him every moment of the stupidity and cruelty of his tormentors. The result is a disorderly incoherent potpourri of old but still unfinished songs.

CHEKHOV, *Ward No. Six*

Gleb Uspenskii was the intelligentsia's chronicler of despair. While other *belletristy* of the seventies and eighties—Naumov, Zasodimskii, Zlatovratskii, Karonin—sought out and tried to depict phenomena consoling to the radical mind, Uspenskii's eyes focused on the unregenerate reality of Russian life that defied the intelligentsia's urge for change. The shafts of hope that occasionally illuminated his writings were lost in a grim landscape of futility, peopled by pitiful, ludicrous characters, whose aspirations inevitably clashed with their own inadequacies. His characteristic humour was the humour of helplessness and resignation, Gogol's 'laughter through tears'. In the sixties, when he appeared on the St Petersburg literary scene, he evoked the sadness and suffering of the petty bourgeoisie and petty bureaucracy, the world of 'Lost Street' (*Rasteriaevaia ulitsa*) that he had known as a child. In the early seventies, he turned his attention to the members of the intelligentsia and their doomed efforts to transform Russia.

Uspenskii yearned to liberate himself from the oppressive spirit of the life he described, and his writings are an account of the strenuous and, in the end, impossible struggle that this involved. He felt the evil and vulgarity that suffused Russian reality in himself, and his life was spent in single-minded pursuit of a new personality, capable of looking beyond the sordid truths of the present into a perfected future. This striving for

[61]

self-renovation, however, could never be consummated in action. A profound sense of inadequacy and personal weakness always lingered in him and left him too full of doubt to play an active role in the work of transformation. Instead, he lived vicariously in the deeds of others, participating in the movement to change Russia with his eyes and his soul, and leaving a record of hopes and disappointments that comprises a veritable spiritual autobiography of his generation of intelligentsia.

He first looked to the intelligentsia for a way of life he could idealize. In the capital, he sought individuals whom he could both esteem and emulate—who would guide his emergence as a new man. His emotions never progressed beyond the rapt admiration for heroic accomplishments that awakened in him when he first set foot in Petersburg. When he arrived in 1862 at the age of nineteen, he was under the heady influence of the spirit of reform and nurtured lofty aspirations inspired by the works of Turgenev, Nekrasov, Chernyshevskii, and Dobroliubov.[1] He vowed to begin life anew, to exorcise the past from his soul and compose 'a new spiritual genealogy'.

When 'the year of '61' came it was absolutely impossible to take any of my personal past forward with me into the future. I could take nothing, not a drop; to live at all I had to forget the past down to the last drop and erase from myself all the traits it had instilled.[2]

But Uspenskii could not exorcise the past from himself. Throughout his life he felt its evil influence in him and witnessed in horror its recurrent apparitions. Unexpectedly, it sprang to consciousness with evidence of his culpability, his sinister involvement with a bygone order. Then hopes of reform and rebirth gained the upper hand, but only for a moment, whereupon the dialectic resumed between old and new, good and bad, salvation and sin. Striving to take leave of his early life and enter the bright domain of the future, Uspenskii lived fettered by the past and saw the present refracted by its memories.

The sense of his complicity in the sins of his ancestors' order hovered at the edge of his consciousness through the sixties and early seventies, threatening him with condemnation and doom. After the failure of the 'going to the people', it broke

[1] V. Cheshchikhin-Vetrinskii, *Gleb Ivanovich Uspenskii* (Moscow, 1929), pp. 30–1.
[2] G. I. Uspenskii, *Polnoe sobranie sochinenii* (Moscow–Leningrad, 1940–54), XIV, 576–7.

through and filled him with a sense of his own worthlessness and degradation. The intelligentsia then no longer appeared to be the model of the new humanity. Its members seemed to suffer from the same frailty and inability to act as he. In his eyes they began to merge with the corrupt civilization that had produced them, destroying his hopes of regeneration. In his thirties, he felt himself the same ashamed youth who had come to Petersburg a dozen years before.

Every sight of everyday life seemed to attest to his contamination. When he served briefly in a railroad office in the town of Kaluga in the spring of 1875, he was overwhelmed with disgust for the cruel and ruthless methods of the managers and the submissive obedience of the educated individuals working under them.[1] Capitalism appeared to him as a polluting greed for wealth, money as the obscene object of accumulation.[2] He felt himself implicated in the immorality and inhumanity of the old life, stained by the corruption that he thought he had left behind him long ago. He was haunted by visions of childhood humiliation and sorrow, and his writings of the mid seventies tell of the terrible struggle with his past that raged within him.

His mind fixed on the original ancestral sin and on its perpetrator, his maternal grandfather Gleb Fomich Sokolov, the individual who had dominated his early life. The son of a poor rural priest, Sokolov had abandoned the church to serve in the bureaucracy and by selfless and unstinting dedication to his work had risen to the post of chief of the Tula bureau of the Chamber of State Lands. Uspenskii saw Sokolov's desertion of the church as the fatal step that determined the destiny of all his descendants. He had forsaken the simple life of the countryside and had brutally imposed new and alien values on his family. All vital and spontaneous impulses had been sacrificed to his overriding lust for money.

Profit, material prosperity, was the single genuine, unaffected motivation in all this mass of lies, and the generation of the grandsons inevitably and instinctively absorbed this trait—they imbibed it with their mother's milk. The thirst for crude animal pleasures boiled like a spring in these would-be pious families. Bestial (I do not lie in using this word) motivations awakened early in the children and in the strongest form.[3]

[1] *Ibid.* IV, 48–52.   [2] *Ibid.* XIII, 192.   [3] *Ibid.* IV, 137.

Uspenskii recalled the funereal atmosphere of the colony around Sokolov's home, where the patriarch had settled his children and in-laws after their marriages. The same strict discipline that prevailed in his bureau was maintained in his family. All who came into the family were ground under the old man's relentless demands for obedience and cut off from their roots in the outside world. When Sokolov's daughter Nadezhda married her tutor, a young seminary student by the name of Ivan Iakovlevich Uspenskii, the couple received a home nearby. Ivan Uspenskii worked under Sokolov's authority in the bureau and lived under his authority at home. A kind but spineless individual, he lost his independence, individuality, and ultimately his manliness to the old bureaucrat. His memory was eclipsed in the mind of his son by the stern and threatening figure of Gleb Fomich.[1]

Sokolov understood only state interests. He would fulminate over the failures of Russian foreign policy, the treachery of Austria and Napoleon III. Personal matters could not be discussed in his presence. He brooked neither frankness nor familiarity from his underlings and would flare into a rage at the slightest manifestation of personal initiative.[2] Uspenskii's parents, uncles, and aunts cowered slavishly before the old man. The grown-up world of his childhood was inhabited by down-trodden, emasculated lackeys.

His children from earliest childhood, and his wife, from the first day of marriage, had to renounce every right to any kind of freedom, any kind of organically independent desire. No one could disturb him in the discharge of his duties...either by a shout, a rap, or attachment to anything or anyone, or a particular characteristic or disposition—anything that would be the slightest manifestation of individuality.[3]

Uspenskii recalled his own terror of Gleb Fomich's shrill rebukes. He felt continually guilty before his grandfather; the sense of sinfulness followed him into the outside world and beset him even in the most trivial everyday occurrences. 'In church', he wrote, 'I was guilty before the saints, the images, the chandeliers. In school I was guilty before everyone from the guard (Hey, where're you going?) to the hanger for my coat;

---

[1] *Ibid.* IV, 132–3.
[2] A. S. Glinka-Volzhskii (ed.), *Gleb Uspenskii v zhizni* (Moscow–Leningrad, 1935), p. 9.   [3] Uspenskii, IV, 134–5.

on the street every dog (so it seemed to me!) awaited my appearance, if not to devour me completely then at least to take a bite.' His schoolmates likewise seemed devoid of a sense of human dignity. Without exception, they 'overflowed with every kind of cowardice, were trained to think and feel fearfully, and in general had become unaccustomed to take any step, to act in any way.'[1]

But Uspenskii felt a strong attachment for his grandfather. Gleb Fomich had been the only vital individual in his early life, and the household the old man kept had, in many ways, been pleasant for little children. There was music, dancing, and singing, piggy-back rides on the uncles' shoulders, and good things to eat from his grandmother's kitchen. Sokolov took a liking to little Gleb, and his affection was deeply gratifying to the child. Uspenskii, down to his declining years, nurtured fond recollections of his grandfather, though no mention of his parents ever appeared in his memoirs. 'Gleb Fomich loved me', he wrote in his autobiography, 'and wanted to take me away from my family.'[2]

Uspenskii at once dreaded and loved the wrathful patriarch. His infant emotions attached him to the despoiler of human feelings, who had crushed his father; they filled him with guilt for complicity in the order he despised. In the late seventies, as the prospects of regeneration dimmed, doubts about his true affiliation began to assail him. He again felt the confusion of childhood loyalties. He remembered his affections being torn between his grandfather and the only other person he admired —a holy fool (*iurodivy*) by the name of Paramon.

'Holy fools' were bizarre, deranged individuals, usually of humble background, who performed miraculous ascetic feats. Their impassioned mortification of the flesh delighted the Tula dwellers, who otherwise frowned upon freely expressed emotions. Paramon wore chains around his waist and back, which had been fastened tightly in his youth and now separated his bones and cut deeply into his skin. He pricked his fingers with needles and held his hand in a flame until it burned. He walked the streets of the town barefoot, summer and winter, and the skin on his feet cracked and bled. But, while he suffered, his lips formed a beautiful smile, which momentarily dispelled the dismal

---

[1] *Ibid.* VI, 94–5.
[2] Glinka-Volzhskii, *Gleb Uspenskii*..., pp. 17–23; Uspenskii, XIV, 581–2.

atmosphere and awoke sincere and happy emotions in the hearts of the observers. 'All felt the awakening of a childlike joy, something light, bright and eternal.'[1] Their fear disappeared, and their numbed sense of personal dignity reawoke. They began to talk of subjects other than punishment and misfortune. The petty concerns of everyday life gave way to speculation about God and the universe. To Uspenskii, Paramon epitomized freedom from society and defiance of the morality that oppressed their lives. He had attained his godliness and displayed his piety with the permission of no one, yet even the dour Sokolov enjoyed and approved of his expression of feeling. The children began to believe in the possibility of redemption and the happy life that would come in the next world. They followed Paramon around town, fasted, put nails in their shoes, and the child whose shoes first leaked blood became the envy of all the others. With Sokolov's consent, they settled Paramon in a shed on the old man's property and decorated the walls with pictures of saints, angels, and devils.[2]

But the passion of the holy fool inevitably came into conflict with the spirit of bureaucratic Russia and Uspenskii was forced to decide his true allegiance. In 1877, sensing his association with an order he hated, Uspenskii relived all the pain and guilt of his childhood choice. He recalled his betrayal of Paramon as the primal revelation of his degradation and involvement in the order he loathed. One evening the police visited Paramon, and when the officer knocked on the door, the 'holy fool' not only remained unperturbed but refused to admit him. Uspenskii's latent desire to emulate his grandfather in the role of oppressor and dehumanizer then rose to the surface. Instead of indignation at the invasion of the police, he felt anger at Paramon's 'fearless confidence in his own rightness', his audacity in the face of authority. 'We could not understand such faith in oneself; we considered it stupidity.'[3] When the police led Paramon away, Uspenskii experienced great relief. The next day, at his grandfather's command, he joined two other children in razing the decorations in the shed, desecrating

---

[1] Uspenskii, VI, 112.

[2] It is interesting that Uspenskii shifted the scene of the episode with Paramon in his story from his grandfather's to his uncle's home, though it is clear that both in reality and in Uspenskii's mind the incident involved his grandfather. See Gosudarstvenny literaturny muzei, *Gleb Uspenskii* (Moscow, 1939), pp. 438–9; Uspenskii, VI, 102–3.   [3] Uspenskii, VI, 112.

the one asylum of freedom and dignity in his life. Then remorse descended upon him. He felt himself an accomplice in his grandfather's evil and was tormented by the awareness of his own unworthiness and contemptibility. 'After this, I became a person alien to everything, needed by no one, a person who did not respect himself. From this day I knew that I could not consider myself worth anything; the fact was at hand.'[1]

Now, when there was no longer a grandfather, and when Uspenskii clearly stood opposed to the existing order, the drama of inculpation and punishment again enacted itself within him. Detesting the frigid, deadening world into which he had been born, he detested himself for being congenitally a part of it and for sharing responsibility for its horrors. He felt guilty for all the evil his grandfather's order had perpetrated. His conscience craved wrong to suffer for and hunted it desperately.

I felt that I had to encounter something revolting, to come across something that would poison my existence...My thought, beginning to torment me again, sought something distressing, some outrage, if only to relieve the unpleasant sensation of the awakening pain by paining me in more or less the right way...[2]

He could remember the horror he had felt as a child at the sight of suffering. In school he ran from the classroom window to avoid the sight and the piercing screams of prisoners being flogged in the adjacent square.[3] He shuddered at the beat of the drum as the inmates of the jail near his home were marched to punishment or penal servitude—mute, chained figures with blank, sallow faces. The melancholy and gloom of the prison became part of his everyday existence, and he was seized by fits of cold, terrifying fear.[4] He sometimes burst into tears suddenly, without knowing why.[5]

In the sixties and early seventies, Uspenskii had justified himself by the renovation that he thought had occurred and was proceeding within him. The belief that he had detached himself from the world that had produced him helped to quiet his sense of responsibility. But now, when he felt himself unchanged, his pervasive guilt returned and shattered his mental peace. His conscience restlessly penetrated to the underlying matrix of injustice, overwhelmed him with disgust and drove him into

---

[1] *Ibid.* vi, 116.   [2] *Ibid.* viii, 197–8.

[3] Glinka-Volzhskii, *Gleb Uspenskii...*, p. 25.

[4] *Ibid.*; Uspenskii, viii, 380.   [5] Uspenskii, xiv, 576.

fits of merciless self-castigation. Relief came only in the oblivion of constant motion, in incessant travel; and in the years 1875–7 he journeyed continuously through Russia and Europe, frantically avoiding contact with his environment.

It was at this time that Uspenskii began to turn to the peasantry for a new source of salvation. In Paris, under the influence of *émigré* revolutionaries, he came in contact with the current *narodnik* ideology and attitudes. He began to look upon the peasantry not as another group of benighted and suffering men, but as a milieu that was congenial, unsullied by the old order, and, by vicariously participating in their life, he tried to recapture the feeling of his worth as an individual. 'On Russian soil it is not so merciless,' he wrote from Paris in 1875. 'Our peasants love to act, not each for himself, but together in the *mir*.' The true force of Russian life, he affirmed, resided in 'the chimneyless Russian huts'.[1] He began to feel that his ideals were already widespread among the people and that the realization of the new life had to await neither the intervention of the intelligentsia nor the culmination of secular historical trends. In the story '*Neizlechimy*' ('The Incurable'), written in 1875, he showed a simple deacon coming to consciousness of the moral truth himself, independent of the futile efforts of the Lavrovist *intelligent*. It concluded with Uspenskii's most optimistic statement of faith in the processes of nature.

With quiet, quiet, imperceptible steps it is penetrating to the deadest corners of the Russian land and insinuating itself into the souls most unprepared for it. Everything around is quiet, sleepy, boring, wherever you may look... Not one great phenomenon in the realm of the soul is visible on the surface of Russian life; it seems that everything is sleeping or has died. But meanwhile in this silence, this apparent muteness, grain by grain of sand, drop by drop of blood, slowly, inaudibly, the broken and forgotten Russian soul is reconstituting itself along new lines, and, most important, is reconstituting itself in the name of the strictest truth.[2]

In the gloom of the Kaluga railroad office at the end of 1875, Uspenskii dreamed of an idyllic rural life untouched by the influence of civilization. He exhorted the peasants to protect their children's purity and innocence, to safeguard them from the hypocrisy of education and mental work.

[1] Cheshchikhin-Vetrinskii, pp. 119–20.
[2] *Ibid.* pp. 120–3; Uspenskii, IV, 218, 609.

Peasant! Give these little children, these fledgling free-loaders [*neplatel'shchiki*: literally those exempted from taxes due to privileged status], give them your tales, your simple country tunes! Regale them with little flowers, little animals, little rabbits...Play with them, spoil them a little!...Otherwise they will wilt in this atmosphere of insincerity, pretence, and untruth—in this costly void! Save them with your simple truth. Have them breathe the fresh, healthful air, hear frank words. They will be deeply unhappy and deeply vile without you, without your true and bitter experience, without your sincere playfulness, oblivious of all evil.[1]

As his personal crisis deepened, the countryside tempted him like a mirage from the distance. He envisioned a world that would offer new possibilities of escaping from himself and of achieving a fresh and better identity. His memories of Paramon told him of his other self, the unrealized self of free, uninhibited feelings, of natural warmth, love, and justice.

In 1877 Gleb Uspenskii, who as a youth had fled the provinces to seek a new life in the city, left the city to seek redemption in the countryside. He accepted an invitation to spend the summer on a friend's estate in Novgorod province. 'The genuine truth of life drew me to the source,' he wrote in his autobiography, 'to the peasant.'[2]

Standing on a village street in Novgorod province in the spring of 1877, Uspenskii contemplated the mournful tenor of rural life. He watched peasants going about their dreary pursuits, indifferent to him and to the civilized society he represented. The issues that stirred the intelligentsia seemed completely irrelevant in the midst of this drab, laborious existence. No newspaper was to be had, and almost no one knew of the Balkan war. He took refuge from the forlorn village street in a small store, where he could draw comfort from the few amenities among the wares upon the shelves.[3]

To Uspenskii the peasant village appeared no less bleak than the town suffering from the ravages of the railroad. 'I ended up in the wrong place, where the source was not to be found,' he wrote in his autobiography.[4] The account of his experiences, '*Iz derevenskogo dnevnika*' ('From a Village Diary'), which began to appear in the October 1877 number of *Otechestvennye Zapiski*,

---

[1] Uspenskii, IV, 60–1. [2] *Ibid.* XIV, 579.
[3] *Ibid.* V, 13–15, 39–41. [4] *Ibid.* XIV, 579.

revealed a strikingly new approach to the countryside. Rather than present another evocation of peasant poverty or of the workings of the commune, Uspenskii turned his critical eye toward the peasant's everyday life. What he saw and what he recorded would make it impossible for the members of the intelligentsia ever again to look upon the peasantry with their former innocence.

Yet one can hardly accept Uspenskii as an objective reporter, or his observations as indicative of general trends in the countryside. Soviet commentators customarily characterize him in this light—as an acute analyst of the rural scene who gave the lie to current *narodnik* myths. It would be difficult to argue, however, that his descriptions of the countryside were significantly more accurate and balanced than other radical writings of the time. His disposition to seek out evil did enable him to perceive sides of rural life to which others had remained blind, but by the same token it led him to ignore the positive qualities of the peasantry. The places where he chose to seek the 'source' that had brought him to the countryside were hardly those where one might expect it to reside. Least of all was the source likely to be found in the province of Novgorod, where, it was well known among the intelligentsia, a money economy was flourishing. Bisected by the Petersburg–Moscow railroad, the province felt the influence of both major urban markets. The land, covered with swamps and thick foliage, offered the peasants little incentive to devote themselves to farming, and by this time roughly one third of the population lived by non-agricultural pursuits.[1] If Uspenskii was ignorant of these conditions on his first visit, he soon learned the truth, yet he returned repeatedly and eventually even settled there.

Longing for the source of elemental purity, Uspenskii actually pursued a spectacle of defilement. His vision of a life free of lascivious impulses was merely a fantasy that enabled him to survive in a world he detested—an existential dream. Enacting the drama of his ancestral sin, he cast himself in the dual role of inflicter and victim, and went in search of the act of violation. In the city he had ascribed his own virtuous impulses to the peasants, and had tried to live vicariously in their experience.

---

[1] B. P. Koz'min, 'Spravka ob ekonomicheskom sostoianii Novgorodskoi i Samarskoi gubernii v 70-kh godakh', in G. I. Uspenskii, *Polnoe sobranie sochinenii*, v, 413–15.

Now he saw in them the evil he felt in himself. The members of the intelligentsia would discover in his writings a countryside that was a negative of the image they held in their minds, and peasants who embodied their failings rather than their aspirations.

Uspenskii saw the villagers succumbing to civilized values. They followed the example of the representatives of civilization they knew—the grasping tax collectors and petty clerks that served in the local administration. Money seemed to have profaned all of their thoughts. It had become their sole sign of status, and those who had accumulated it, no matter by what devious and unscrupulous means, stood high in their regard. They especially admired Adolf, a rich German who had recently purchased an estate from a humane but impecunious nobleman. Adolf prospered by paying his workers exceptionally low wages which they usually took in overpriced vodka.[1] Another village hero, Mikhail Petrovich, had decided that the peasant's hard lot was not for him and had resolved to become rich. His comely wife shared his ambitions and, with Mikhail's consent, set about acquiring primary capital, first by selling herself to the surveying students practising in the area, then by easing a retired army officer out of part of his fortune. With this capital, Mikhail bought a house and cattle. The peasants, dazzled by his wealth, elected him village elder, *starosta*. In this position, he further enriched himself and enhanced his reputation by embezzling communal funds.[2]

The whole village knew that his wife was consorting with the devil, but the very ability, the knowledge of how to go about it, how to turn things to one's own advantage—this conquered everyone. Everyone realized that the job was done intelligently and skilfully, not foolishly or haphazardly, or just for its own sake.[3]

Those peasants who lacked this talent received neither respect nor sympathy and faced impoverishment and ruin. Ivan Afanas'evich, who lived in perfect symbiosis with the land and devoted himself wholeheartedly to agricultural work, was forced to leave his plot in search of outside earnings. Devoid of cunning and ruthlessness, he failed at whatever he attempted. He tried to sell cloth, but the peasants would only exchange for other kinds of cloth and not pay money. Then he sold cookies,

---

[1] Uspenskii, v, 42–6. [2] *Ibid.* v, 110–14. [3] *Ibid.* v, 114.

but after brief success was driven out of business by competitors. Without the acumen and capacity for deceit of a Mikhail Petrovich, he was left helpless and indigent.[1]

Uspenskii's confrontation of rural reality made him aware that the peasants, too, were suffering the pains of civilization and hardly represented a source of virtue and strength. His venture into the real world merely yielded more cause for revulsion and impelled him to retreat into the world of the ideal, where he again sought the impetus to improvement in the moral consciousness of the intelligentsia. Like Engel'gardt, he responded to the sight of the real peasantry by conceiving an ideal intelligentsia that embodied the qualities of both groups and the shortcomings of neither. These educated individuals would bring the benefits of civilization to the peasantry rather than the ills. They would work not for money but to help the people. Instead of serving in the state employ, they would go as teachers and doctors to lead the life of the people, and would support themselves, like village priests, from voluntary contributions, given by the peasants in true gratitude.[2] Thus, like a gyroscope, Uspenskii's mind maintained its frail equilibrium: shifting its weight from reality to dream, it conjured up the image of a mythical peasant when the real *intelligent* appeared repellent, and the image of a mythical *intelligent* when repelled by the real peasant.

Indeed, the deeper Uspenskii penetrated the countryside, the more sordid became his revelations about the peasantry and the more insistent his call for a new kind of intelligentsia. His second attempt to study peasant life took place in Samara in the following year. This time he tried to follow the *narodnik* practice of settling in one place for a long time and occupying a responsible post in which it would be easy to make contact with the peasants. While his stay in Novgorod had lasted only a few months, he remained in Samara for about a year, one of the rare sedentary spells in his life. He took a post as a clerk in the office of the 'Savings and Loan Cooperative' (*Ssudo-sberegatel'noe tovarishchestvo*) in the village of Skolkovo. His longer residence and closer association with the peasantry gave him greater scope for finding wrong in rural life.

Once again he chose a region where social relationships were disintegrating under the pressures of change. The breakdown

---

[1] *Ibid.* v, 53–9. [2] *Ibid.* v, 107–10.

of the economy in Samara and the suffering that was evoked among the population had made the situation in the province the most dire of the whole black earth zone. The desperate need for land of the Samara peasants had forced them to rent from speculators, who controlled large areas of the province. They farmed the land to exhaustion, trying to squeeze out of it the means to pay their exorbitant rents and taxes, and the crops yielded by the once fertile soil declined sharply through the late sixties and seventies. Lacking non-agricultural sources of income, the peasants borrowed from usurers, and many mortgaged their harvests as long as two years in advance. The series of crop failures and famines that followed staggered educated society and stirred heated polemic.[1]

In Novgorod, Uspenskii had observed individual peasants who seemed to be the victims of changes over which they had no control; in Samara, he had the opportunity to examine peasants who ran their own institutions, and he discovered that even where they could influence their own fate, their acts were selfish, inhumane, and unilluminated by morality. Despite the widespread misery in the province, the commune seemed to take no responsibility for the plight of its members. A calamity might deprive a family of its breadwinner and leave wife and child destitute, but the commune would intervene only to free them of land and taxes. The victims of misfortune, left to their own resources, often returned to plague the villagers as brigands. Such was the case of Fedia the horse thief, who, early in life, had been orphaned and abandoned without food or shelter. The members of his commune succeeded in catching Fedia, whereupon they proceeded to beat him to death.[2] 'No, he isn't guilty,' Uspenskii exclaimed at a morality that allowed a man to starve and valued his life at less than that of a horse. Not only did the peasants fall short of the image of a higher form of humanity, but, concerned only for their own material welfare, they seemed bereft of elementary human decency.

The economic halo of the horse obscured all considerations of human suffering, obscured them to such an extent that in the name of the equine aureole, it became permissible to slaughter a man like

---

[1] Koz'min, in Uspenskii, *Polnoe sobranie sochinenii*, v, 416–25; P. Lavrov, *Po povodu samarskogo goloda* (London, 1874), *passim;* Mordovtsev, 'Deistvitel'nye prichiny samarskogo goloda', *Otechestvennye Zapiski*, no. 211 (April 1874), pp. 365–90.

[2] Uspenskii, v, 167–79.

a dog, and not feel anything but the consciousness that, as they say, 'it's now gotten quieter on this account'.[1]

Uspenskii found no evidence of the vaunted fraternal spirit and solidarity in the communes he observed. Each family seemed indifferent to the fate of the others and fended for itself in the struggle for survival as if on its own desert island.[2] So great was the distrust and enmity among the peasants that they were unable to act in concert even when it befitted their interest. One commune received an offer from a landlord proposing to sell some land at advantageous terms, but only if the purchase was made by the entire commune. The commune as a whole failed to reply, but the landlord was deluged with requests from the individual members. Each refused to trust his brother and all believed that, if the *starosta* made the arrangements, only he would profit, while everyone else would suffer. The poor feared that the rich would end up with all the land and reduce them to servitude.[3] Each was concerned only with his own self-interest and feared any form of collective action. They all reasoned, 'In all these undertakings there is no direct benefit worth a *grosh* to me. This is all we think of because we know of no other benefit.'[4]

The only tasks that the commune undertook responsibly were the distribution of the land and the awarding of the saloon concession, and it discharged neither in the members' best interest. It divided the land with niggling thoroughness, but neither justly nor equitably. The saloon transaction customarily proceeded in the midst of wild bacchanalia—the drink being donated by the hopeful merchant. The more each peasant imbibed, the less he troubled himself about the details of the agreement and in the end the concession went for a paltry sum. Other business was dispatched in similar fashion. At *volost'* meetings the heads of the respective communes would partake in riotous drinking, merrymaking, and unseemly behaviour, while they bartered away such profitable items as forests and rights to coach services.[5]

Indeed the peasants who had achieved sufficient independence of mind to think for themselves thought only of drink. They painstakingly devised elaborate pretexts for celebration and

---

[1] *Ibid.* v, 180.   [2] *Ibid.* v, 135.   [3] *Ibid.* v, 145-8.
[4] *Ibid.* v, 137.   [5] *Ibid.* v, 136, 139-40.

techniques for equal distribution of vodka.[1] The resourcefulness they had developed at these tasks, however, was applicable to nothing else.

In these cases the peasant's mind works and works well, observes all possible trivial details, knows a person and sees through him, is not sparing of the back, arms or energy, does not attempt to do anyone in or to cheat anyone. But once it is a question of truly social interest, which would bring the commune substantial benefit, alleviate its condition and help the members to act in accordance with God's will, in such matters, as it might be, everything vanishes: attentiveness, power of observation, even the very shadow of justice.[2]

Uspenskii perceived the same egoism in the peasants of Samara that he had felt in himself and observed in educated society. His writings pictured them not as blameless victims of the social order, but as mortals, with all too patent failings of their own. He neither attributed their behaviour, as he had in Novgorod, to external influences of civilization, nor excused their actions by pointing to their abject condition. Their problem, he stated bluntly, was moral, not economic, for, even where they were in possession of adequate resources, they stupidly squandered their wealth and disregarded the general welfare.

By assigning full responsibility to the peasants for their poverty, ignorance, and depravity, Uspenskii blasphemed against the *narodnik* faith, and brought forth sharp retorts in the radical press of the capital. Iosef Kablits, the chief publicist of the newspaper *Nedelia*, asserted that such characterizations of the people, to be expected from a conservative, could be regarded as nothing less than apostasy from a member of the radical intelligentsia. Though acknowledging Uspenskii's gifts of perception, Kablits questioned his ability to assess the material he had gathered.[3] Georgi Plekhanov, the elegant young leader of Land and Freedom, elaborated this position in the pages of *Nedelia*. 'In spite of the centuries-long struggle with completely opposed principles,' Plekhanov wrote, '*artel*' and communal principles still permeate the peasant's thinking... "the commune pities everyone"'.[4] Drawing upon the works of noted authorities on rural life, he affirmed that the commune fostered 'a high level of altruistic feeling', which forced the peasant 'to

---

[1] *Ibid.* v, 231–6. [2] *Ibid.* v, 238–9.
[3] I. Kablits (Iuzov), 'Liberal o serom muzhike', *Nedelia* (1878), no. 13, pp. 283–7.
[4] G. Plekhanov (Valentinov), 'Ob chem spor', *Nedelia* (1878), no. 13, p. 1740.

take a more humane attitude toward crime'. He extolled the 'direct feeling' ('*neposredstvennoe chuvstvo*') which gave the peasant a natural comprehension of morality, without guidance from books. The commune, he contended, contained the embryo from which a just form of production could spring, and its present imperfect state was the fault of the existing economic system. He referred the reader to Nikolai Zlatovratskii for a more sensitive and accurate rendering of life in the countryside.[1]

Uspenskii replied by deriding his critics' 'sickly sweet' and 'slobbering' attitudes towards the people[2]. The peasants' natural 'direct feeling', he pointed out, often manifested itself in brutal and criminal behaviour that could not be explained by their poverty. In one case a group of peasants had agreed to murder their employer for twenty-five rubles.

> The job was finished the same night and I humbly asked someone to explain to me what relationship the smallness of the strip, the excesses in taxes, arrears, etc., have to the magic significance of the twenty-five rubles. It is not hard to see that in sinning for twenty-five rubles there was no such reason, for twenty-five rubles were not enough to either buy land or pay their taxes, in other words not enough to straighten themselves out.[3]

Rather than the economic system, the 'pedagogical conditions' in the countryside were the source of the peasant's misfortune. The bonds of the old commune had dissolved and the landlord's tutelage had been removed, leaving the peasant to withstand the hardships of rural life alone. Allotting land according to the number of 'souls' (male members of each family) the existing commune deprived many households of both security and rights.

> An old woman with daughter and granddaughter—these three creatures, not including a worker, cannot even be counted in the number of souls, and thus all three are left without a part of the woods, water and land, and are left to freeze and beg their way in the world.[4]

Many left the commune and tried to secure their material well-being by their own wits. Since they were wedded to no 'stern moral system', these new entrepreneurs pursued their own interest with unabashed ruthlessness.[5] In reply to his critics,

---

[1] *Ibid.* pp. 1740, 1744–5. [2] Uspenskii, v, 195.
[3] *Ibid.* v, 200. [4] *Ibid.* v, 204. [5] *Ibid.* v, 205–6.

Uspenskii depicted a helpless disoriented peasantry in dire need of the intelligentsia's guidance.

Why is it that in general only the problem of arrears is considered calamitous? Is it not also calamitous that the mass of the people neither 'hears nor gives an answer' and every moment is spawning nothing but robbers, *kulaki*, *miroedy*, those who (like horse thieves) raise the plundering of their brother to an industry...[1]

Yet Uspenskii's works offer scant indication of where those who were to answer the peasants' problem could be found. The numerous *intelligenty* depicted in his writings at this time were absurd and pathetic figures, divorced from real life—characteristic 'superfluous men'. They yearned to change themselves, but their inner weakness ensured that they would forever remain the same. Their longing to fuse with the people grew out of false notions of the nature of the countryside, and the ludicrous misunderstandings that arose from their contacts with the peasants filled them with bitterness and chagrin. Uspenskii described them ironically, but his irony often had a tinge of melancholy. Only with difficulty could he distinguish himself from his characters and keep the roles of narrator and leading personage apart. The lost intellectuals of his stories were third-person images of himself who dramatized the futility of his own hollow rationalizations. By depicting them he was able to inveigh more eloquently and unabashedly against himself.

Typical of the figures reproducing Uspenskii's attitudes and reactions to the countryside was Mikhail Mikhailovich, the 'gentleman' (*barin*) in the sketch '*Ovtsa bez stada*' ('Sheep without a Flock'), written during Uspenskii's visit to Novgorod. Mikhail Mikhailovich had always felt ill at ease in educated society and believed he had little in common with his privileged friends. By virtue of his strong childhood attachment to his peasant nurse, he thought himself more akin to the peasantry. But when he went to the countryside, life among the peasantry proved even less to his liking. He was shocked at the brutality of peasant judges in *volost'* courts who ordered punishment by beating for minor offences. The spectacle of peasants exploiting peasants and enriching themselves appalled him and caused him to raise his voice in protest. When he learned that one peasant, in the service of a German landlord, was ruthlessly preying upon his

[1] *Ibid.* v, 191.

fellow villagers, he summoned them to resist. Their indifference
to his exhortation stunned him. They regarded him, clearly,
not as a brother, but as an officious stranger. They chafed at his
flamboyant, bookish language and his pretentious manner.
'This is the real tragedy!' he exclaimed angrily when they
refused to follow his lead. 'Everyone is out for himself. This is
what is eating itself into the countryside. And with every day,
it goes deeper.' To his rebukes, the peasants replied tersely, 'We
are bad, that's all there's to it'.[1]

Uspenskii could not trust his own hope that men like himself,
born infected with the ills of civilization, could suddenly take
on the traits that would enable them to bridge the gulf between
themselves and the peasantry. He could nourish none of
Engel'gardt's faith that such men could be created by re-
education. Uspenskii's peasant *intelligent* was an individual who
had been endowed with the necessary qualities to work in the
countryside, one who grew up near the peasants and from childhood felt an affinity towards them. But such men, he knew, were
rare, and there was no way to increase their numbers. When
one appeared, his example put the whole intelligentsia to shame,
for the natural course of his life realized what for others remained an unattainable dream.

In Samara, Uspenskii saw a young *intelligent* who seemed to
embody his ideal. This was A. A. Aleksandrovskii, a participant
in the 'going to the people' movement and one of the accused
in the Trial of the 193. Aleksandrovskii came to Skolkovo to
serve in the local branch of the Savings and Loan Cooperative
and rapidly became a part of the life of the village. Uspenskii
was amazed at his ease in mingling with the peasants and
winning their sympathy. The son of a poor rural priest, he was
well educated, but remained uncorrupted by a privileged upbringing. Illiterate till the age of fourteen, he had been reared
with peasant children, and, Uspenskii believed, knew the
peasant 'better than the peasant knew himself: knew his crude-
ness, callousness, and desire to do others in. But he also knew
the strength of the peasant's magnanimity and his understanding of others' need and misfortune.'[2] Within two weeks
of his arrival, Aleksandrovskii had learned everything about
the village and had begun to share the inhabitants' interests.
When his work in the cooperative ended, Aleksandrovskii re-

[1] *Ibid.* VI, 121–65.   [2] *Ibid.* V, 246–8.

mained to help the peasants. He learned the elementary facts of medicine and prevailed upon the sick to accept medical aid. He took a post in a local bank, and exposed those who had been swindling the peasants. When local merchants and kulaks began to conspire to avenge themselves, he led the villagers in their own defence.[1]

But Aleksandrovskii, Uspenskii realized, was an isolated exception who could, by himself, cope only with a small part of the task to be accomplished in a single peasant village. Once he returned to the city, the peasants would relapse into apathy, and the kulaks' grip would tighten upon them again. If he stayed, the petty but unremitting demands of work in the countryside would crush him. The countryside would eat him alive 'with nothing left over'. A few months after leaving Samara, Uspenskii summed up the prospects for men like Aleksandrovskii working among the peasantry.

The countryside, devouring him with such an appetite, of course would enjoy some benefit, but this benefit, in comparison with the immensity of the personal sacrifice of the one who had been eaten, would be trifling, hardly noticeable...And if this benefit is to be great enough to lead the countryside out of its impenetrable darkness and into the brilliant light of God, the number of victims that it will have to devour will be great indeed![2]

By the end of 1879, the single ground for hope that remained from Uspenskii's visit to Novgorod had also disappeared from view. Men like Aleksandrovskii, heartening as was their example, were merely an intimation of what might be. No intelligentsia existed that could change the peasants, and the peasants in their current state merely reproduced the ills of civilization. Uspenskii's observations of the countryside had left no populist idol intact. In his writings, reality, so long shrouded in pleasant illusion, suddenly appeared with an inimical face.

The psychology of the intelligentsia of the seventies rested on a faith in the beneficence of reality. This was not the sensory reality of squalor and injustice; it was the reality of the future, the antithesis in their dialectic which was embodied in the concealed forces that would overthrow the existing society. The revolutionaries regarded the life and institutions around them

---

[1] *Ibid.* v, 248–56, 267–78.   [2] *Ibid.* v, 269–70.

as unfortunate but transitory expressions of human irrationality, doomed to extinction. The ignorance and poverty of the peasants, the grinding weight of the autocracy, the lack of freedom—all these represented aspects of a system that had lost its *raison d'être* and that would disappear with the rise of the new world. This philosophical optimism sustained their revolutionary *élan* and their confidence in the future before the sombre appearance of Russian life. As we have seen in the first chapter, this faith survived Land and Freedom's disappointments in the countryside. Returning to the city, the revolutionaries engaged in the more spectacular strategy of terrorism, but they in no way relinquished their earlier hopes or conceptions of the world. Terror was justified merely as a means of defence, which would remove the bureaucracy from the countryside and allow them to pursue their agitation unhindered. Their assassinations, they hoped, would paralyse the government 'like an electric shock' and render it unable to impede their work in the village.[1]

But in late 1878 and early 1879 the autocracy stiffened its resistance and the struggle in the city took a turn for the worse. Answering the revolutionary challenge, the government installed new, more ruthless, and more efficient administrators at the top levels of the provincial bureaucracy and stepped up police measures. In October 1878 all members of the 'basic circle' of Land and Freedom except Aleksandr Mikhailov were arrested. A few months later, police descended on the Kiev terrorist centre, the major group of revolutionaries in the south. In retaliation, the members of Land and Freedom voted to attempt the assassination of the tsar. Their initial effort was met with the imposition of martial law in the major cities of European Russia and with the summary execution of the southern revolutionaries. At the same time the workers' movement in the cities subsided and the nascent *Severny Soiuz Russkikh Rabochikh* (Northern Union of Russian Workers) was infiltrated by *agents provocateurs* and disbanded.[2]

Now when both rural and urban struggles had met with defeat, the revolutionaries, like Uspenskii, felt themselves overpowered by the antagonistic forces dominating Russian life and their faith in a beneficent reality began to wane. This change

---

[1] Iakovlev, *Revoliutsionnaia zhurnalistika*, pp. 497–8.
[2] Franco Venturi, *Roots of Revolution* (London, 1960), pp. 626–35.

in mood marks the onset of the crisis of Russian populism, the turning-point in the thoughts and feelings of the intelligentsia. For at this point the intelligentsia ceased to view existing reality as ephemeral and arbitrary and began to admit that it had a logic and force of its own that were not easily controlled or fathomed. The problem of adjusting reality to ideals now became a more troubled one. The hopes of the post-reform generations had been dampened with the realization that old Russia, with all its associations and memories, could not be willed away.

In the late seventies, the awareness of the prevalence of evil that Uspenskii expressed in his writings spread among the members of the intelligentsia. But their reaction to the problem was not at all the same as his. For while he turned all his aggressions inward, abusing himself for the manifold injustices he encountered, they placed the blame on the system and their faculty of hate remained alive. The system had always been something diffuse that pervaded Russian reality, but now, after their successive rebuffs and frustrations, they sought and found a defined object upon which they could focus their anger and against which they could actively fight. The arrests and executions that decimated their ranks pointed to the true source of their discomfiture. The bitterness that grew as they became aware of their inability to cope with the disembodied evil of Russian life welled up and poured out at the Russian autocracy, the principal antagonist of their designs, whose presence beset them in all their endeavours. The condescension toward political struggle as something unworthy of the socialist's concern now began to disappear. The revolutionaries relinquished their notion of the state as the product of unjust social relationships that had to be destroyed before it would topple. In their eyes it now began to appear as the begetter of those social relationships, a self-perpetuating apparatus responsible for the misery and ignorance of the population.

The attitudes toward the peasantry current among the intelligentsia also began to change. They could now admit the dissatisfaction and frustration with village life that many had experienced and which Uspenskii had evoked in his writings. It became possible to take into account, even to emphasize, the frailty of the peasantry, for all the flaws in *narodnik* ideals could be laid to the autocracy, to underscore its guilt. The ideologists of the movement began to stress the debasement of the peasant, rather than his virtues, and their writings bore unmistakable traces of Uspenskii's influence. In April 1879 Lev Tikhomirov, writing in *Land and Freedom*, showed the world of the peasant commune engaged in an unequal struggle with the Russian government. The state crushed the peasants and turned them into starving work animals. It forced them to devote their lives to the acquisition of bread and money and thus killed their sense of human dignity and their ethical feeling. It deprived them of land and independence, leaving them at the mercy of the bureaucracy. It perverted them 'in a thousand ways, each one more dreadful and hideous than the last'.[1]

The transference of all responsibility for Russia's condition to the autocracy rejuvenated revolutionary hopes, for if, in one heroic feat of destruction, the state could be levelled, then all the concomitant injustice would fall with it. On the verge of total defeat, the revolutionaries conceived of spectacular victory. By the time of the Voronezh conference of Land and Freedom in June 1879, only a few, like Plekhanov and M. P. Popov, remained faithful to the old programme of agitation in the countryside. The majority advocated a direct attack on the fount of political authority, the assassination of Tsar Alexander II, and insisted that all other revolutionary activity be subordinated to this goal. At the end of the summer of 1879, the two approaches could no longer coexist in the same organization. The spokesmen of the old view broke off to form the weak and short-lived Black Partition (*Cherny Peredel*); the rest united in The People's Will (*Narodnaia Volia*) to execute the death sentence upon the tsar.

The inception of The People's Will marks the revolutionary movement's rediscovery of the political struggle. For the first time, the ideology of the seventies recognized that social revolution in Russia presupposed the overturn of the tsarist state. In the history of the movement this was a departure of momentous significance. For by making their attack on the government the pivotal point of their plans, the revolutionaries allied their cause with the cause of political freedom, thereby paving the way for the ultimate unification of political forces under the banner of opposition to the autocracy. This has led many to see in The People's Will the forerunner of later constitutional tendencies.

[1] Iakovlev, *Revoliutsionnaia zhurnalistika*, pp. 400–3.

But, besides a common adversary, there was little in common between the objectives of The People's Will and those of the socialists of the end of the century, who strove for a transition period of Western-style liberal government. Two decades of political and economic maturation separated the two outlooks and made the mentality of the members of The People's Will alien to those revolutionaries who looked to them for inspiration. Constitutional government remained abhorrent to most of the *narodnovol'tsy* and the freedom of the individual figured in their ideology only in so far as it was a prerequisite to further revolutionary action. The organization's programmatic statements never consistently spelled out the nature of the political system to be introduced and, indeed, no defined general view on this subject seemed to have existed among the members.[1] Only later, in defeat and exile, did its spokesmen view its activities in terms of Western-style democracy. In its doctrinal statements The People's Will recognized the theoretical necessity of a new instrument of government. But the organization's emotional appeal was above all negative—to the spirit of vengeance and destruction. Most of the members envisioned not the building of a new system of government but the killing of an incubus.

The first programme of The People's Will, drafted in the fall of 1879, depicted the Russian state as no ordinary political institution. It was the most powerful capitalist force in the country, 'the single oppressor of the people thanks to which all the minor predators are able to exist'.[2] Methodically despoiling the population, it resembled the Mongols of Genghis Khan more closely than any European polity. Lev Tikhomirov, the chief ideologist of the new organization, wrote in the lead article of the first issue of *Narodnaia Volia* (*The People's Will*),

Our government is not a commission of plenipotentiaries of the ruling class as in Europe, but an independent organization, existing only for itself, a hierarchical, disciplined organization which would hold the people in economic and political bondage even if there were no exploiting classes here. Our state owns as a private proprietor half the territory of Russia—over half the peasants rent its land. It is the principle of our state that the whole population exists mainly for its benefit. State assessments absorb all the labour of the populations,

[1] V. A. Tvardovskaia, 'Problema gosudarstva v ideologii narodnichestva, 1879–1883', *Istoricheskie Zapiski*, no. 74 (1963), pp. 179–84.

[2] V. Ia. Iakovlev (B. Bazilevskii) (ed.), *Literatura partii Narodnoi Voli* (Paris, 1905), pp. 162–3.

and, a characteristic feature, the peasants' *groshi* flow into the pockets of our stock-brokers and railroad entrepreneurs through the state treasury.[1]

The assassination of the tsar, the programme affirmed, would deliver the people from the burden of the state edifice and allow them to shape their way of life according to their sound instincts. The *narodnik* ideal could then flourish unmolested. 'The development of the people from that time on will proceed independently, according to its own will and inclinations... many purely socialistic principles, common to us and the people, will be recognized and upheld.'[2]

Balked as the organizers of the people, the revolutionaries stepped forward as its avengers. Self-effacement gave way to self-assertion and their ethos became one of hate. They beheld themselves in the guise of the fearless killer who gives no quarter to his opponent in a duel to the finish.[3]

On the horizon appeared the outlines of a sombre figure, illuminated by some kind of hellish flame, a figure with his chin raised proudly in the air, with his gaze breathing provocation and vengeance. He began to make his way through the frightened crowd so as to enter, with firm step, onto the arena of history. He is wonderful and awe-inspiring, irresistible, charming, for he unites the two most lofty kinds of human grandeur, the martyr and the hero.[4]

This was the *narodovolets'* ideal self. Immortalized in the words of Stepniak-Kravchinskii, it would excite the imagination of later generations of radical youth with a model of implacable revolutionary courage. But here, too, myth embellished reality. The dashing hard-boiled type represented by Aleksandr Zheliabov, the leader of the organization and one of the few revolutionaries of peasant origin, was approached by few of the others. Most of the members were bewildered and desperate youths, who struck out, not in cold-blooded determination, but in panic when all other resorts had failed. Their gazes 'breathed', not 'provocation', but the sad confusion of personal turmoil.

Sofia Perovskaia, the engineer of the assassination of Alexander II and the first woman in Russian history to go to the scaffold

---

[1] *Ibid.* 7.   [2] *Ibid.* 163.

[3] For excellent accounts of the events leading up to the assassination of the tsar, see Venturi, pp. 633–720, and David Footman, *Red Prelude* (New Haven, 1945).

[4] Kravchinskii, *Podpol'naia Rossiia*, pp. 25, 34.

for a political crime, was a meek and retiring woman, whose saintly compassion was appreciated by both her fellow revolutionaries and the peasants she devoted her life to helping. The daughter of a former governor of St Petersburg, she threw over her civilized existence to live a simple life among the people. Without pretence or concern for her own-well being, she dedicated herself to caring for the ill and suffering, whether peasants in the village or revolutionaries in prison. Never an exponent of terrorism, she joined The People's Will only when the movement seemed threatened with destruction. Her face, before she met her death at the age of twenty-eight, was still that of a little girl, with full baby cheeks, small pursed mouth, and large eyes that stared forward, focused on nothing, in the child's stubborn unwillingness to see evil.[1]

Aleksandr Mikhailov, the disciplinarian of Land and Freedom, turned to terrorism when the organization he had built crumbled under the blows dealt to it by the autocracy. In desperation he summoned agitators to return from the provinces to join him in defending the core of Land and Freedom. When this failed, he abandoned the hope of immediate social revolution in order to participate in the concerted effort against the state. On the surface he resembled the terrorist ideal: suave in demeanour, he was harsh and demanding in the pursuit of his calling. But the severity of this young martinet—twenty-two when he was arrested in 1880—arose from an anguished struggle to protect the single congenial milieu he had found in life. His moist grey eyes expressed the loneliness he felt when he saw that milieu collapse in ruin.[2]

Aleksandr Barannikov, the son of an officer, left military school at the age of 17 in 1875 and joined the revolution to participate in a different, more noble form of combat. Violence was the only means of expression that this tall and powerful youth had inherited from the past, and he could deal with reality in no other way. Deemed the organization's 'angel of vengeance', he lived only to inflict the final blow upon the tsar. But he was not the hard-boiled killer of Kravchinskii's

[1] V. I. Figner, 'Sofia Perovskaia', *Byloe*, no. 32–3 (April–May 1918), pp. 3–11; V. I. Figner, 'Portrety narodovol'tsev', *Byloe*, no. 32–33 (April–May 1918), pp. 71–4; 'K biografam A. M. Zheliabova i S. L. Perovskoi', *Byloe*, no. 8 (1906), pp. 116–29.
[2] Figner, 'Portrety...', pp. 74–5; Valk, *Arkhiv Zemli i Voli i Narodnoi Voli*, pp. 92–5, 319–21.

imagination. A shy, withdrawn individual, he spoke rarely and with great difficulty. At meetings he would listen mutely, staring wildly forward. His portrait shows a large strong face, tense with anxiety, as if about to burst into screams. Huge eyes gaze out with a fanatic incomprehension akin to madness.[1]

Revolutionary optimism had provided the single source of faith for these rootless youths. When reality appeared bleak and discouraging, challenging the presumption that they were superior to the unjust and unilluminated world around them, they desperately fought back, in defence of their own self-respect. Each was endowed with a sense of his own personal worth that inspired him to rise in combat when his ideals were beleaguered; each had the trust in himself to regard his life and his cause with pride.

It was precisely this sense of personal worth that was alien to Gleb Uspenskii. Nikolai Mikhailovskii, Uspenskii's friend and most acute critic, was the first to point out this failing in him. Uspenskii, Mikhailovskii observed, suffered from an over-developed 'sick' conscience that insistently asserted his guilt and the need for repentance. The other side of his character, the quality of 'honour', was correspondingly stunted, leaving him devoid of the strength to stand up against provocation and defend what he cherished.[2] His upbringing and early life, as we have seen, had instilled in him a sense of frailty so strong as to make him doubt the justice of any cause that he embraced. This lack of a sense of honour estranged Uspenskii from the narodovol'tsy, and though he sympathized with them and knew many of them personally, he shrank from their methods and self-confident ways of thought.[3] When, at the end of 1879, his faith in the peasantry began to fail, he responded instead by idealizing the existing countryside, and by venting the indignation for the flaws he perceived in reality upon himself. The narodovol'tsy had spared the people responsibility for the condition of the countryside by casting all blame on the autocracy. He would spare the people responsibility by casting all blame on himself; he would absolve the people by taking on their sins.

[1] A. I. Barannikov, *Narodovolets A. I. Barannikov v ego pis'makh* (Moscow, 1935), *passim*; M. F. Frolenko, 'Lipetskii i voronezhskii s'ezdy', *Byloe*, no. 13 (1907), p. 70; Figner, 'Portrety...', p. 76.
[2] N. K. Mikhailovskii, *Literaturno-kriticheskie stat'i* (Moscow, 1957), pp. 356–7.
[3] A. I. Ivanchin-Pisarev, *Khozhdenie v narod* (Moscow–Leningrad, 1929), pp. 387–412; Uspenskii, VII, 485.

Uspenskii's striving for a posture of acceptance began in the summer of 1880, when he again visited his friend's estate in Novgorod province. The chief object of his idealization was a peasant working on the estate, whom he called in his account Ivan Ermolaevich.[1] There was little enough that was attractive about Ivan, and Uspenskii at first took a strong dislike to him. He was a morose, solitary, and apparently shiftless peasant who went about his tasks oblivious of all other concerns. He worked from morning till night with the primitive techniques of his ancestors, his only goal being to secure enough to eat, 'to be full'. Moral problems and the feeling of communal solidarity awakened no enthusiasm in him. He could not be bothered with 'friendship, comradeliness, or the mutual consciousness of the benefit of communal labour', Uspenskii's cherished values. Human beings in general held no interest for him. He looked upon other peasant households as economic units and could tell the precise number of cows in each and the exact quantity of grain and milk each produced, though he knew absolutely nothing about the people in them. When Uspenskii attempted to explain the advantages of collective labour to him, he always had a convenient pretext for slipping away.[2]

Ivan seemed to embody the moral apathy and shiftlessness that Uspenskii saw everywhere in the countryside. There was no arguing with him. He had no mind for lofty ideals and made no pretence of leading a model life. His was the alien mind of the people that had coldly rejected Uspenskii's advances. In Ivan, Uspenskii's conscience discerned the image of everything opprobrious in the world. The peasant's silence attested to Uspenskii's utter isolation, the failure of his attempt to find spiritual comradeship. But at this point, when his conscience had seemingly denigrated all sources of hope, Uspenskii's critical faculties stilled. He suddenly saw Ivan as the ideal and discovered the other self that had been lurking so long in his fantasy.

The revelation came upon Uspenskii as a result of an apparently petty incident on the farm. Ivan had been chagrined to find that a calf he had just purchased was sickly and weak.

---

[1] Uspenskii's Ivan Ermolaevich sketches were later collected under the title *Krestianin i krestianskii trud* (*Peasant and Peasant Labour*), in *Derevenskaia neuriaditsa* (St Petersburg, 1881–2), II, III.

[2] Uspenskii, VII, 7–8, 18–23, 27–9.

The peasant's distress over such an insignificant matter at first seemed unreasonable to Uspenskii; he could not comprehend why the peasant had become so exercised. But then understanding dawned upon him. He recalled an episode of six years before, that struck him as similar to Ivan's distress about his calf. While in the Louvre, examining the Venus de Milo, an artist friend had flown into a rage over the patchwork on the statue's leg. Uspenskii had been baffled then by the fury provoked by what appeared to him a minor flaw. In both cases, he now realized, he had failed to appreciate the other person's values. Both peasant and painter had been animated by an injured sense of artistic pride, unfathomable to him. His failure to sympathize with the misgivings of the peasant and the painter merely reflected his own lack of sensitivity. He could not sympathize with the peasant because the peasant possessed peculiar endowments that he lacked. Ivan Ermolaevich, who had seemed crudely and obtusely materialistic, thinking only of the fullness of his stomach, now appeared with the halo of the idealist, indifferent to mercenary cares and interested only in the perfection of his product. He harboured an artist's love for a task that absorbed all his energies and that dominated his thinking completely. Like the artist, he was prepared to sacrifice his well-being for his beloved work: his devotion to his trade was total and could spare no personal need.[1]

The artist who takes *his own personal advantage*, material gain, as his goal ceases to do ceremony with his conscience and paints only what is needed. He may lower himself to the drawing of signs for tailor and vegetable shops and this happens for the same reason that the peasant slips dung into his pressed hay.[2]

What Uspenskii had construed as a sluggish adherence to habit and tradition now appeared to be the arcane logic of art, justifying any sacrifice on the part of the creator. The peasant was motivated by an esoteric 'poetry of agricultural labour', and the *intelligent*'s attempts to tamper with it could only mar its beauty.[3] The peasant's life realized a perfect esthetic unity and harmony of proportion (*stroinost'*)—the wholeness and serenity so lacking in Uspenskii's broken, strident existence.

In the thoughts, acts, and words of Ivan Ermolaevich, there was not one petty detail that did not have the most real basis that was not

[1] *Ibid.* VII, 31–5.   [2] *Ibid.* VII, 35.   [3] *Ibid.* VII, 39–40.

completely intelligible to Ivan, while my life is continually burdened by thoughts and acts which have no link between them.[1]

Tormented by doubt, he looked enviously upon Ivan's unerring confidence, as the peasant, in communion with nature, attained complete freedom from uncertainty. Heeding nature's dictates, Ivan had been endowed with enormous power. Unlike the functionary, who had to storm and rage to cope with petty matters, Ivan, in tune with nature, knew what was and what was not impossible and acted with ease and assurance. He milked the cow because the cow had to be milked; sheared the lamb because the lamb had to be sheared; and, in exchange for accepting nature's dominion, he was accorded the same absolute authority over his animals and family.[2]

In answer to the intelligentsia's locutions, Ivan had only to say, 'It can't be done in any other way.' Ruling his family as the despotic agent of nature, he knew what was best for it, though his conduct seemed cruel and unjust to the educated. One head of family refused to allow his sister to marry because the family could not afford a dowry; another forced a young man to marry an idiot because it was economically advantageous; all was ordered according to the rule of nature.[3]

Uspenskii came to admire the very traits in Ivan that he had previously deplored. Ivan's hostility to communal methods suddenly appeared in a favourable light. Prospering by his own laborious efforts, he distrusted any arrangement which might permit poorer and lazier brethren to profit from his efforts. When asked about collective work, he replied laughingly, 'How is that possible? One person has one character, another, another! It's like trying to write one letter for the entire village.' Now, yielding to Ivan's logic, Uspenskii agreed that equalization of land holdings in the commune would be unfair, and even found fault with the poorer members for not forming a special co-operative among themselves.[4]

He comforted himself with the assurance that everything that disturbed him was inevitable. He met the poor shepherd, Eremei, who moved from job to job, unable to find steady employment. Ordinarily, Uspenskii would have fallen into remorse. Now he simply reasoned that Eremei could not live otherwise. 'You may pity him', Uspenskii wrote, 'but willy-

[1] *Ibid.* VII, 42.
[2] *Ibid.* VII, 44–7.
[3] *Ibid.* VII, 49–52.
[4] *Ibid.* VII, 62–5, 69–70.

nilly he must follow the course of life which is predetermined for him and is explained by the conditions found in his nature, his breed.' Rebelling against his own uncontrollable pity, Uspenskii bowed before the dominion of nature, which ordained that creatures must die so that new ones might be born.

Life and death for a person who is close to nature are fused together in one...A horse perishes, and before you have time to lament this deceased worker, she, the dead horse, momentarily begins to live a new life. How many lives she produces in one day! How many worms perish, for their own good! And what a wonderful mood the flocks of birds, crows, jackdaws and all kind of charming wood bird are in! How they clean the bones, giving them the most marvellous white colour with the aid of their sharp beaks and the wind and rain. By spring, there is no horse, and not even a drop of memory remains, for everything has run, crawled, flown away in the form of a thousand living creatures.[1]

Uspenskii's greatest enrapturement with the countryside thus followed his devastating exposures of rural life. As the countryside appeared more oppressive, his yearning for identification with the peasant received gratification in a succession of bizarre and contradictory fantasies. Unable to reconcile the real with the ideal, he idealized reality and renounced all claims to judgement. The material concerns of the peasantry which had revolted him in Samara were now justified by the incontrovertible sway of nature and became another object of adulation. The intricate process of land division, which only months before had seemed a perversion of communal principles, he now vindicated as a method of ensuring the distribution of land in proportion to each family's work force. The Russian state now became part of the greater hierarchy of nature, whose authority the peasant recognized in his everyday phrases, 'one cannot live without the family elder (bol'shak)', 'one must pay one's taxes', 'the tsar also needs money', and 'the tsar gives land'.[2]

But Uspenskii achieved no spiritual repose in his worship of nature. The perfection of the countryside merely attested to his own worthlessness. Recognizing the sway of nature, he became a mere spectator, a defective by-product of civilization, who could not presume to participate in the pure life of the peasantry. Watching Ivan go about his daily tasks completely

---

[1] *Ibid*. VII, 76.   [2] *Ibid*. VII, 52–3.

oblivious of him, Uspenskii thought that the peasant was re-
buking him for his clumsy meddling. Ivan seemed to be saying,
'Keep out!' (*Ne suicia*), 'Keep out and beat it!' He seemed
to be yelling, 'You have no reason to be messing around in
someone else's business.'[1] The words stunned the writer. Never
uttered by the peasant, engendered in his own mind, they were
an apocalyptical statement of the indifference to his values that
he had sensed since 1877. They recurred, jeering at his proud
aspirations and consigning him to doom.

All my books in which hundreds of various views are expressed about
one and the same question; all these rags of newspapers, these
brands of humanitarianism, nurtured by spare time *belles-lettres*,
all this, like dust borne by gusts of wind, was stirred by the 'natural
truth' breathed by Ivan Ermolaevich. Having no soil beneath my
feet but bookish humanitarianism, and split in two by humanitarianism of thought and parasitism of action, I, like a feather, was
lifted upward on Ivan Ermolaevich's breath of truth, and felt
irresistibly that I and all these books, newspapers, novels, pens and
proofsheets—even the calf that refuses to do Ivan's bidding—we,
this disorderly, disgraceful mass, are the whistle and din, flying
into a bottomless abyss...[2]

The only task the members of the intelligentsia could fulfil in
the countryside was to protect the natural harmony of peasant
life. They had to relinquish their hopes for far-reaching transformation, and become the peasants' guardians rather than
their preceptors. Then they could defend them from the incursions of civilization disrupting the primeval balance of the
countryside, and resist the introduction of farm machinery,
which, Uspenskii feared, would bring the abolition of the
communal system of land division. They could stand opposed
to the use of all farm implements and such household items as
tea, sugar, and kerosene lamps.[3] Having forestalled the breakdown of the commune, they could use peasant ideals to reform
themselves and introduce 'the natural demands of communal
life' into the 'mutilated, robbing, lying course of civilization'.[4]

Yet the possibility of thwarting the march of civilization,
Uspenskii conceded, was remote. Civilization had to be halted
if the ideal was to be saved, yet action was impossible. Uspenskii's summons incriminated the intelligentsia and himself in

---

[1] *Ibid.* VII, 40–1. [2] *Ibid.* VII, 54–5.
[3] *Ibid.* VII, 55–60, 485–6. [4] *Ibid.* VII, 486.

the ills of the countryside, ills over which they admittedly had no control. The challenge he sounded was merely a new note of masochism that suggested fresh and more unreasonable grounds for self-reproach. 'No, he [Ivan] is not guilty. I the educated Russian, I am most decisively guilty.'

I intentionally tried to benight the people, to sow confusion among them, to keep land and knowledge from them and to prevent the slightest alleviation of their toil. I familiarized them with civilization in a way that could only make them groan.[1]

Uspenskii's idealization of peasant life modulated very quickly into a diatribe against the intelligentsia that ended in a flood of self-abuse. The strange gyrations of Uspenskii's thought in his writings of the early 1880s left his friends, in whom hopes of change still remained alive, perplexed. His editor, the austere and exacting Mikhail Saltykov-Shchedrin, demanded in irritation that he delete the most strident of his passages and tone down others.

Your article has made a very bad impression on me and I am seriously beginning to think that you have been carried away by the ideals of Aksakov and Dostoevskii. . .The chief thing that you complain about is, in your own words, inevitable, and these complaints, consequently, are in large measure futile. Perhaps you are surprised that I understood your work in this way, but, *indeed, it is impossible to understand it in any other*.[2]

Uspenskii's message was heard more clearly after the ultimate revolutionary stratagem had failed. Once the autocracy had withstood the assassination of Alexander II and the forces of reaction began to gather strength, his sense of enraged helplessness before a hostile reality took on a meaning it did not have when sudden and total transformation was still adjudged possible. Then the members of the intelligentsia had to face a world they were powerless to change but unable to accept. Uspenskii's writings revealed the pathology of their outlook— the growing discrepancy between the ideals they lived for and the reality they had to live in.

In Uspenskii's final, major work, *Vlast' zemli* (*The Dominion of the Land*), published in 1882, the ideal bore almost no relation to

---

[1] *Ibid.* VII, 104–5.

[2] N. I. Mordovchenko, 'M. E. Saltykov-Shchedrin—redaktor G. I. Uspenskogo', I. I. Veksler, ed., *Gleb Uspenskii, materialy i issledovaniia* (Moscow–Leningrad, 1938), pp. 418–19.

the real. The strained idealization of reality in his Ivan Ermolaevich sketches was abandoned. Instead, resplendent fantasies alternated with pictures of squalor and degradation, and
Uspenskii, lapsing into myth and rhapsodic speculation, sought
refuge in a world of hallucination.

In 1881, Uspenskii purchased an estate and settled with his
family in Novgorod province. But permanent residence in the
countryside merely made peasant life more abhorrent to him
and deepened his despondency. The leading figure of *Vlast'*
zemli, Ivan Bosykh—the only living peasant in the work—
embodied all the sordidness that Uspenskii had perceived. Gone
were the transparent, idealized features of Ivan Ermolaevich.
Ivan Bosykh was a rural proletarian or, more accurately, a
tramp, who had severed his ties with the land and set himself
adrift in an alien, incomprehensible world. Although intelligent, strong, and a good worker, he drank so much that he
was incapable of doing any kind of labour. He beat his wife and
his children, who wandered through the village starving and in
rags. Indifferent to his present and future state, he was a person
'without prospects' and 'without a tomorrow'.[1]

Ivan said that he had gone to ruin because of freedom and
independence (*svoevolie*). He had left his land to work on the
railroad, where he earned more money than he had ever
possessed before. He drank cognac and lemonade, and, he
admitted, was spoiled. He could not become accustomed to the
new life. 'Our peasant nature just isn't this way,' he said. 'Our
nature is a working nature.' The more he earned, the more he
craved, and he did not come to his senses until he received a
sound beating at the hands of the local police captain. At the
mention of this punishment, Ivan's face became radiant. He
began to speak of his resurrection and told how he had run
home, repented, and vowed to begin farming again.[2] But it was
too late: by deserting the land, Ivan had forsaken the peasant's
sound ethos and doomed himself to a broken, dissolute life.

Ivan had lost his original innocence by being lured away
from his work on the land. Uspenskii's idealized peasantry
existed under the 'dominion of land', where peasants lived by
farm work and knew nothing else. This idyllic state was comparable to the rule of nature in his Ivan Ermolaevich sketches.
But in 1880 Uspenskii had sought out the manifestations of the

[1] Uspenskii, VIII, 7–9.   [2] *Ibid.* VIII, 18–22.

rule of nature and tried to shape his understanding of reality to take it into account. 'The dominion of the land', on the contrary, seemed to have no real existence at all. In describing it, Uspenskii relied on his fantasy, not his perception. It was inhabited by the peasantry of his imagination, 'patient and powerful in misfortune, young in heart, manfully strong, yet gentle as a child, the people who bear everything on their shoulders, the people that we love, the people that we go to for the cure of our spiritual ills'.[1] Though pervaded by bestiality and injustice, their untouched life knew neither artifice nor deceit. It was led according to the dictates of nature and even the most brutal acts happened spontaneously and therefore without sin. It was a condition where 'one devours another, though without base motivation', but where the commune functioned according to its original just principles.[2] Agricultural labour imposed similar conditions on all who performed it, fostering a natural sense of equality. Those differences that did arise were easily understandable to the peasant, for they stemmed from obvious disparities in intelligence and prowess.[3]

But the dominion of the land had been broken and its levelling influence had disappeared with it. Many peasants had left farming, and money now fell to the members of the commune arbitrarily. While the inept prospered, many strong and effective workers became impoverished. The logic of rural life had been destroyed and Ivan Bosykh epitomized the new conditions. Once a staunch worker, he had left his state of grace, and now found himself without values, in a moral void: 'Only the hollow machine of the human organism remains. Spiritual emptiness has set in—full freedom, i.e., unknown, empty expanses, limitless, empty space, a terrifying "go where you please"'.[4] The communal spirit had vanished from his soul. Although he had no wealth to fear for, he scoffed at the commune, declaring that he would not suffer for the good of 'the rascals and other rats'.[5]

In *Vlast' zemli* the intelligentsia appeared to be cast in its hallowed role of 'enlightener' of the people. The honest life under the dominion of the land, Uspenskii acknowledged, was unilluminated by morality, and even acts performed without evil intent could be horrifying in their unabashed savagery.

[1] *Ibid.* viii, 25.   [2] *Ibid.* viii, 78–84.   [3] *Ibid.* viii, 32–5.
[4] *Ibid.* viii, 25.   [5] *Ibid.* viii, 23–4.

One person skins another alive and feels nothing: it is enough for him to know that it can't be otherwise...Another, regarding this spectacle from afar, not only feels the pain of the torn skin, not only feels the suffering of the skinned individual, but has the effrontery to consider this inevitable act shocking and cruel.[1]

Uspenskii thus seemed to be upholding Herzen's classical formula for intelligentsia action in Russia: the intelligentsia was to combine its civilized justice with the peasant's natural truth.

But it was not the contemporary Russian intelligentsia that Uspenskii was thinking of when he expressed these hopes. The ideal intelligentsia in *Vlast' zemli* appeared through the mists of fantasy and illusion. The existing intelligentsia, like the existing peasantry, was degraded and unregenerate; it 'wallowed in some sort of old national and European rubbish, in old national and European trash heaps'.[2] The ideal intelligentsia lived in a remote and idyllic past. He saw them in the guise of ancient Russian missionary saints (*bozhie ugodniki*), whom he had learned of from the writings of Herzen. Understanding the needs of rural life, the missionary saints had won the peasants' confidence with bread and seeds, and spread the truth of Christ through the countryside. Neither guilt nor hopes of eternal salvation had impelled them. They had acted out of a sincere desire to help the people. 'Although *our peasant* saint withdraws from worldly cares, he lives only for the world,' Uspenskii wrote. 'He lives in the masses, the people, and rather than talk, he really does his task.' The *ugodniki* had inculcated moral strictness in the peasant, reared him in 'the education of the heart'. From them the peasants, then living like beasts, had learned the difference between right and wrong, and love for their brother. They were taught not to slaughter wives and children who were unfit for work.[3]

At the end of *Vlast' zemli*, as Uspenskii's eyes began to focus on reality, both the mythical peasant and the mythical *intelligent* faded from view. In place of the former he saw the people exemplified in the enigmatic figure of Platon Karataev, from Tolstoy's *War and Peace*. Inseparably joined to the great mass of the peasantry, Karataev was bereft of all individuality and incapable of experiencing simple human emotions like friendship and love. Alone he had no importance and he was aware of his

[1] *Ibid.* VIII, 84.   [2] *Ibid.* VIII, 85.   [3] *Ibid.* VIII, 84-6, 36-7.

insignificance. Besides the millions of Platons, there were only the 'predators', *khishchniki*, whose individualism was as developed as Platon's was suppressed. The countryside presented a distressing scene of ignorant, shiftless, helpless peasants victimized by a grasping, petty bourgeoisie.[1] Only the *bozhie ugodniki* could help and they were no more. Despairing of human agents, Uspenskii, in the last lines of *Vlast' zemli*, invoked the divine. 'Do not drive the need for God's truth among men from the peasant milieu,' he pleaded. 'It is as necessary to them as land. Do not forget that, though not in the near future, God, without fail, will speak the truth.'[2]

Uspenskii's writings from 1877 to 1882 provided a corpus of material on the peasantry and the intelligentsia's attitudes toward the peasantry that all radical writers on the countryside would have to take into account. For some his works would serve as a rich source of information on the breakdown of peasant institutions and the loss of primitive innocence, the unpleasant truths of rural life that the intelligentsia now had to acknowledge and to assess. Studies such as Kravchinskii's *The Russian Peasant* drew heavily on Uspenskii's accounts and analyses to show the advanced stage of disintegration that peasant life had reached. The character types, the situations, and the rich dialogue of Uspenskii's sketches became standard illustrations of the economic and spiritual revolution occurring in the countryside. Other writers, like Nikolai Zlatovratskii and Georgi Plekhanov, refused to accept his conclusions and took his experience as evidence of the confusion reigning in the thought of the intelligentsia. To them his works revealed the deep malaise that prevented the educated individual from fathoming the true meaning of the phenomena of rural life.[3] I will deal with this opposing viewpoint in the subsequent chapters.

After 1882, Uspenskii wrote less frequently about the peasantry. He tried to shun the disquieting scenes of rural life.

My nerves were long ago frayed by rural life, that life which is continually destroying, and, at the same time, continually disappearing into oblivion. This infinite vitality, having neither end nor limit, submerging the moment just past, can horrify you and

[1] *Ibid.* VIII, 119–21.
[2] *Ibid.* VIII, 564.
[3] G. V. Plekhanov (Bel'tov), *Za dvadtsat' let* (St Petersburg, 1906), pp. 26–61.

kill the very concept of your right to reflect on life and to build your plans according to some of those reflections. Thus 'the eternal life' of the countryside has vitiated my spiritual activity and aggravated and undone my nerves...[1]

He turned away from the outside world that had denied him consolation to contemplate his own inner world and to create his own comforts. In the years from 1882 till his confinement in a mental hospital in 1891, he gradually lost his grip on reality and his writings betrayed growing evidence of his ailment. His portraits show a sad and tired face, with knitted brows and large round eyes that stare out plaintively, expressing the grief and turmoil in his soul.[2]

Writing came with increasing difficulty. Family life began to oppress him and he fell into sieges of melancholy more frequently. He wrote to his wife, in early 1883, 'I was truly unable to take advantage of the moment when I was needed as a writer, and I fear that this moment has passed. I am weary...In my soul there is a total void...'[3] Rebelling against the sedentary existence he had imposed upon himself, he again sought relief from introspection in movement. The number of trips he took rose sharply through the eighties: in 1881, there were twelve; 1882, fifteen; 1883, twenty-four; 1884, twenty-two; 1885, thirty-seven. The time spent travelling increased, while the period spent in each place became shorter and shorter. Many trips seemed to have no rational purpose.[4] He would travel in phobic flight to new surroundings, only to find the same evil lurking there.

As the reaction took its toll, Petersburg too ceased to be an asylum. Many of his close friends had been imprisoned or exiled; others had died or committed suicide. An atmosphere of fear and hopelessness prevailed in intelligentsia circles. Nowhere finding relief, Uspenskii travelled back and forth between countryside and capital. 'For the lack of a place to stay, I have spent the last few months in the following manner: I live in Petersburg, get tired, go to the country, get tired and return to Petersburg...thus I have knocked about, back and forth for four months, and have become tired, more tired and more tired.'[5]

---

[1] Uspenskii, VIII, 518.   [2] Uspenskii, VIII, frontispiece; IX, frontispiece.
[3] Cheshchikhin-Vetrinskii, pp. 290–3; Uspenskii, XIII, 306.
[4] A. S. Glinka-Volzhskii, 'Opyt itinerariia G. I. Uspenskogo (1880–1900 gg.)', Gosudarstvenny literaturny muzei, Gleb Uspenskii, pp. 225–40.
[5] Uspenskii, VIII, 321.

Once he arrived in Petersburg at eleven at night and left at two the next afternoon, without seeing anyone, doing anything, or even knowing his original reason for coming.[1] He went to the Caucasus to visit a group of communal sectarians. His initial enthusiasm for their rigorous morality, however, was quickly dispelled by close observation of their life and he left after a stay of only a few days.[2] Disillusion and depression now overcame him almost immediately: at sight each new environment degenerated into immoral chaos.

As his faith in the peasant disappeared, his conscience insistently declared its terrible judgement. The old seemed to have survived the onslaught of reform and remained intact within the unjust life around him. He felt it insinuating itself into his soul and extinguishing the last flickering of optimism. Guilt, distrust, and hatred re-emerged from his past. Visions of his relatives and scenes from childhood passed before him. He remembered the sad, grey faces of the inmates in the prison and their mournful groans. The image of a tyrannical school inspector who demanded total obedience from his pupils flashed through his mind. He again felt the fear of his grandfather and the certainty of wrongdoing that had poisoned his life and allied him with evil.[3] Denied redemption, incapable of atonement, Uspenskii now bore the full burden of his past and was haunted by the presence of festering sin. He remembered the unrelenting dread of retribution, 'the cruel punishment that awaited all of us for this grave, inexpiable sin...hellish torment, hooks driven into the ribs, the fire, the flame and the stench'.[4]

He recalled the buoyant figure of Paramon, the joy the holy fool had awakened in him and his initial failure of strength. Now his baby daughter replaced Paramon in his mind. Untainted by life, she too seemed to demand courage that he did not possess. It evoked the images of Bradlaugh and Parnell, men who could unite personal and social aspirations and act with determination in defence of individual as well as group rights. Uspenskii, too, yearned to accomplish a *podvig*, a great, heroic deed, but he felt the need for a command from a higher authority, and felt unable to act in the absence of a greater cause that would engulf his person.[5] 'Yesterday, today, I am ready to perish

---

[1] Mikhailovskii, *Literaturno-kriticheskie stat'i*, pp. 411–12.
[2] Uspenskii, VIII, 291–315; XIII, 304–8.   [3] *Ibid.* VIII, 379–84, 387–92.
[4] *Ibid.* VIII, 386.   [5] *Ibid.* VIII, 416–19, 424–5.

"for them", for the general harmony, for social beauty (*bla-goobrazie*), and justice, but to defend this harmony for myself—that I cannot do!"[1] The mute independence of the infant seemed to reproach him for his impotence, and, filled with rage, he felt the vile impulse to murder it, and deliver himself from his own unrelenting self-deprecation.[2]

As he retreated from the outside world, he lost awareness of the limitations imposed by reality and set upon himself with ferocious violence, his self-castigation rising in a merciless tempo. Now surcease came not in images of an ideal peasant but in visions of virginal women, who enjoyed a state of grace and perfection beyond the reach of ordinary mortals. In 1885 he described the apparition of a beaming farm girl with long flowing hair living in joyous harmony with the fields of wheat, in the perfect unity with nature that he had once thought he had discovered in Ivan Ermolaevich. Then he saw the resplendent figure of Vera Figner, who had been sentenced to death by the autocracy, and in his mind she assumed the form of a martyr who by her sacrifice could redeem his polluted soul. She appeared as a girl of 'strict, nearly monastic type', whose face and gestures bore the imprint of deep sadness, not for herself but for others. The sadness was in perfect accord with her character and seemed to be an intrinsic part of her. She displayed a composure in her suffering, a 'harmony of self-sacrifice'. Her sacrifice sprang not from a sense of guilt but from her natural goodness, and beholding her gave Uspenskii the courage to suffer. 'With one look at her all suffering lost its frightening aspect and became simple, easy, pacifying and, mainly, *alive*, so that instead of the words "how awful" one felt impelled to say, "How fine, how glorious!"'[3] Then the perfection of Vera Figner and the peasant girl suddenly were embodied in the Venus de Milo. The flawless female statue radiated the total purity forsaken by the fallen human male, and gave Uspenskii, 'the mutilated contemporary individual', the strength to rise above himself, 'for the bright but hazy future penetrated to the soul'.[4]

But this exaltation would give way to bitter despondency and renewed consciousness of his unworthiness. During the late 1880s his depressions became longer and more hopeless, and

---

[1] *Ibid.* VIII, 410.   [2] *Ibid.* VIII, 423.   [3] *Ibid.* X, part I, 251.
[4] *Ibid.* X, part I, 270–2; Mikhailovskii, 372–5.

his hallucinations more vivid and ecstatic, his mental imbalance turning into derangement. The clash between good and evil rose to consciousness and rent his personality in two. When the evil in him gained the upper hand, he was Ivanovich, his patronymic, the father figure, the evil of the existing order, the defiler and transgressor. The swinishness (*svinstvo*) that he had felt in himself and observed in the world took possession of his mind and he would believe he was a pig, turn his face into a snout, and behave accordingly.[1] At other times the yearning for good would clear his soul of evil, and he would become Gleb, the name his mother had given him, the violated feminine self. He would behold Marguerite, a saintly woman in a snow-white dress who approached him and placed her hand on his shoulder. The world then would overflow with love and he would feel himself divine. But this would last only a few moments. Gloom, fear, and self-hatred would gradually descend upon him. The memories of his past would reawaken and recall the nightmare of his life.[2]

The works of Gleb Uspenskii portrayed the fate of an *intelligent* at odds with reality, one whose conception of the ideal ran counter to the order of nature and who found reconciliation inconceivable. His writings foretold the demise of progressive hopes, the spiritual doom of the intelligentsia. He was the populist 'martyr of the pen' whose personal disintegration epitomized the tragedy of a generation whose ideals of life had proved to be false. But many were unable to accept so pessimistic a view and sought a less disconsoling rendering of the events in the countryside, one which would yield the necessary reconciliation between real and ideal. To create this was the task of Nikolai Nikolaevich Zlatovratskii, who sought the good in reality with the same determination and passion as Gleb Uspenskii sought the evil.

---

[1] B. N. Sinani, 'Dnevnik doctora B. N. Sinani', Gosudarstvenny literaturny muzei, *Gleb Uspenskii*, p. 520.

[2] P. M. Zinov'ev, 'Bol'noi Uspenskii', Gosudarstvenny literaturny muzei, *Gleb Uspenskii*, p. 495.

4
NIKOLAI NIKOLAEVICH ZLATOVRATSKII AND THE NECESSARY RECONCILIATION

This free heart,
That lived through bondage,
The heart of the people,
Is a heart of gold!

The force of the people,
Is a force that is mighty,
A conscience that is tranquil,
A truth that is alive!

NEKRASOV, *Komu na Rusi zhit' khorosho*

During the 1870s and 1880s the writings of Nikolai Nikolaevich Zlatovratskii were an unremitting source of faith for the intelligentsia. Even when depicting the social and economic dilemmas of the countryside, they effused optimism. Zlatovratskii's trust in his ideals always remained firm. Never for a moment did he doubt that what he believed was right; only in rare instances did he doubt that it would triumph. If Uspenskii's world was incomprehensible in its flux, Zlatovratskii's was predictable in its certainty. His works were pervaded by an unctious moralism—a dogmatic consistency that yielded neither to divergent opinions nor to contrary facts.

The painful ideological evolution of the intelligentsia, the heated debates between conflicting theories, held little interest for Zlatovratskii. He never regarded himself as an *intelligent*, and intellectual talk and philosophizing always remained alien to him. He presented his image of himself in the character of Bashkirov, the young hero of the novella *Zolotye serdtsa* (*Hearts of Gold*), published in 1877. An ugly youth, a bastard by birth, Bashkirov was unadorned by civilized nicety. Like Zlatovratskii, his language was an incongruent blend of seminary jargon, classical phraseology, and peasant argot that struck the ears of the educated harshly. Bashkirov felt alienated from the students at the university and uncomfortable during their discussions.[1] But he loved the people and knew them well. 'I am not a theoretician but a practical individual,' Bashkirov declared. 'Not an abstraction but life, not generalization but fact, not dogma but faith, not mind but heart, not reflex but sensation. I am an old reflection of everything that is the people.'[2]

Rather than a member of the intelligentsia, Bashkirov was an integral part of the '*ustoi*', the 'foundations' of rural life that embodied the virtue and wisdom of the peasantry. Zlatovratskii considered himself a product of these 'foundations'. Although he, like Uspenskii, was the son of a bureaucrat of clerical background, he felt himself bound 'by living nerves to the living material' of the people.[3] The 'foundations' were the subject of most of Zlatovratskii's work, and in describing them he wrote with a colour and passion that won the attention of the reading public. The 'foundations' represented the underpinnings of his mature identity, the source of good in himself that proved that he was not isolated and alone like the intelligentsia, but capable of drawing strength directly from the matrix of Russian life. Many members of the intelligentsia agreed with Zlatovratskii's conception of himself. In their midst this sickly, irascible, pompous man seemed a strange, almost foreign, figure who must have come to them from the people. The literary critic Protopopov wrote:

No matter how he berated us—the intelligentsia—Uspenskii was still a bird of our flock, while Zlatovratskii among us was like a Canaide among Trojans. Questions of politics were not alien to Uspenskii, and were even close to him, but Zlatovratskii did not even wish to know about them. Although Uspenskii passionately loved and pitied the people, observed and studied them, and in excitement told about them, he did so as a person apart from the people, an educated individual. But Zlatovratskii is a pure-blooded Russian peasant like Turgenev's intellectual Khor who has 'learned all about our knowledge' and what is in our books, but has remained true to his nature and is ready at any moment to trade the company of Darwin and Spencer for that of Grandpa Mitayai or Grandpa Minyai.[4]

[1] N. N. Zlatovratskii, *Sobranie sochinenii* (Moscow, 1897), III, 17–19; N. S. Rusanov, *Na rodine 1859–1882* (Moscow, 1931), p. 251.
[2] P. N. Sakulin, 'Narodnichestvo N. N. Zlatovratskogo', *Golos Minuvshego* (January 1913), no. 1, p. 122.
[3] Zlatovratskii, *Sobranie sochinenii* III, 19–20; Sakulin, p. 122.
[4] M. A. Protopopov, *Literaturno-kriticheskie kharakteristiki* (St Petersburg, 1896), p. 475.

To be sure, Zlatovratskii was not a peasant nor did he feel much more comfortable in the peasant village than others reared on civilized values. Though he forswore the society of St Petersburg, once his writings began to bring him a steady income in the mid seventies, he spent all his falls and winters there.[1] Most of the rest of the year he lived not in the countryside, but in his Vladimir home, where his contact with rural life was limited to chats with visiting peasants from the vicinity. Yet it is also true that his background had bred in him a much stronger attachment to the peasants than most other educated individuals of his time possessed. Zlatovratskii's personality, like his speech, was an ill-proportioned amalgam of disparate elements. He had grown up too close to the common people to feel a part of the intelligentsia; yet he had become too educated and his thinking too refined for him to fit in easily with the peasantry. In many ways he, like his character Bashkirov, was a bastard, set apart by his confused heritage from the rest of the world.

Only in childhood had Zlatovratskii felt that he belonged to the life around him. In the warmth of his parental home, he had been imbued with ideals and aspirations that could find no gratification in later life. Zlatovratskii's longing for the 'foundations' was a nostalgia for his own lost past and his writings were the account of his lifelong search for his original innocence.

In childhood, Zlatovratskii had felt himself graced with a majestic heritage. He grew up in the historic town of Vladimir, where the ancient churches and cathedrals that lined the streets and dotted the countryside recalled the era of the foundation of the Russian state. As a boy, he regarded himself as a descendant of men of prowess and stature who had created Russia's past. His grandfather, the deacon of the Church of the Golden Gates (*Zolotye vorota*—whence the name Zlatovratskii), exemplified to him all of this ancient glory. Smelling of wax and incense, the old man would play with him and spoil him with communion bread and honey cakes. Zlatovratskii would always remember him worshipping: eyes fixed on the church ceiling, arms aloft, body quivering, he shouted his prayers to the heavens.[2]

The life in Zlatovratskii's home was one of rich sensuous

[1] N. N. Zlatovratskii, 'Pro memoria', Zlatovratskii archive, Pushkinskii dom, no. 37, p. 16.
[2] N. N. Zlatovratskii, *Vospominaniia* (Moscow, 1956), p. 41; N. N. Zlatovratskii, 'Biografiia i bibliografiia', Zlatovratskii archive, Pushkinskii dom, no. 49, p. 1; Zlatovratskii, *Sobranie sochinenii*, I, 229.

experience, and as a child, he learned the delight of intense and ecstatic emotion. He remembered the pleasures of his mother's caress. He marvelled at the mystical dreams and legendary tales that she and his nurse told him. He craved 'religious-idealistic exaltation', when he could rise to inspired communion with nature and humanity.[1] He had watched his mother attain this state when she prayed before one of her old ikons. At such times he imagined that she had achieved a mystical understanding of the world.

For her this was not something that was simply external and formal. It was a vast and unified world view, which encompassed in one vast harmonic system all the facts of the human soul. It embraced the answers to the most complex demands of life, the most elevated problems of morality, and the satisfaction of all aesthetic needs...It was actually a kind of religious romanticism...[2]

Zlatovratskii believed that his relatives' natural spontaneous feeling arose from their nearness to the people. Both of his grandfathers were members of the poor rural clergy, and his family, unlike Uspenskii's, cherished its simple origins. His home was frequently crowded with peasants, who came to pray or to receive comfort and advice from his mother and grandmother. He heard them lament their hardships and voice their religious feelings. Many of them, he thought, harboured the same vague spiritual yearnings as he.

In the majority of cases these were either people suffering deeply from the burdens of life, seeking consolation, healing and escape from their torment in religious quest; or they were true peasant romantics, a spontaneous peasant intelligentsia whose souls were not content with the petty commotion of life, who were continually striving toward freedom, breadth and spiritual contact with the people of the boundless world of the divine, where they sought the answers to the disturbing demands of their souls, a broadening of their horizons.[3]

In Zlatovratskii's eyes, the advent of reform in Vladimir boded the triumph of his own mythical past. He saw the outside world being redeemed by the kind of emotional exaltation he had experienced in his own home. Change meant the revival of an ancient heritage for Zlatovratskii and in him the psychology of change was expressed as a relentless dreaming of the

---

[1] Zlatovratskii, *Vospominaniia*, p. 104.   [2] *Ibid.* p. 43.   [3] *Ibid.* p. 45.

great apocalyptic process by which that heritage would come to prevail.

His uncles, returning from the university, brought with them the ideas and the enthusiasm of the youth of the capital. 'How buoyant and joyous they were, how many illuminating and transfiguring revelations they bore, how many unknown pearls of "free thought" and poetry they imperceptibly introduced into our souls.'[1] They showed him a copy of Herzen's *Kolokol* (*The Bell*); he heard them talk of Belinskii and Shchedrin, and he read the poems of Nekrasov. Impressions, only half comprehended, poured into his mind 'like a cascade'. He revelled in the sound of the strange words, and though he was too young to fathom their meaning, they inspired him. When his uncles gathered at his home, he concealed himself behind a screen and overheard their whispered conversations. He sensed the conspiratorial excitement of their lives. The daring radical figures they discussed reminded him of ancient martyrs and heroes.[2]

You only have to imagine that all this was said in subdued voices, in broken phrases and subtle hints, to understand the strange form in which this was grasped by my consciousness: a series of fanciful, legendary images were evoked in my imagination, which still preserved in its depth cloudy reflections of other, just as fanciful, images, the 'martyrs', the 'passion sufferers' (*strastoterptsy*), about whom I had learned from hints in the religious legends told to me in childhood, in the cooking hut of our small provincial house.[3]

Once, through a chink in the screen, he caught a glimpse of Nikolai Dobroliubov, who had come to visit one of his uncles. The sight of the critic's face thrilled the boy, and later in life, his idol's portrait would always hang on his wall, a memento of a lost race of men, next to whom the members of his own generation would seem feeble and impotent.[4]

Zlatovratskii's father, Nikolai Petrovich Zlatovratskii, though only a minor bureaucrat, played an active role in the reform movement in Vladimir. He founded and organized Vladimir's first public library. When the preparations for emancipation began, he was chosen secretary to the marshal of the provincial nobility and entrusted with the task of assembling information about the economic condition of the Vladimir peasantry.

---

[1] *Ibid.* pp. 76–7.   [2] *Ibid.* pp. 80–3, 85–6, 102–3.   [3] *Ibid.* p. 102.
[4] *Ibid.* pp. 133–4; N. Teleshov, *Zapiski pisatelia* (Moscow, 1952), p. 129.

Accompanying him to several meetings of the gentry, Zlatov-ratskii rejoiced at the excitement of the debates interrupted by angry shouting and stormy bursts of applause.[1]

Emancipation was decreed shortly after Zlatovratskii's fifteenth birthday, and the terms jarred him like a cold douche. "The Manifesto of February 19" and especially the publication of the rescript drew a final line between the past and the imminent future: there was suddenly a definite end to all the lofty hopes and to all the fears.'[2] The line also marked the boundary between Zlatovratskii's childhood and youth, the time when the exaltation of his fantasies gave way to frequent and painful encounters with reality. The world began to appear not as an expression of his family's ideals of heroism and piety, but as something inimical and menacing. For Uspenskii the emancipation represented a beginning, a moment of liberation when an inviting future seemed to beckon; for Zlatovratskii it represented an end, a moment of failure, when the inspiration of the past seemed to lose its force.

In Vladimir, conservative nobles succeeded in gaining the strength to oust their liberal marshal, and Nikolai Petrovich lost his post as secretary. He could find no other position, and the family fell on hard times. The old expansive and bounteous spirit disappeared, and Zlatovratskii's life became meagre and austere. The beloved ikons were sold to secure the means for subsistence, and the family was forced to move to dingy quarters. Zlatovratskii's father was a member of the first generation to be broken by Russian reality, to fail the heroic image of the past. Zlatovratskii always preserved the memory of the decline of this active, talented man into a taciturn recluse. He recalled his father sitting gloomily in his bathrobe from morning till night, doing nothing but smoking his pipe and composing futile pleas for work to important bureaucrats.[3]

In his own ventures into the outside world, Zlatovratskii met with drabness, sordidness, squalor, and a general contempt for everything he considered beautiful. At the gymnasium, which he attended from 1855 to 1864, he underwent a series of painful and disquieting experiences. He found the classrooms harsh and dank, and the cold intellectual material oppressed him. 'The dry lifeless formalism killed in me the direct poetry of religious

---

[1] Zlatovratskii, 'Biografiia i bibliografiia', p. 1.
[2] Zlatovratskii, *Vospominaniia*, p. 145.   [3] *Ibid.* pp. 151–6.

feeling.' Knowledge became 'a terror, like the penance for some awful guilt'.[1] He felt completely apart from his schoolmates. The upper-class students told stories that sickened him, and brought the younger boys under their sway. Even he felt himself surrendering to their influence: impulses alien to his nature began to stir. 'Hour by hour, day by day, the malignant disease of this atmosphere pervaded my soul as well and brought vile animal instincts up from its depths.'[2]

The great emotional and spiritual needs awakened in him in childhood were suddenly left without sustenance. The downfall of his father deprived him of someone to guide him in the tradition he revered. Deep in melancholy, Nikolai Petrovich could offer his son little help. To his son's questions, he answered with feeble maxims about studying and bettering oneself.[3] Zlatovratskii's coming of age was marked by the realization of his own weakness and inferiority. He felt himself deprived of the strength and virtue of the past, cut off from the heritage he considered his own. Throughout his life he strove to recapture the lost warmth, colour and courage of his childhood. He pursued affection that simulated his mother's caress, the company of benign old men who resembled his grandfather, and heroes whose lives had the glitter and sweep of his childhood tales.

He first sought answers to his problems at a circle of seminary students who met to discuss science and religion. Though he attended the gymnasium, he found youths with theological and mystical interests more to his liking. He was intrigued by a theory some of them advanced about a new higher religion based on transcendental good which could replace the dry, formalistic teachings of the church. Their ideas recalled the sincere devotion of his home, and when he spoke, he spoke of his family life. With artless candour, he unburdened himself to the students, telling them of his mother's passionate form of worship. He described the chagrin that had overcome him when he realized that her faith was mixed with superstition. He voiced his belief that the pure religious feelings could be separated from the profane and be preserved.[4]

As the other youths elaborated the tenets of a new religion, Zlatovratskii punctuated their arguments with examples from his own life. The circle became a sounding board for his attach-

---

[1] *Ibid.* pp, 47–8, 57–8.　　　[2] *Ibid.* pp. 58–9.
[3] *Ibid.* pp. 156–7.　　　[4] *Ibid.* pp. 170–5.

ment to his family, rather than an opportunity to establish comradeship and a new identification. Zlatovratskii's commitment to his past discouraged rapport with people of his own age and education.[1] It diverted him from all the concerns of the intelligentsia, and the events of the day held little interest for him. He rarely read newspapers, and politics entered his life only when news came of the persecution of leading radical figures. Then his mind would again entertain visions of heroes and their legendary deeds.[2]

In 1864 Zlatovratskii left Vladimir to pursue his education and to seek his livelihood in the city. First he attended Moscow University, then the Technological Institute in Petersburg. But after a year at each, he found it impossible to support himself and finally had to terminate his studies and go to work. His stay in Petersburg from 1865 to 1872 was a period of intense anguish and poverty, when he engaged in a lonely and fruitless struggle to establish a literary reputation.

The capital oppressed the young Zlatovratskii. While Uspenskii felt moved by its pulse and intellectual ferment, Zlatovratskii was repelled by its stern impersonality, the aloofness and indifference of its urban population. He took a job as a proofreader in a printer's shop, where, in a damp, chilly cellar, he worked until five in the morning, his body warmed by large quantities of vodka which steadily undermined his health and stamina.[3] His first literary works appeared at this time—typical *raznochintsy* sketches of the sixties with a sardonic, lightly humourous contempt for Russian reality. They briefly furnished him with means to live, but his inspiration soon ebbed and he was again left penniless.

In the winter of 1872, Zlatovratskii, suffering from cold, hunger, and excessive drinking, collapsed in the streets of Petersburg. When he emerged from the hospital, he was, at the age of twenty-seven, physically broken and crippled for life. Directing a pen across paper became a difficult task and fits of dizziness would strike him at the moments of highest creative excitement.[4] His condition hobbled him, depriving him of the ability to climb stairs and to walk out of doors without assistance.

---

[1] N. N. Zlatovratskii, 'Zolotaia rota i eia predvoditel'', *Remeslennaia gazeta*, no. 1 (1876), p. 10.   [2] Zlatovratskii, *Vospominaniia*, pp. 178, 184.
[3] N. N. Zlatovratskii, 'Pro memoria', pp. 6–8.
[4] *Ibid.* pp. 6–12; *Literaturnoe nasledstvo* (Moscow, 1949), no. 51–2, p. 302.

By the end of the seventies, he was a prematurely old man who could be seen shuffling through the streets of Petersburg hunched over his cane with his wife at his side. Pierced by the damp, icy wind, he would burst into paroxysmic coughing and rush for shelter.[1]

During 1872 and 1873 Zlatovratskii recuperated from his illness in his Vladimir home under his parents' care.[2] It was there, in the quiet and warmth of familiar surroundings, that his mature viewpoint took form. Crippled and disabused by the Russian capital, he turned against all that urban life represented —society, civilization, and knowledge. He began to see the city as the incarnation of the sinister forces endangering his home, and the countryside as the womb of all that was natural and benevolent. It was there that the identity of his own fate and that of the peasants dawned upon him. He realized that they too were buffeted by a soulless world, and he perceived in their communal institutions the warmth and protection of the hearth.

Perhaps it was here that for the first time the thought took root in Nikolai Nikolaevich's soul of the terrible helplessness of the lonely existence of the toiling people, and of the great importance for them of brotherly communal solidarity, which alone can secure material and spiritual independence for them.[3]

At home, Zlatovratskii recalled the assistance an *artel'* of water-carriers had given him when he had been evicted from his room in Petersburg and had gone to sleep hungry in the basement of a saloon. The members had fed him and cared for him as one of their own. Zlatovratskii remembered their robust vigour and their natural physical effervescence. He wrote of their leader Selifan:

Selifan was a peasant of such gigantic height, such healthy muscles that one could regard him only with admiration. The soul rejoiced, looking upon this incarnation of health and strength, particularly in comparison with the worn-out Petersburg worker folk...[4]

[1] Rusanov, *Na rodine*, pp. 250–1; *Literaturnoe nasledstvo* (Moscow, 1934), nos. 13–14, p. 366.
[2] Zlatovratskii, 'Pro memoria', p. 12; Zlatovratskii, 'Biografiia i bibliografiia', p. 3.
[3] Zlatovratskii, 'Pro memoria', p. 11; V. V. Bush, *Ocherki literaturnogo narodnichestva 70-80 gg.* (Leningrad–Moscow, 1931), p. 22.
[4] Zlatovratskii, *Sobranie sochinenii*, I, p. 102.

The peasants possessed the spiritual solidarity and vitality lacking in the ailing, lonely writer. He was aggrieved by his own debility, his inadequacy before the vital heritage that the peasants, it seemed, had preserved.

And how in these moments I wanted to be invested with the powerful flesh and blood of my benefactors, to feel in myself the healthy strength of iron muscles in order to receive the sanction for 'equality of rights' and the 'legal capacity' to bear the horrifying hardships and adversities of life. I stretched my arm, squeezed my fist, and fresh blood began to run through me, but my fist was weak and my arm hung limp like a leash...I was ashamed and tears rushed to my eyes...[1]

In 1873 and 1874, when the youth in the capital were contemplating a popular, socialist revolution and trying to arrive at a conception of the nature of the peasantry, Zlatovratskii reached his own personal understanding of rural life. Alone in a harsh and unfeeling world, he dreamed of 'foundations' that were an extension of himself, the realization of his beliefs and values, and he conceived of a peasantry that could succour him in his despair. He felt himself rejoining his tradition. He tried to shed the hated features of the *intelligent* and to return to his original purity. He let his beard grow long and introduced peasant phrases into his otherwise bookish speech.

In his writings, Zlatovratskii turned his new view of the world into a picture of rural reality. He portrayed his ideals at war with the ruthless and menacing forces of civilization. He described good peasants, faithful to the 'foundations', victimized by city people pursuing their own profit. In '*Krestiane-prisiazhnye*' ('Peasant Jurors'), his first major story, the simple and virtuous peasants who came to Moscow as jurors were derided mercilessly by the crass Muscovites and in the end were left embarrassed and confused.[2] Zlatovratskii made no pretence at artistic detachment in his fiction. His works were elaborate justifications of himself and of what he stood for, and his peasants embodiments of his own aspirations and fears. Though couched in the realistic idiom of the day, his fiction was a prolonged act of narcissism, a contemplation of himself, depicted on the broad canvas of Russian reality.

[1] *Ibid.* i, p. 105.

[2] N. N. Zlatovratskii, 'Krestiane-prisiazhnye', *Otechestvennye Zapiski*, no. 219 (March 1875), pp. 147–203. It is interesting that Uspenskii's first story about the peasantry also appeared in this issue.

Since his return home in 1872, Zlatovratskii had dreamed of a work of epic proportions that would describe the fateful social changes taking place in Russia. At first he tried to write a play with this as its subject, but as the results proved unsuccessful, he changed his *genre* to the novel, and in 1877 began work on *Ustoi* (*The Foundations*), the major creative effort of his life. *Ustoi* absorbed most of his energies for the next six years and became the vehicle for all of the ideas about the countryside which he held during his period of greatest influence. A sprawling, chaotic work with an involuted plot, transparent characters, and numerous, wearisome sermons, *Ustoi* was almost completely devoid of literary merit. But the rich tableau of the countryside that Zlatovratskii presented appealed to the intelligentsia, for whom the peasantry remained something remote and unknown. He brought to the urban reader a close-up view of village life and insights into the actual thoughts and feelings of peasants caught in the vortex of social change.

The scene of *Ustoi*, as of most of Zlatovratskii's works, was his native Vladimir. There Zlatovratskii could easily observe and describe the impact of the new economic forces upon the countryside. Located in the Moscow industrial region, Vladimir in the 1870s was experiencing a rapid growth of trade and commerce, and traditional rural ways were yielding to the spreading individualism. Peasants in growing numbers went off to work for part or all of the year in the city, and those who remained devoted an increasing part of their time to trade. Farm work devolved largely upon women or children. A leading expert on Russian agriculture, Prince Vasil'chikov, wrote in 1876, 'In the province of Vladimir there have been cases where whole villages with all of their members have surrendered their land, turned it over to the Bureau of Crown Lands (*Udel'noe vedomstvo*), and registered as members of the petty bourgeoisie (*meshchanstvo*).'[1] Zlatovratskii viewed Vladimir as a microcosm that revealed the early stages of a conflict which would ultimately engulf all of Russia. In Vladimir, the foundations could be observed under stress, and their triumph, if triumph it was, could be heralded.[2]

[1] Kniaz' A. Vasil'chikov, *Zemlevladenie i zemledelie v Rossii i drughikh evropeiskikh gosudarstvakh* (St Petersburg, 1876), II, 628.
[2] N. N. Zlatovratskii, 'Krasny kust'', *Otechestvennye Zapiski*, no. 254 (January 1881), part II, p. 6.

The first instalment of the novel appeared in the May 1878 number of *Otechestvennye Zapiski* with the subtitle 'The History of a Settlement' ('*Istoriia odnogo poselka*'). It began with a revealing indication of Zlatovratskii's approach. He would try to describe all, including the most disturbing, trends in rural life. But he warned the reader not to take the signs of breakdown seriously. The variety of settlements in Vladimir was not, he contended, a sign of genuine economic differentiation. The countryside, he acknowledged, was in flux, but on the strength of a metaphor he assured the reader that the apparent diversity would flow back to its original uniformity, and that the communal tradition would, in the end, prevail.

Thus it is more a process of searching for the channel that the sea of peasant life, turbulent and tossed by the interaction of new and varied forces, is trying to pour into, just as a river, breaking through the dam restraining it, flows across the plain in a thousand tiny streams, twisting and gliding, striving to find a common channel so that, pouring together once again, they can flow majestically in a mighty current.[1]

The plot line of the first section of *Ustoi* followed the pattern set out at the beginning, recording the collapse of the old way of life, yet stressing its great vitality. The general picture of social change was offset by Zlatovratskii's descriptions of the peasants themselves. The figures who inhabited his landscape were creatures of his nostalgia, elaborated from the tales told him by the kindly old peasant men who sat and chatted with him in his Vladimir home. In his characters, 'the foundations', although embattled, lived on and stalwartly resisted the corrosive new influences. The hero of the first part of *Ustoi* was old Mosei Volk, the wise patriarch of the Volk family, who in the sublime past had shown that it was possible to adapt the 'foundations' to meet the new challenges. Although Mosei had purchased land deep in the forest outside the commune—and thus was likely to mislead the untrained eye of the *intelligent*—he remained an exemplary member, a champion of communal principles and of traditional peasant values. He forbade his sons to go to the city. Since he had acquired too much wood for his own use, he invited the members of the commune to share it

---

[1] N. N. Zlatovratskii, 'Ustoi (Istoriia odnogo poselka)', *O echestvennye Zapiski*, no. 238 (May 1878), p. 120.

with him. He voluntarily boarded soldiers' widows and continued to discharge his usual communal obligations. But he was not sacrificing his own interests, for the arrangement was mutually beneficial, though 'in the old way'. The *starosta* told him, 'If you need any help from the commune do not be afraid to ask for it. It won't be refused you...We are living with you as if in common.' 'In common, that's the best!' Mosei replied.[1]

Mosei's creative involvement with the *ustoi* placed him in the category of 'peasants with ideas'. There were many such individuals in the countryside, Zlatovratskii claimed, 'and perhaps no fewer than in civilized society'.[2] 'The people know that the "peasant with ideas" rarely goes astray, and, therefore, that what is permissible for the "peasant with ideas" is not for the ordinary mortal.' The thought of such peasants as Mosei, however, was not the private possession of single individuals. It was the cumulative product of centuries of peasant experience, an integral part of the 'economic and moral or intellectual system of the people', which the 'peasants with ideas' merely had the gift to express.[3]

In the first part of *Ustoi* Zlatovratskii traced the decline of the Volk family from pristine grace to its current confusion and dissension. Mosei's oldest son Vanifantii, who had once defied his father's injunction against going to the city, was weak-kneed and unsure of himself, and after Mosei's death the mantle of defender of the *Ustoi* passed to Vanifantii's sister Ul'iana, who, in Zlatovratskii's grandiloquent rhetoric, was an 'honour-able-minded person of the village' (*blagomyshlenny chelovek derevni*). Ul'iana, though sincerely devoted to the family's tradition, lacked her father's creative spirit. Whereas Mosei had been a brilliant innovator who had overhauled the foundations, Ul'iana was a conservative, sustaining a beneficent legacy and resuscitating it when she found it failing: she was 'the directing organ, the adviser and preserver of her forefathers' foundations'. She lived according to justice (*po pravde*), and all her words were laden with 'justice and conviction'. She possessed a great capacity for renunciation that enabled her to rise to heroic feats of altruism. She counselled the poor, helped the sick and brought husbands home to their wives from the tavern.[4]

Ul'iana led a holding action in defence of the communal

---

[1] *Ibid.* no. 238, pp. 135–6. [2] *Ibid.* no. 238, pp. 121–3.
[3] *Ibid.* no. 238, pp. 124–5. [4] *Ibid.* no. 238. pp. 172–4.

ideals. When a poor peasant, who had gone astray and become a thief, reformed and petitioned for re-entry to the commune, the members voted almost unanimously to accept him back and to return his land. The *starosta* cried, 'We must not violate the old precepts,' and Ul'iana joined him in shouting down those who opposed the decision. After the meeting, the peasants merrily rejoiced and exchanged warm congratulations. 'For a long time, mutual greetings and assurance of mutual aid resounded. Everything is in common as it has been for all time and as it ought to be forever.' When a visitor from Moscow jeered at the commune's decision, Ul'iana answered stoutly, 'We live the way we feel—in the communal way.'[1]

Several months after the appearance of the first instalment of *Ustoi*, Uspenskii described the incident of Fedia the horse thief, perhaps in response to Zlatovratskii's account.[2] Uspenskii showed each family living 'on its own desert island', indifferent to the fate of the others; Zlatovratskii had peasants patting each other on the back for upholding their forefathers' traditions. The ideals of the two writers were identical; their conceptions of reality were absolutely irreconcilable. Fedia's murder confirmed Uspenskii's sense of the prevalence of evil in the world. Mosei and U'liana expressed Zlatovratskii's belief in the vitality of the traditional good. And just as Uspenskii could not discern the sources of cohesion and strength surviving in peasant life, Zlatovratskii found it impossible to appreciate the nature of the forces of disruption. Though he depicted the social disintegration taking place in the village, he could never fathom the reasons for such a development. The elements endangering his ideal remained clothed in the diabolical aura of the unknown and preternatural spirits that had threatened his childhood security. The onslaught of civilization seemed to take its strength not from a rational dynamic of history, but from the sinister machinations of people outside the commune, who contrived to subvert some of the members within.

Zlatovratskii embodied the powers of destruction in the sinister figure of Petr Volk, the son of Vanifantii. Won to the cause of evil by a Moscow merchant, Petr turned against his grandfather's heritage and entered the civilized world to pursue his own material interest. Zlatovratskii's Satan, he was cast from heaven to hell for his proud rebellion against the existing

---

[1] *Ibid*. no. 238, pp. 156–62.   [2] See chapter 3, pp. 73–4.

state of grace. Zlatovratskii spared no venom in his portrayal of Petr. He appeared as a wretched, wicked youth, who was suddenly consumed with the malicious determination to break away from his family traditions and wreck what Mosei had created. He was ashamed to be attached to 'the foundations' and tried to suppress his peasant mannerisms. He sauntered through the village street attired in fancy city clothes, which he brushed continuously. He avoided contact with his former brethren and when addressed responded curtly. When Filaret, a simple peasant lad, asked him how people lived in Moscow, he replied, 'A smart person always gets along well, and even in the capital it's tough for fools.'[1]

Zlatovratskii expressed his own sentiments about Petr in the naive reactions of Filaret. Filaret disliked Petr, but his dislike was tempered by disbelief: he could not admit that a fellow villager had actually deserted to the enemies of the commune. His dreams pantomimed the wish in Zlatovratskii's soul that the prodigal one day would realize his error and return as a supplicant to the old ways, that the threat to the commune, terrible though it seemed, would ultimately prove transitory. Filaret dreamt that the *kulaks* were swept from the commune and that Petr came back from the city imbued with communal spirit; then the two became good friends and began to work for the village, he as a *volost'* clerk, Petr as a leader of the commune.[2]

Petr's aloofness and his new airs awakened the suspicion and antipathy of the villagers. The peasant, Zlatovratskii explained, could not tolerate privacy and liked people who were frank and ingenuous. 'He assumes that perhaps things are not completely clean when they cannot be laid out in the open for all to see.' In Petr's seclusiveness he recognized a threat to his traditions, and he determined to defend them.[3]

When something new, something alien to him shook the foundations of his life, he raced into the breach and held fast to the foundations, as 'his own', since in this 'his own' he found satisfaction for his mind, his heart, and his age-old ideals.[4]

And, indeed, these premonitions soon proved accurate. Petr was bent on detaching the Volk land from the commune,

---

[1] Zlatovratskii, 'Ustoi...', *Otechestvennye Zapiski*, no. 240 (October 1878), pp. 279–93.　　[2] *Ibid.* no. 240, pp. 294–8.
[3] *Ibid.* no. 240, pp. 310–12.　　[4] *Ibid.* no. 240, p. 299.

mortgaging his property, and purchasing an estate, which he intended to rent to the peasants at high prices. Under the leadership of Ul'iana, the villagers trooped through Moscow seeking an official who would prevent Petr from going through with his plans. Shunted from bureaucrat to bureaucrat, they spent lavish sums on bribes, but to no avail. The first part of *Ustoi* ends with Petr, helped by his weak father, removing the Volk land from the commune and severing his ties with the 'foundations'.[1]

In the first section of *Ustoi*, Zlatovratskii used his fictional licence to create characters, situations, and an outcome that corresponded with his conceptions of reality. But once his image of the peasant began to be taken seriously by the members of the intelligentsia, he found himself drawn into polemics and called upon to support his views with more than his imagination and intuition. Almost monthly, Uspenskii, in his reports from Novgorod and Samara, issued challenges to his characterizations of the peasantry. Orthodox *narodniki* like Plekhanov cited Zlatovratskii's works in defence of their position. Zlatovratskii now felt impelled to go forth into the countryside to seek factual corroboration for his notions of rural life.

Zlatovratskii believed himself to be exceptionally well qualified to carry on such a study. His superior familiarity with the countryside, his deep understanding of the peasant's way of thinking, he believed, put him at a great advantage over the 'novices' ('*svezhie liudi*') who left the city only for a brief sojourn and then 'flitted from village to village, district to district, and province to province, gathering their droplets of honey while in flight'. He resolved to make a serious and prolonged effort to penetrate to the real 'everyday life' of the countryside, and for this purpose he believed it necessary to settle in a single spot. In late 1878, Zlatovratskii arrived in Yamskaia commune, a small village deep in the forest and far from the influences of urban centres, and took up residence with an old peasant by the name of Grandpa Matvei.[2]

In March 1879 Zlatovratskii's account of his impressions of peasant life began to appear in *Otechestvennye Zapiski* under the

---

[1] *Ibid.* no. 241 (December 1878), pp. 455–84.
[2] N. N. Zlatovratskii, 'Derevenskie budni', *Otechestvennye Zapiski*, no. 243 (March 1879), pp. 229–30.

title '*Derevenskie budni*' ('Everyday Life in the Countryside'). This is a strange and confusing work, part description, part invective. On one hand Zlatovratskii tried to reveal the true nature of peasant life, and to make contact with the 'foundations'; on the other he was intent on excoriating those with opposing views, and exposing their ignorance and irresponsibility. But despite the violence of his polemic and his elaborate and tortuous argumentation, the countryside that Zlatovratskii described in '*Derevenskie budni*' conformed not to his views but to the conceptions of those he was determined to refute. His candid report immediately made it clear that things were not peaceful or orderly in Yamskaia. Grandpa Matvei, who served as his cicerone in the village, had numerous complaints about recent changes in the village. He told how his two sons spent most of the year in the city, leaving him to farm the land for three by himself, and acquainted Zlatovratskii with the fact that his situation was not exceptional. As families became involved in trade, Zlatovratskii learned, individual members often went into business for themselves and many of the old family *arteli* were dissolving.[1]

Zlatovratskii was dismayed to see that, with trade, economic differentiation had come to Yamskaia. The commune was divided into rich and poor, each living in a separate section of the village. The degree of poverty of the less fortunate was something that he had failed to anticipate. The sight of the scrawny peasant children appalled him. 'To tell the truth,' he wrote, 'the poor peasant's child is not quite as healthy compared to the children of the urban proletariat as is usually believed'—a startling admission from a *narodnik*. They were 'sickly and puny from want'; they suffered from 'vile living accommodations, disgracefully poor food, backbreaking toil at an early age'. 'All of this in spite of the country air and of the fact that, in general, the peasants pity and are tender to their little children.'[2] Dishonesty, too, was common in Yamskaia. Grandpa Matvei told of widespread grain theft, and when Zlatovratskii asked in astonishment why the commune had not organized some form of protection, the old man could only answer, 'What are you to do if there is nothing?'[3]

Yet Zlatovratskii did not consider his ideals impugned by

---

[1] *Ibid.* no. 243, pp. 246–52, 261–2.   [2] *Ibid.* no. 243, p. 265.
[3] *Ibid.* no. 243 (April 1879), pp. 481–3.

the conditions he had observed in Yamskaia. His conscientious reporting in no way indicated an open mind, for his willingness to depict honestly all sides of rural life arose not from a desire to discover an unknown truth or to maintain a scientific objectivity, but from his utter certainty that, no matter what was revealed, his conception of the countryside would prove correct. Indeed Zlatovratskii considered his observations confirmation of his initial feelings about the countryside. The signs of breakdown, he contended, were merely surface phenomena that obscured real village life. Only by probing beneath the surface could one follow the progress of the struggle between old and new, and gauge 'how vital the beloved eternal ideals were'.[1] It was precisely 'the novice' who took the disturbing appearances for reality. Clearly alluding to Uspenskii, Zlatovratskii ironically characterized those who came to the countryside merely to cure their psychological ills.

For the novice there are untold possibilities [in the countryside]: no prior knowledge about it is available, yet there are infinite reasons to fly into indignation or into ecstasy. In the end, the observer finds either an arcadian idyll, or a mass of the stupid, wild, bestial, spontaneous, and unilluminated, depending on his own temperament—whether he is optimistic or pessimistic. Thus error, both intentional and unintentional, reigns in the intelligentsia—that strange division of thought that anyone studying the materials of the novices inevitably notices.[2]

The essential nature of peasant life, Zlatovratskii asserted, was so prosaic and unobtrusive that it had eluded intellectual investigators, who were seeking sensational discoveries. The matrix of communal relations had by now become so habitual and accepted in the village that the peasants were prone to take its existence for granted. They maintained an elaborate system of aid for orphans and travellers in distress, but they considered this too commonplace to warrant discussion.[3] A 'novice' witnessing each peasant working on his own plot would surmise that individualism was rampant in the countryside. But, staying a while longer, he would see those who finished their strips early move over to help others. And the peasant would think nothing of this: 'Assistance without promise of refreshments or remuneration on this earth—that is the everyday life of the countryside.'[4]

[1] Ibid. no. 243 (March 1879), p. 264.   [2] Ibid. no. 243 (April 1879), p. 483.
[3] Ibid. no. 243, pp. 485–6.   [4] Ibid. no. 243, pp. 486–7.

Having established the existence of an immutable, almost imperceptible system of fraternal practices, Zlatovratskii proceeded to dismiss the signs of individualism he saw around him. In the breakdown of the large families, he discerned not a portent of the growth of the proletariat but the nascent spirit of human dignity. The peasant was simply expressing the urge for personal freedom that had been awakened by the reform; to take umbrage at this development was merely to deny him his right to self-respect, and his wife the right to her own home, husband, and child. The peasant, in breaking away from the family, consciously forfeited his material advantage for the values of privacy and personal dignity.[1]

Zlatovratskii, of course, was not trying to justify private ownership in the name of personal liberty. The old form of familial land holding would disintegrate, he held, but only to be recreated as a new, perfected institution. The dialectical triad, probably drawn from Plekhanov's writings of 1878–9, turned Zlatovratskii's dream image of the past into a prognostication of the future. The old communal order, negated by its antithesis, the spirit of individualism, had produced the present stage of disintegration. But this, too, would be negated, to produce the third and highest stage, embodying the communal features of the first and the freedom of the second. Thus, the material sacrifices made by the peasants who broke off from the large families would become increasingly difficult to bear. With their tiny plots and inadequate cattle and equipment, they would become impoverished and would recognize the advantages of coalescing in larger units. In place of the troublesome family ties there would grow up a new 'free communal union', in which each person would be supplied with an individual plot—'his cozy corner'—and also would be guaranteed freedom. There would be equal resources for all, equal right to the commune's assistance, and, where possible, the land would be cultivated collectively. The traditions evolved by the people 'at the dawn of civilization' would rise to the fore and govern peasant society.[2]

Disposing of the fact of the growing individualism and differentiation in the countryside, the dialectic enabled Zlatovratskii to conceive the countryside completely in terms of faith. 'Once we accept this, once we are imbued with the conviction

[1] *Ibid.* no. 243, p. 491.   [2] *Ibid.* no. 243, pp. 491–2.

that these are the ideals of the people, we will have under us the firmest (*ustoichivy*) basis, which at once will illuminate all the varied and contradictory occurrences of contemporary life.'[1] One then would have the strength to find the ideal that was concealed in reality. 'No matter how lost these pearls may have been under the yoke of all possible external influences, no matter how difficult it is to find them now, with the honourable and honest observation of the peasants' life, their presence comes to be sensed everywhere...'[2] Thus, when Grandpa Matvei could not explain the process of allotment in the commune, Zlatovratskii reasoned that the old man actually understood the workings of the commune but could not verbalize his thoughts and that the existing system of plots and souls, in any case, ran counter to his communal mentality.[3] Zlatovratskii discovered cases of peasants trying to revise the system of land division, and, while their changes often accentuated the old inequality, he took their attempts as a sign of the peasants' dissatisfaction and craving for a better life.[4]

At the meeting of the commune, Zlatovratskii was completely bewildered. 'These people are completely different from you,' he wrote. 'Their speeches are beyond your comprehension; from their premises emerge conclusions which are precisely opposite to those forming in your mind.'[5] Indeed, in the raucous chattering and yelling, the commune's decisions seemed to be reached without any kind of logical consideration, and often they proved completely at odds with Zlatovratskii's sense of justice. A poor woman, whose husband had died, leaving her with two small children, petitioned the commune to relieve her of her land and tax burden. The commune obliged both her requests, depriving her of land and setting aside the empty plots for her children when they came of age. A peasant who had gone to ruin through drink reformed and asked the commune to return his plots. The commune consented, but only on the condition that he pay all his accumulated arrears, which, of course, was impossible. After pondering the commune's decisions, which at first seemed unjust and irrational, he concluded that the fault lay in himself and that the commune had acted as equitably as possible under the existing tax system.[6]

---

[1] *Ibid.* no. 243, pp. 492–3.
[2] *Ibid.* no. 243, p. 493.
[3] *Ibid.* no. 243, pp. 502–4.
[4] *Ibid.* no. 243. pp. 505–7.
[5] *Ibid.* no. 244 (June 1879), p. 508.
[6] *Ibid.* no. 244, pp. 511, 517–24.

After the meeting, he talked with several of the peasants. Grandpa Matvei pined for the olden days and told how the youth were now forsaking the commune, compelling it at times to hire its own wage-labourers. Other joined in and complained about the private individuals who were buying up the land in the area 'in private ownership'. All voiced their hopes for 'a black partition', a division of all the land they did not own among them. Zlatovratskii was delighted to hear them predict that this would happen through the offices of the commune, with the land to be held in common.[1] Those who dissented were vehemently shouted down. Even Matvei's son Yakim, who had been working in the city, agreed; he declared, 'The holding of land by private owners will bring no good!' He warned that each proprietor would yell 'Keep off my land!' to the others. He told how peasants who left the commune went to ruin from drink and illness and abandoned their children. When asked, Zlatovratskii, with proper humility, ventured his own opinion.

To tell you the truth, I don't know. I'm afraid to give you advice. We know your life very poorly. From your conversation I can see that you favour the old ways, that you think it would be better to live in the communal manner.[2]

Then Zlatovratskii prepared to observe the actual partition of land in the commune. 'Is it possible', he asked, 'that this factor did not leave its unique mark on the peasant soul, and did not permeate his whole world view, did not accompany him from the cradle to the grave?'[3] The current practices, he admitted, could be but a faint shadow of the original 'division of the product' and consequently it demanded 'an extremely attentive and honest attitude on the part of the observer' to detect the communal spirit amidst the incredibly complex, apparently petty machination of the distribution.[4] But even with his 'extremely attentive and honest attitude', he was unable to discern the elements of primeval justice in the procedure he observed or, for that matter, make any sense of it whatsoever. He saw that each peasant vigorously defended his own interest and that the measurements were performed with great care and exactitude, but the bargaining shortly became too complex for him to follow.[5]

---

[1] *Ibid.* no. 244, pp. 530–6.　　　　　　[2] *Ibid.* no. 244, pp. 538–41.
[3] *Ibid.* no. 245 (August 1879), p. 274.　[4] *Ibid.* no. 245, pp. 276–9.
[5] *Ibid.* no. 245, pp. 280–3.

Yet Yamskaia commune was relatively untouched by the influences of civilization. Surrounded by woods and swamps, it was cut off from urban centres, and at the time of the spring muds became all but inaccessible. When Zlatovratskii pursued his investigation in less isolated villages, the elaborate tissue of ideology that had enabled him to reconcile real with ideal in Yamskaia disintegrated. He moved to Lopukha, a village experiencing the direct impact of recent changes. Located in the midst of a heavily populated region crisscrossed by roads and train tracks, Lopukha displayed conditions contrasting sharply with those in Yamskaia. Most disturbing were the obvious signs that the Lopukha peasants were prospering in spite of the incursions of civilization. Their houses were sturdy and attractive, and many of them were roofed with metal rather than straw. Their dress was so fine as to make them indistinguishable from merchants. When Zlatovratskii asked one of them whether he had earned his wealth by tilling the land, the peasant replied caustically, 'The land! Even if there were plenty of land, that couldn't happen. The land is dirty work, for idlers and women.' 'Well, then,' Zlatovratskii continued, 'where did you acquire all of this?' 'By my own wits...,' he impudently answered, 'because I know how to farm economically (*khoziastvovat*').'[1]

Zlatovratskii was aghast at the peasant's crass candour. The verb *khoziastvovat*', denoting farming for profit, conjured up in Zlatovratskii's mind the sordid, calculating, profiteering aspects of commercial agriculture. Uttered by a peasant whose mind, he believed, harboured saintly thoughts, it was like obscene words from the mouth of a child. It implied that a peasant could introduce large-scale farming, conduct rational agriculture, exploit the poor, and live better than he could have by docilely following the old ways. It contradicted his most sacred notions of how a peasant should think.[2]

Progress seemed to be moving not towards but away from Zlatovratskii's ideal. Individualism, it seemed at Lopukha, was engendering not the increasing poverty he had predicted, but economic well-being and signal technological advances. Further investigation confirmed his initial impressions. He observed that the enterprising peasants (*khoziastvennye muzhiki*) drank less and used fertilizers more intelligently than other peasants. They

---

[1] *Ibid.* no. 246 (October 1879), pp. 442–6.   [2] *Ibid.* no. 246, pp. 446–7.

were compelling the commune to lengthen the period between divisions, and seemed in general to be taking control of the village and directing its life in a rational manner that did not at all accord with the ancient 'foundations': communes were exploiting other communes, and peasants were supporting themselves by wage labour.[1]

Zlatovratskii was consoled only by the fact that the enterprising peasants themselves seemed concerned about their own methods of acquiring wealth. He saw them not as empty shells, innocent of knowledge and morality, who had been filled with the corrupt stuff of civilization, as Uspenskii depicted them. For him they were thinking beings aware of their own descent into evil. He showed them driven by forces beyond their control to betray their ideals. They were beset, he believed, by the same spiritual dichotomy that pained the educated individual: 'In the peasant soul, the same dualism, the same struggle between altruistic and egoistic drives exists as in ours.'[2] One wealthy peasant with extensive holdings pleaded, 'What kind of justice do you expect to find here? No justice at all. The times are simply that way... You try to get ahead the best you can.'[3] The enterprising peasants had no choice: they were forced to become agents of values antithetical to their own, and to live in 'an atmosphere of moral duplicity and doubledealing'.[4]

But as time passed the peasants were showing diminishing resistance to the new trends. Ruthless predator types who manipulated the commune to victimize the poor were winning the respect and admiration of the other peasants. The villagers adulated those who had made out in the world and could mingle with the rich in the city, and began to look to them for guidance and advice. In their fascination with material success, they forgot the ancient 'foundations' which brought neither repute nor wealth. They lost interest in the division of communal land, which either was discontinued or assumed the character of a commercial bargaining session.[5]

Zlatovratskii had come to the countryside seeking the firm, underlying stratum of ideals that he believed had been preserved by the peasantry. The mass of evidence he gathered, however, led inescapably to the conclusion that no such stratum

---

[1] *Ibid.* no. 246, pp. 451–4.   [2] *Ibid.* no. 247 (December 1879), p. 527.
[3] *Ibid.* no. 246 (October 1879), pp. 459–60.   [4] *Ibid.* no. 246, pp. 457–9.
[5] *Ibid.* no. 246, pp. 460–2; no. 247 (December 1879), pp. 545–9.

existed. The documentation of the distintegration of the communal system in '*Derevenskie budni*' was complete—indeed, so complete that Georgi Plekhanov, whose *narodnik* views the work was supposed to substantiate, was able, when he became a Marxist four years later, to use it as ammunition for his famous critique of the *narodnik* view of the commune in '*Nashi raznoglasiia*' ('Our Differences').[1] At the end of 1897, Zlatovratskii, who had set himself apart from the other members of the intelligentsia and dismissed their dilemmas as psychological aberrations, entered upon his own psychological and ideological crisis. The world that he had envisioned as the reflection of his own virtue suddenly appeared to be suffused with evil, and the elaborate structure of his personal beliefs and justifications began to totter.

Disoriented and confused by his experiences in Lopukha, Zlatovratskii briefly turned for guidance to the views being aired among the intelligentsia. The ideological explanations of the two new revolutionary organizations, however, afforded him little assistance. In temperament and outlook he was clearly closer to the members of The Black Partition, who shared his faith in the great potentialities concealed in the people. He knew several of them personally, most notably Plekhanov, who often hid out in his home. But The Black Partition, avowedly adhering to the original precepts of Land and Freedom, presented much the same diagnosis of Russia's ills as The People's Will. Its spokesmen also attributed sole responsibility for recent economic changes to the state. In the lead article of the first issue of *Cherny Peredel* (*The Black Partition*), Plekhanov flung the same accusations at the autocracy as had his rivals. He took issue only on revolutionary strategy. Denying the efficacy of a purely political revolution of the intelligentsia, he stressed the necessity of a peasant uprising if genuine change was to be accomplished. Only the masses, preserving the communal heritage of centuries, could successfully resist the alien force of the government, he contended. Then, under modern conditions, conducive to large-scale production, communal exploitation of the land could flourish. But Plekhanov was unable to show how the peasantry, corrupted and impoverished by the government, could suddenly acquire the force to rise and overthrow it. Such

[1] G. Plekhanov, *Sochineniia* (St Petersburg, 1920), I, part 2, pp. 283–309.

an eventuality seemed unlikely indeed in 1880, and, with it excluded, his analysis offered only the gloomy prospect of continued change for the worse.[1]

Thus to Zlatovratskii the explanations of The Black Partition were hardly more comforting than those of The People's Will. He was searching for a vindication of the peasantry; casting the blame for a disturbing situation on a single institution could hold little appeal for him, for he did not believe that a single external factor could so easily erode the strength of popular tradition. His hostility turned not on the Russian state but upon all those who had divorced themselves from the people: his hatred was diffused through all civilized society and he never saw fit to differentiate among those people and those institutions that existed beyond the 'foundations'. His animosity was directed above all at the intelligentsia itself. In his only contribution to the ideological debates of the moment, '*Narodny vopros v nashem obshchestve i literature*' ('The Peasant Problem in our Society and Literature'), he bitterly derided the members of the intelligentsia for their ignorance of the countryside and for their inability to help the people. He exhorted them to make an honest effort to live with the peasants and to learn from their wisdom, rather than debate false problems in the capital. In the end, he added his voice to those clamouring for political change, for he believed that only greater freedom of thought and action would permit the intelligentsia to attain a close relationship with the people.[2]

Unenlightened by the doctrinal controversies of the day, Zlatovratskii finally relied for his solutions on his own introspective devices. When observation of 'everyday life' failed to corroborate his dreams, he merely retreated into a world of his own making. His discoveries in Lopukha occasioned, not a reevaluation of his view of the world, but a renewed attempt to confirm it, based on the insights of his imagination rather than on his experience. He allowed his fantasy the free rein of fiction and resumed work on *Ustoi*.

Zlatovratskii overcame his crisis of ideals by virtue of his native propensity to see reality through the prism of wish. His

---

[1] *Cherny Peredel* (Moscow–Petrograd, 1923), pp. 107–16.
[2] N. N. Zlatovratskii (N. Oranskii), 'Narodny vopros v nashem obshchestve i literature', *Russkoe Bogatstvo*, no. 1 (March 1880), part II, pp. 25–48; (May 1880), part II, pp. 1–19; (June 1880), part III, pp. 1–20; Rusanov, *Na rodine*, p. 254.

portrayal of rural life became a subtle blend of the real and the fashioned that created the comforting impression of truth both for himself and for his readers. Thus, though Uspenskii, too, withdrew into fantasy when discouraged by his observations, the illusions of the two writers differed radically both in meaning and in impact. Zlatovratskii's dream world was depicted as a higher form of reality transcending actual developments in the countryside; Uspenskii's appeared as a hallucinatory escape from grim facts, the significance of which he was unable to deny. And while Uspenskii's works gave expression to the terrifying doubts besetting the intelligentsia, Zlatovratskii's presented a monumental visage of confidence, a picture of the ideal alive in the midst of squalor, breakdown, and change.

The second section of *Ustoi*, published during 1880, portrayed the inner life of those individuals in conflict with the 'foundations' rather than the disconsoling life of the village as a whole. The subtitle was accordingly changed from *The History of a Settlement* (*Istoriia odnogo poselka*) to *A Novel of the New Man of the Countryside* (*Roman novogo cheloveka derevni*). Zlatovratskii now indulged the longing, expressed in Filaret's dream, to turn his adversary into a friend and to absorb the hostile world into his narcissistic self. He portrayed the 'new men' as tragic figures who suffered the torment of the clash of old and new in the village, who lived through dilemmas similar to his own. They appeared as anguished, lost, peasant types who, though good at heart and true to the ideals of the commune, felt themselves impelled to turn against the ancient traditions. They engaged in interminable soul-searching and acted precipitously and irrationally, as Zlatovratskii thought befitted those in so turbulent a state.

He described the miller Strogii, whose suddenly awakened moral sense made him dissatisfied with his native village. Unable to obtain guidance from the local intelligentsia, he was forced to formulate his ideas by himself. He said, 'One must be just because everyone is guilty. And the cause of all this [trouble] is liquor. And he who drinks is guilty, and he who gives to drink is guilty.'[1] He vociferously criticized the conduct of the other peasants, to their embarrassment and indignation. He strongly objected to the operations of the commune, and Zlatovratskii admitted that his strictures were in large part just.

---

[1] N. N. Zlatovratskii, 'Strogii (Ocherk iz Ustoev)', *Russkoe Bogatstvo* (April 1880), pp. 147–8.

The more [the villagers] became impoverished and the more they became entangled in the various sticky but elusive and fine webs of the *mir*'s affairs, and the less consciously they lived, as if only on hope and faith, half instinctively, not caring about anything, the more Strogii began to drift away.[1]

No longer able to tolerate the drunkenness and disorder in the village, Strogii decided to leave for the city. Ul'iana Volk, now a querulous old woman, helpless to save the commune, screeched futilely at him, 'In old age you are fleeing your native parts. Shame on you, old man! Shame! You love your own soul too much...You self-lover...'[2]

Strogii enacted the stark tragedy of the abandonment of home, the poignant and irreversible severance of roots, that was Zlatovratskii's primal and central life experience. As Strogii prepared to depart from his birthplace, he felt his deep attachment to the 'truth' of peasant life and was overcome with sad longings for the honesty and innocence of his past.

And why shouldn't he feel 'the truth'? A person who leaves his native region *forever*—just like that, *forever*—surrenders all possibility of attending endless series of peasant feasts, weddings, public prayers, name-day festivals, the great church holidays, the patron saints' holidays, the holidays of the saints' churches and all the ancillary holidays. He surrenders all possibility of receiving the benevolent gifts and treats; he gives all of this up not only for himself but for all his descendants...[3]

The second of the 'new men' was Petr Volk, the villain of the first section of *Ustoi*. Now Petr appeared not as an example of unalloyed wickedness, but as a pathetic victim of the new circumstances. Strogii's godchild, he was strongly influenced by the old miller and also felt the dichotomy between old and new. Alienated from the peasants, he moved to the city. Once there, he could not even live with an *artel'* of his fellow villagers, whose ways struck him as messy, vulgar, and too familiar. He endeavoured to adapt to urban life, and at first his efforts met with some success. He took a room in a nobleman's house and began to work in an office. A group of students adopted him as a 'son of the people', and taught him science. But Petr soon

[1] *Ibid.* no. 1, p. 155.
[2] N. N. Zlatovratskii, 'Ustoi (Roman novogo cheloveka derevni)', *Otechestvennye Zapiski*, no. 252 (October 1880), p. 345.
[3] *Ibid.* no 252, p. 348.

learned that he was as out of place in the city as he had been in the village. The callous dishonesty and bribery in the office appalled him and he blushed when his boss snickered at the common people. Confused and without values, he began to keep evil company and fell into debauchery. When he tried to return to the *artel'*, the members rejected him. He was evicted by his landlord and the students lost interest in him. The chilling feelings of isolation and helplessness that had settled over Zlatoratskii eight years before now pained his arrogant hero. Confused and frustrated, Petr indiscriminately attacked everyone around him, and finally was apprehended by the police and thrown into jail.[1]

In the throes of mental breakdown, Petr, stricken with remorse, suddenly saw the truth and realized that his roots were home in the village, with the 'foundations' he had wantonly deserted. Zlatovratskii's 'enterprising peasant' now became the protagonist of his own aspirations. The 'enterprising peasant', contrary to all appearances, was pining for a return to the old ways, for, even as he was destroying the 'foundations', they lived on in his heart. The wishes of Filaret's dream were suddenly fulfilled as Zlatovratskii transformed the enemies of the 'foundations' into their firmest defenders.[2]

On his next venture into the countryside, Zlatovratskii went in search not of concrete economic or social conditions but of these elusive promptings of peasant souls. The record of his impressions, published under the title '*Ocherki derevenskogo nastroeniia*' ('The Mood of the Countryside') in early 1881, was devoted explicitly to the psychic phenomena of the countryside. The intellectual and moral sides of peasant life, he asserted at the beginning, had been omitted from the *intelligent*'s purview, which encompassed only questions of an economic nature. The intelligentsia's economic investigations, he argued, had simply confirmed the already known existence of exploiters and exploited in the countryside and narrowed the scope of interest to these two groups. But the people, he stated, could not be viewed as a sacred cow: they possessed their own world view; they could think and be conscious.

[The people] are not a colourless, amorphous mass living by the primitive instincts of the stomach, but a mass developing harmonious

---

[1] *Ibid.* no. 252, pp. 355–91; no. 253 (November 1880), pp. 7–9, 24–36.
[2] *Ibid.* no. 253, pp. 39–40.

traditions, living by known ideals and striving to realize them, and to the extent of their ability, trying to save them from ruin...[1]

An 'invisible psychological process', he believed, was transfiguring the old ideals, and an awareness of this imperceptible change could give the *intelligent* hope and revive his confidence.

Believe in the existence [of this process] and with sympathy try to perceive and unravel the general meaning of these subtle psychic moods, and without fail you will find firm ground under your feet. Hope will replace despair and the mysterious sphinx will, perhaps for a moment, open his soul to you.[2]

This change transpired in the thought of the rising generation. While the old men accepted everything that existed in the commune, the young men were developing an awareness of their own rights and personal dignity. Not only did they resent administrative arbitrariness, but they were beginning to chafe at all forms of privilege. 'Indignation with "arbitrariness" is giving way to indignation with their "unjust position"'. Accepting the traditional communal institutions as the sole means to secure land, they were eager to change them to fit their needs, and their ambition grew with their evolving consciousness. They were able to discuss every detail of rural life 'with reason' (*ot razuma*) and were applying new, advanced methods in their work. Their farms were orderly, their houses neatly patched, and all of their actions seemed to show considerable intelligence.[3]

But though the young men respected 'intelligence' rather than 'the truth' of their elders, they had not forgotten their ancestral values. The intelligence they evinced was not simply native peasant shrewdness and practicality: it was a rudimentary form of the progressive thinking that characterized the intelligentsia: it was a 'peasant rationalism', 'ability to think' (*umstvennost'*), 'satisfying the needs of the soul, answering the demands of the consciousness of human dignity, capable of existing independently of practical goals as an inalienable "spiritual mood" in itself; this is *the people's rationalism*'.[4] The 'people's rationalism' promoted humane conduct among the

---

[1] N. N. Zlatovratskii, 'Ocherki derevenskogo nastroeniia', *Otechestvennye Zapiski*, no. 254 (February 1881), p. 229.   [2] *Ibid*. no. 254, p. 231.
[3] *Ibid*. no. 255 (March 1881), pp. 115–20.   [4] *Ibid*. no. 255, p. 121.

young men. Rather than swindle their neighbours, they tried to win their respect and consequently were fastidious in their means. They were thus not incipient kulaks, and their intelligence was not the kulaks' cunning, but a constructive beneficial force.

The ability to think (*umstvennost'*) can be as much of a binding moral cement as tradition...not only 'sufferings' can unite people but any other 'mood' that can, in favourable circumstances, meaningfully and with plenty to spare, replace the vanished moral binding elements; and instead of unconscious traditions, rationally conscious ones evolve...[1]

Like Engel'gardt and Uspenskii, Zlatovratskii was fascinated by the successes of the prosperous new peasant, even when they were gained at the expense of the communal tradition. But in Engel'gardt's and Uspenskii's writings, this admiration always remained anomalous, a symptom of their inability to reconcile real with ideal. Zlatovratskii, unable to accept an unpleasant reality, projected his hopes on those who were devastating the ancient traditions and claimed that they were actually advancing the ideal.

The reconciliation, however, occurred only in his mind. The rational consciousness he extolled reflected itself but elusively in rural reality, and its presence could be confirmed only by the signs of disintegration and discontent. He overheard peasants arguing about the commune and took this as evidence of a nascent moral consciousness.[2] Once again, the task of confirming his view of the countryside fell to the dialectic. The Hegelian triad transformed the individualistic instinct of the peasantry into an urge for a perfected commune and made the discordant life of the countryside a mere prelude to future harmony. It showed that the most sordid reflections of reality concealed the same longing for the womb of primeval purity that acted in him. But now his use of the triad no longer depended upon a decline in the peasants' economic well-being, as it had in Yamskaia, for the impulse to return to the communal system was not supposed to be apparent, but instead concealed in the soul of the prosperous peasants. With their growing moral consciousness, they would cease their competitive struggle and form groups which would vie with each other until the strongest and most homogeneous absorbed the others in a greater communal organization. Zlatovratskii believed that the stage

---

[1] *Ibid.* no. 255, pp. 122–3.   [2] *Ibid.* no. 256 (May 1881), pp. 81–5.

of disintegration had been completed and individuals were beginning to enter new associations. 'The struggle of individuals
has given way to the struggle of groups,' he declared em-
phatically.[1]

Zlatovratskii illustrated his conclusion in the final section of
Ustoi, which appeared in *Otechestvennye Zapiski* during 1882 and the
beginning of 1883, under the subtitle 'The History of a Village'.
Placing the peasants of his imagination in a social context, he
presented a total view of life in the countryside. He peopled his
village with honest and far-sighted peasants who were aware of
the problems the future held in store. The leading characters
were old and stately grandfather figures who sustained the
moral strength and stability of the past in the face of grim events
transpiring around them. 'Happy Grandpa Piman' was a hard
worker and led the best team (*vyt'*) when the *mir* performed its
common labour. He arose early each morning, worked till late
at night, and never touched drink. An old-fashioned peasant,
he lived in symbiosis with nature and in keeping with the
ancient foundations. He lived with the river, the cow, the horse,
in a greater harmony of labour, according to nature's dictates.[2]

In the completeness of his arcadian existence, Piman rivalled
Uspenskii's Ivan Ermolaevich, who had preceded him in the
pages of *Otechestvennye Zapiski* by only a few months. Like Ivan,
he profited well by his labour, and was even parsimonious. But
while Ivan was Uspenskii's desperate and unsuccessful attempt
to find comfort in a bleak reality, Piman fulfilled all of his
author's ideals. Ivan enacted his role only instinctively, while
Piman appreciated the perfection of his life and stood prepared
to defend it. He was an active upholder of communal ideals
and one of its most influential members. He would reminisce
about the idyllic pre-emancipation period, before the countryside was molested by the new influences. He remembered how
the *mir*

watched over everyone and bred the feelings of love, justice, equality,
how it strictly rendered the peaceful and assiduous their due honour,
and defended the frail and weak, while severely punishing the wild
and irresponsible. Thus from olden days a common life developed
kind feelings in the wild soul of the tiller of the land.[3]

---

[1] *Ibid.* no. 256, pp. 88–91.
[2] N. N. Zlatovratskii, 'Ustoi (Istoriia odnoi derevni)', *Otechestvennye Zapiski,*
no. 261 (March 1882), pp. 200, 209–11.   [3] *Ibid.* no. 262 (May 1882), p. 168.

Through Piman's mind passed Zlatovratskii's apprehensions. The old man remembered the alien forces that had destroyed the old harmony of feeling when the bureaucracy came to impose its authority on the isolated commune. He watched with dismay as the commune's lands were traded away and the youth left for the city.[1]

Piman's attachment to the commune was governed primarily by its material advantages. The other side of communal life—the creative, ethical impulses of the peasantry—was reflected in the figure of the 'peasant romantic', Piman's friend, Grandpa Min. Min was a hero, the embodiment of Zlatovratskii's legendary men who had achieved great feats with no concern for their own well-being. Energetic and longing to express himself, Min found farm work tedious and unrewarding, and once he had even left the village to work in the city.[2] While Piman's strength lay in his ability to bend with nature and in his interest in the welfare of his land and animals, Min was a born fighter for justice, who sought the way to the good life. His family lived in a common household with his brother Karp, and although their wives were constantly bickering and the families had separated five times, they strove to continue the relationship. Min would advise his son never to be greedy, even greedy for work. 'If there is greed in labour, then there is no happiness in it for you,' he told him. Min was the *vol'nitsa*, the free spirit of the countryside, whose forefathers, thousands of years before, had created the poetry, faith, and love of the commune. While Piman's ancestors were fighting the struggle for survival, Min's were building the commune's peculiar spiritual heritage, which 'imparted roundness (*okruglost'*), wholeness and sense to millions of human lives, in order to mitigate the effect of the backbreaking struggle for subsistence'.[3]

Despite their disparate characters, both Piman and Min agreed that the commune was in grave condition. Min said, 'Our commune is not so big, and yet we are already fighting among ourselves. There is envy everywhere.' 'I think so too', Piman answered. 'This is because it has become freer for everyone, but more cramped for the *mir*. Before, it was cramped for us, but the *mir* had plenty of room.' Min, however, sensed

[1] *Ibid.* no. 262, pp. 169–82.
[2] *Ibid.* no. 261 (March 1882), pp. 211–12, 202.
[3] *Ibid.* no. 263 (August 1882), pp. 505–6, 510.

that the future would bring an end to the commune's difficulties and told Piman not to worry. He envisioned the time
when a *prikaz* (decree) would establish peace and justice in the
commune and provide equal land for all.[1]

In Piman, Petr Volk discovered all of the virtues he had
sought in civilization—intelligence, prudence, efficiency. He
was impressed by Piman's orderliness and respectability, and
marvelled at the cleanliness and spaciousness of the old peasant's
home; in everything he perceived 'the consciousness of strength,
righteousness, and firmness'.[2] In his own dwelling, Petr sensed
the absence of the 'foundations'. Cold and empty, it symbolized
the hollowness of the person who had abandoned his ancestral
traditions. In Zlatovratskii's most pathetic and personally
gratifying scene, punishment was inflicted on the desecrator of
the ideals, who now returned supplicant to the forsaken womb.
Petr, Zlatovratskii asserted, was one of those who had

rushed headlong up the stairs to somewhere on top, who had im-
petuously torn themselves from the land, the stable ground beneath
their feet. But having reached the top, they, forthright natures, had
bumped their heads against locked doors, and when they regained
consciousness, they had suddenly *come to themselves*...[3]

Yearning for people of his own kind and for the feeling of the
'foundations', Petr frequented Piman's home regularly and
finally fell in love with and married the old man's daughter,
Annushka. Then Petr took upon himself the defence of the old
traditions. He declared his intention to work to restore the
foundations he had once foolishly renounced. 'Grandpa made
an effort, tried,' he said. 'He wanted to make real peasants
out of all of us, and we in our stupidity overthrew him and went
to ruin...How fine it would be to restore those foundations!'
Petr proposed to build a steam-driven lumber mill, where the
members of the commune could work. Piman and his sons were
receptive to the idea, which diverted them from their gloomy
thoughts of the commune's disintegration.[4]

Petr's ideas, however, were forgotten as dissension struck the
commune. At the end of *Ustoi*, in describing the social discord
that arose, Zlatovratskii tried to scale the heights of epic drama.

[1] *Ibid.* no. 261 (March 1882), pp. 213–15.
[2] *Ibid.* no. 264 (September 1882), pp. 173–5, 178–9.
[3] *Ibid.* no. 265 (November 1882), p. 168.
[4] *Ibid.* no. 265 (December 1882), pp. 499–503, 507–10.

But conflict was alien to his nature, and he could render it only by making the narrative itself frenzied and incoherent. From this point the plot became increasingly tortuous and obscure. The poor members demanded an equalization of holdings in the commune. In the absence of other authority, Petr came to the defence of the 'foundations'. He used his power to force the *kulaki* to return the land they had usurped and rallied the villagers to defend themselves against their exploiters. The chaos, however, continued to mount. The poor did not relent in their complaints, asserting that Petr's redistribution of land was unjust. Then Petr became embittered, lost his sense of balance, and turned into a vicious despot. Having abandoned the foundations, he was unable to re-establish rapport with peasant life; his rule lacked real roots in the village. The *kulaki* and the poor united to drive him back to Moscow, whereupon the feud between them resumed with new vigour.[1]

The involutions of the final sections of *Ustoi* soon lost all sense, leaving the reader in doubt about the author's meaning. The confusion was compounded by the outpourings of turgid prose, occurring often in completely inappropriate situations. Shchedrin could not contain the irritation he felt at these sections and wrote to Zlatovratskii:

You are simply digressing and deceiving yourself with all these episodic contrivances. You must finish this thing—that is what you must, in my opinion, keep in mind. It has become so drawn out and episodic that it is already impossible for the reader to put the different pieces together...In the last chapters the language you use is, in general, awkward, and in respect to peasant life even unthinkable. Please abstain from these Latin constructions, which Karamzin could employ successfully, but which have long been obsolete.[2]

But to those members of the intelligentsia sensing a loss of their ability to comprehend the countryside, Zlatovratskii conveyed a message of hope. Despite the confusion of the narrative and the numerous scenes of social strife and disintegration, the closing chapters of *Ustoi* contained an emphatic affirmation of faith, a statement that, in spite of the bleak tenor of events, the good would triumph. The 'peasants with feeling', the 'peasant

---

[1] *Ibid.* no. 265, pp. 517–30; no. 267 (March 1883), pp. 194, 207–10.
[2] N. Shchedrin (M. E. Saltykov), *Polnoe sobranie sochinen ii*(Moscow–Leningrad, 1933–41), XIX, 276.

romantics', Zlatovratskii believed, would perpetuate the ancient ideals. He placed his hopes in Min and his son Iania, with their 'infinite, unswerving faith in the truth of life, a faith that this truth must exist, even though we are unable to find it. . .'[1] This faith overshadowed all the discord in the village. It quieted all doubts and permitted Zlatovratskii to be content with himself and the course of social change.

After completing *Ustoi*, Zlatovratskii went to the countryside reluctantly. When he did, he sustained his faith with 'historical consolation' (*istoricheskoe uteshenie*), the certainty that the future would bring a better life. The ferment among the peasantry, the fact that they were asking 'What is to be done?', convinced him that a just world was in the offing. He inquired no further and rested serene.[2]

After 1884 he rarely wrote about the peasantry. He withdrew into himself and relived the happy experiences of his childhood. He recalled the warm kindness of his grandparents and his mother's glowing religiosity. He wrote and rewrote his memoirs about his family, though about his later years, when doubts and difficulties clouded over his initial enthusiasm, he left almost nothing.[3] His conversation, too, dwelled on his early memories, the work of reform, the momentary glimpse of Dobroliubov.[4]

His stooped figure and thickly bearded face became a symbol of deep, unquestioning faith in the people. In informal debates with Mikhailovskii, he defended his position, his heavy demeanour contrasting with his adversary's refined, chiselled features. Mikhailovskii would pose sharp, astute questions, to which Zlatovratskii would answer vaguely and elusively in the manner of his writings. Mikhailovskii challenged him to justify the peasants' involvement in the anti-Jewish pogroms. Zlatovratskii agreed that the Jews deserved equal rights and protection, but refused to oppose his opinions to the people's. 'Who has given me the guarantee that I am right and all the people wrong?', he would ask. 'Wouldn't that be intellectual pride?' To all Mikhailovskii's strictures about the peasantry,

---

[1] Zlatovratskii, 'Dve pravdy', *Otechestvennye Zapiski*, no. 267 (March 1883), p. 210.

[2] N. N. Zlatovratskii, 'V rodnykh mestakh', *Nedelia* (4 September 1883), pp. 1194–6.

[3] Zlatovratskii, *Vospominaniia*, *passim*; Zlatovratskii, 'Pro memoria', *passim*; Zlatovratskii, 'Biografiia i bibliografiia', *passim*.

[4] Teleshov, pp. 128–9.

Zlatovratskii would show the same stubborn reluctance to make any judgement that might upset the delicate reconciliation of real and ideal upon which his psychology rested.[1]

Zlatovratskii's confidence communicated new hope to many of those whose faith had been shaken by the disconcerting appearance of reality and by the mounting reaction. Inspired by his writings, men like Vladimir Korolenko delved deeper into the countryside in quest of 'the secret treasure of peasant thought' and spent many years wandering across the land nurturing *smirenie*, a humble acceptance of all that existed.[2] When their illusions were threatened, Zlatovratskii's work afforded them comfort and strength. On the twenty-fifth anniversary of his literary career, in 1898, they attested their debt to him. 'Confronted by your deep faith in the best sides of the Russian people, our doubts were silenced and our helpless falling hands held the candle of knowledge more firmly.'[3]

[1] V. G. Korolenko, *Vospominaniia o pisateliakh* (Moscow, 1934), pp. 83–4.
[2] V. G. Korolenko, *Istoriia moego sovremennika* (Moscow, 1930–1), II, 442; III, 558.
[3] Teleshov, p. 125.

5

THE INTRUSION OF ECONOMICS

It is hard to endure the contradiction which must torment the soul of a Russian student of Marx at every step, in this or that particular situation. He is doomed to the role of an observer, noting in his chronicle, with the impartiality of Pimen, the facts of a double-edged progress. He can, to be sure, play no active part. For the vile side of the process he is no good at all, and any activity corresponding to his moral impulses simply retards, draws out the process.

NIKOLAI MIKHAILOVSKII, 1877

The members of the intelligentsia of the 1870s saw the real world as a reflection of their aspirations. From the appearance of the first major writings of Lavrov and Mikhailovskii at the end of the sixties, they accorded objective reality little attention and regarded its study as subsidiary to the more imperative task of social change. After the 'going to the people', they conceived of rural institutions embodying their wishes and assigned to thought and perception the function of revealing the collectivistic spirit that they presumed reigned in the village. They envisioned the peasants as virtuous brethren in distress, whose life still preserved the elements of justice and humanity lacking in the urban educated milieu. At the close of the 1870s, when they became aware of the threat posed by the inimical forces in the countryside, they ascribed those forces to the state and managed to preserve their image of a peasant life that was still inherently just. The general devotion to this view muted differences of opinion and made for a rough unity of attitude—a unity that contrasts strikingly with the dissension and mutual intolerance that later prevailed among the intelligentsia. Dispute arose in the latter part of the decade on various doctrinal and tactical issues, but few questioned the soundness of the populist notions of reality or challenged the populist vision of a future peasant society, unmolested by government or civilization, free to function entirely according to communal principles.

Those who went to the countryside at the end of the 1870s went in search of a way of life that could answer their longings. They expected to find a better humanity, one congenial to them in temperament and ideals. When instead they beheld a turmoil of human degradation and misery, they were unable to make sense of what they saw. Baffled and appalled by the sordidness and squalor that confronted them everywhere, they had no conceptual apparatus that could help them explain the meaning of actual conditions—no technique of weighing and relating their myriad impressions. At the sight of reality, the order and symmetry of populist ideology dissolved into a mist of exalted concepts whose meaning was difficult for them to perceive. Consequently, their guides to the interpretation of reality became their individual predispositions, and the knowledge they drew upon, the self-knowledge of their individual life experiences. Each strove to preserve the image that had brought him to the peasantry by forcing his observations into the framework of his own personal world view and, by invoking elaborate personal defences, to exclude what did not fit. Each formulated his own understanding of what comprised Russian reality and what the intelligentsia's relationship towards it should be. The unity of outlook then began to break down into a chaos of conflicting and irreconcilable views.

Aleksandr Engel'gardt, an eminent agronomist and member of the nobility, nurtured a faith in the power of science to transform conditions and to improve humanity. When the peasantry showed the same destructive traits as civilized society, he dreamed of bringing about a reconciliation of real with ideal by remoulding the basic nature of both peasantry and intelligentsia. He imagined that he could create a class of peasant *intelligenty* who would enact his beliefs and set an example for the real peasantry. But since the members of the intelligentsia could not shed their civilized character, Engel'gardt's effort failed, and, without resolving the problems he raised, he withdrew once more into the less trying realm of agronomical research. Uspenskii and Zlatovratskii, who came from the provincial clerical and petty-bureaucratic milieu, were closer to the everyday life of the people and more aware of the deeply ingrained difference between the peasantry and the intelligentsia. Though each of them tried to find individuals who combined the qualities of the common people and the educated, neither could convince himself that they could be created. Instead, they tried to shun the unpleasant implications of what they had seen by rationalizing their experience and by entertaining fantasy images which could blot their observations out of their consciousness. Uspenskii's destructive scepticism, however, swiftly destroyed his rationalizations and, finding reality impossible to reconcile with the ideal, he went through the countryside desperately struggling to deny what he knew to be true. For Zlatovratskii, these defences had always provided a welcome shelter from the world and when in difficulty he merely indulged them more freely. Finding it impossible *not* to reconcile reality with the ideal, he embraced what he knew to be false. Their renderings of rural life expressed their contrasting psychologies. Uspenskii presented the countryside as a nether world, inhabited by primitive, bestial beings, above which hope floated as a comforting but essentially meaningless illusion. Zlatovratskii showed it as a primitive idyll, to which the forces of evil, though alarmingly powerful, remained somehow extrinsic and irrelevant.

According to the current canons of realism, literature was supposed to present a close simulation of reality, and the author to strive to compose works as worthy of credence as those of scholars and statisticians. In pursuing this goal, Zlatovratskii and Uspenskii forsook their fictional artifice and tried to assume the objective pose of the investigator. Yet in the end, it was clear, they achieved just the opposite of their intentions. In their effort to reconcile truth with longing, reality became merely the leavening of personal desires and art a powerful instrument to shape the world in the image of the ideal, rather than a mechanism subservient to perceived truth. They became, despite their realistic pretence, the most subjective of writers, and their works appeared as a strange blend of candour and wish-fulfilment, the boundary between dream and actuality shifting to suit their transient psychic needs.

It was precisely this clash of individual personal opinions in the writings of the *belletristy* that pointed to the inadequacy of the dominant view of the world and raised for the intelligentsia the problem of objective reality. The authors' disparate evaluations of reality revealed the existence of an issue where none had hitherto been recognized and engendered sharp debate about the actual nature of peasant society. The revolutionary ideologist, Petr Tkachev, took note in 1879 of the pronounced biases that marred both Uspenskii's and Zlatovratskii's commentaries. 'These subjective preconceived notions impede the objectivity and impartiality of the observations against the observer's will and desires, that is, they, to some extent, pervert and distort the observed object and display it in a more or less artificial and false light.'[1] The early sections of '*Derevenskie budni*', he thought, displayed a narrowness and onesidedness of outlook that permitted Zlatovratskii to evade disagreeable phenomena. 'Zlatovratskii is always and without fail hammering away at the same point,' and for this reason had not taken into account the forces militating against communal solidarity. But if Zlatovratskii had seen too little and his narrative was but a monotonous reiteration of a single idea, Uspenskii, Tkachev claimed, saw too much, more than he could comprehend, and his ideas changed with each new set of impressions, leaving the reader with no clear conception of the peasantry.[2] Referring to contemporary sources, Tkachev insisted that the communal tradition was more vital than Uspenskii would allow, that Uspenskii had remained blind to the fact that only adventitious social and economic conditions had prevented it from flourishing.[3] The radical critic A. I. Vvedenskii, reviewing the works of the two authors in 1880, also questioned the accuracy of their portrayals of the peasantry. Though accepting many of Uspenskii's observations, he disagreed with his conclusions. Vvedenskii thought that Uspenskii had demanded too much from the commune and had not made proper allowance for the poverty of the majority of the peasants. In regard to the story of Fedor the horse thief, he wrote, 'The rural commune is so poor that it is hard to be concerned with Fedushka, and we doubt that it is capable of the scientific, sociological and political-economic ideas that Uspenskii is asking from it. . . .'[4] Zlatovratskii, on the other hand, had disregarded the centuries of degradation that the peasants had undergone, and consequently had described only the bright side of rural life. Vvedenskii placed the character of the peasant between the extreme images presented by the two writers.[5]

With objective truth an issue, the workings of intellect could no longer respond to the dictates of emotion and a grave dis-

---

[1] P. Tkachev (Nikitin), 'Muzhik v salonakh sovremennoi belletristiki', *Delo*, no. 13 (August 1879), part 2, p. 6.

[2] *Ibid*. no. 13, part 2, p. 12.

[3] *Ibid*. no. 13 (September 1879), part 2, pp. 1–33.

[4] A. Vvedenskii, 'Gleb Uspenskii i N. Zlatovratskii', *Slovo*, no. 3 (July 1880), part 2, p. 88.

[5] *Ibid*. part 2, pp. 83–6.

junction between thought and feeling began to open in the soul of the *intelligent*. On the one hand, he was compelled to try to view the world dispassionately in order to determine which of the pictures of the countryside deserved credence; on the other, whatever his findings, he could not sacrifice his concept of the peasantry. The result was an uneasy mixture of fact, surmise, and wish, with the populist image of reality, once so logically proportioned, turning into an unintelligible blur. 'We see a variegated, formless picture of ferment in which everything is springing and darting like a boiling whirlpool', the literary critic Aleksandr Skabichevskii wrote at the end of 1881.[1] In describing the chaotic tendencies at work in the countryside, he observed, literature itself had become chaotic. The field of agreement had disappeared, and writers with roughly the same outlook could no longer be expected to agree on the nature of rural life. There was

a pronounced uncertainty, lack of definition, at times a pathological duality of views, a disjointedness between the various scenes, a vagueness or even a poverty of evidence and argumentation despite all the signs of great conviction. And, in the same camp, notice that you meet the most flagrant contradictions of ideas on significant problems: on what is meant by countryside, the rural commune, the intelligentsia's attitude to the people, etc.[2]

The same discord between thought and feeling beset those who approached the vast quantities of descriptive and statistical material that began to be published in the late seventies and early eighties. Undigested and unsystematized, the facts and numbers appeared to point in every direction and reveal no clear conclusions. Lacking adequate conceptual tools, the members of the intelligentsia regarded the copious data with bewilderment and tried as best they could to find bits of information that confirmed their beliefs. The works analysing and explaining the new materials lent little assistance, for here, too, it was clear that the authors were selecting and shaping their information to fit their own preconceptions. Such was the case with the *Sbornik materialov dlia izucheniia pozemel'noi obshchiny* (*Compendium of Materials for the Study of the Land Commune*), begun with such *éclat* by the Imperial Free Economic Society and the

[1] Aleksandr Skabichevskii (Alkandrov), 'Zhizn' v literature i literatura v zhizni', *Ustoi*, no. 1 (January 1882), p. 77.
[2] *Ibid.* no. 1, p. 79.

Imperial Geographic Society in 1878 and published in 1880. The unrelated studies of various *volosti* and communes by authorities on the peasantry that comprised the volume were merely elaborations of the author's *narodnik* preconceptions. The single exception, a lengthy study of a *volost'* in Riazan province by the prominent *zemstvo* statistician, A. A. Semenov, detailed the growth of individualistic tendencies among the peasantry and the mounting opposition to communal traditions.[1] The other authors presented synoptic, romanticized pictures of rural life, dwelling on the benevolent influence of the redistribution of land, the peasants' attachment to the land, and the feeling of solidarity that impelled the peasants to assist each other when in need. Indeed, most of this compendium, designed to clear the air of conjecture, reads like fiction and it is indicative of the spirit of the undertaking that Nikolai Zlatovratskii was one of the contributors. His report on another *volost'* in Riazan sounded the same note of fantasy and unreality as the early sections of *The Foundations*. Good-hearted village elders, acting in the interest of the commune, thwarted the efforts of the *kulak* as of old; the commune divided the land in proportion to the work force of each family and secured the welfare of all its members; the rental of land and the maintenance of the forest were carried on happily by peasants working in common.[2]

The flaws in the study drew sharp criticism from the radical press. L. S. Lichkov, writing in *Delo*, pointed out that the authors had concerned themselves with juridical formalities rather than with actual economic relationships. By presenting 'decorative pictures' (*sploshnye kartiny*), they had succeeded in evading the most important questions of village life, such as the problem of differentiation within the commune.[3] The reader, aware that the 'decorative pictures' omitted many of the most striking and disturbing aspects of peasant life, was dubious about their veracity. Lichkov's most severe strictures were reserved for Zlatovratskii.

The presentation is workmanlike, clear and consistent, just as Zlatovratskii always writes...It is not apparent, however, why the author fails to mention a word about the predatory kind of land-

[1] F. L. Barykov, A. V. Polovtsov, P. A. Sokolovskii, ed., *Sbornik materialov dlia izucheniia sel'skoi pozemel'noi obshchiny* (St Petersburg, 1880), pp. 38–128.

[2] *Ibid.* pp. 159–69.

[3] L. Lichkov, 'Pervye opyty po izsledovaniiu pozemel'noi obshchiny', *Delo*, no. 15 (January 1881), part 2, p. 86.

holding. Is this because it does not exist in the commune, as it is necessary to assume? Or is this because he did not explore the problem, which is more probable?[1]

The anonymous reviewer of *Sbornik*... in *Otechestvennye Zapiski* noted the obvious disparities between the factual material presented in the compendium and the authors' general conclusions. The peasants' frequent reluctance to repartition, the inequality that prevailed in many of the villages, contradicted the authors' trust in a commune united in thought and action. To the reviewer, the material indicated, instead, that a bitter struggle was raging between rich and poor in the countryside.[2] The majority continued to oppose private landholding only because of their mistaken notions of the benefits of the communal system.

The principle of the equal right of all to land, in other words, reigns among the people in full force. But meanwhile, in practice, the very individuals who do not want to take a private holding because they think it will be 'worse than the others have' nonetheless remain without any land at all or with disproportionately small pieces (i.e., it turns out anyway to be worse than the others have). Obviously the influence of the rich peasants, who have discarded the old communal theory, is so great that they are always strong enough to defeat the demand for repartition on the part of the dissatisfied. But they cannot compel the mass of peasants to renounce the very principle of communal equality and sanction the factual individual landholding in a formal renunciation of the communal system. Their influence has not reached this stage and the cheated member continues to console himself with the hope of a future equalization.[3]

Even Vasilii Orlov's scrupulous *Formy krestianskogo zemlevladeniia v Moskovskoi gubernii* (*The Forms of Peasant Land Tenure in Moscow Province*) suffered from a disconnection between the material presented and the author's subjective evaluation. Many of his data pointed to the disintegration of the traditional rural institutions of the province. They showed growing economic differentiation in the village, the migration of the rural population to the cities, the invasion of peasant life by a money economy, and the stresses all these changes exerted on the commune. Orlov noted that land purchased by communes was

---

[1] *Ibid.* no. 15, part 2, p. 68.
[2] *Otechestvennye Zapiski*, no. 254 (January 1881), part 2, pp. 89–92.
[3] *Ibid*, no. 254, part 2, p. 91.

almost invariably held in private ownership, and he concluded that both rich and poor were eager to break away from the commune—the former in order to consolidate their holdings, the latter to seek more profitable work in the cities.[1] But at the same time Orlov advanced evidence that the communal tradition was thriving. He found most of the peasants he questioned outspokenly attached to communal forms. Many of those who had formally withdrawn from the commune, he claimed, still maintained their customary ties and continued to avail themselves of members' privileges.[2] He concluded that communal traditions remained so ingrained in the people that they were virtually unassailable.[3] But to many *intelligenty* his material spoke otherwise.

Georgi Plekhanov, for one, found serious grounds for concern in Orlov's work. In two articles published in early 1880 in *Russkoe Bogatstvo*, he expressed serious doubt and apprehension about the fate of the rural commune. The sure and undaunted tone of his reply to Uspenskii was gone, and he stressed the need for a thorough examination of the commune and its origins. 'The problem of the historical succession of relationships to the land, with regard to the entire sum of statistical and dynamic influences upon them, one might say, is a question that is just rising to the fore.'[4] He was distressed by Orlov's evidence of the increasing inequality in landholding and the growth of agricultural and urban proletariats. The disintegration of villages, the constantly lengthening period between repartitions, the spread of private landholding struck Plekhanov as sinister and disturbing signs, in the light of which Orlov's faith in the commune seemed unwarranted.[5]

We are convinced that rural collectivism is not always able to resist the pressures of hostile influences; in particular, in the rural commune we can perceive signs of the distortion of the basic principle itself and even cases of its complete disintegration, although these, fortunately, are few.[6]

Plekhanov still believed that there was time for the intelligentsia to act on behalf of the commune. It still enjoyed the

---

[1] V. I. Orlov, *Sbornik statisticheskikh svedenii po Moskovskoi gubernii: Formy krestianskogo zemlevladeniia v Moskovskoi gubernii.* (Moscow, 1879), pp. 275–6.
[2] *Ibid.* p. 295.   [3] *Ibid.* p. 319.
[4] G. Plekhanov (Valentinov), 'Pozemel'naia obshchina', *Russkoe Bogatstvo* (January 1880), p. 35.   [5] *Ibid.* pp. 44–5.   [6] *Ibid.* (February 1880), p. 34.

support of the majority of the peasants, and if the effects of the current money economy could be temporarily staved off, then the commune might last until the advent of the next historical stage, when collective forms would become economically more advantageous and individualism would naturally vanish. But Plekhanov was most uncertain about its chances of survival and his prescriptions for action were vague and weak: its future now hinged in large measure upon 'the correctness of our intelligentsia's understanding of the economic problems of our native land'. Yet how the members of the intelligentsia were to achieve this understanding, and how it was to enable them to influence reality, Plekhanov did not intimate, either in this or in any of his earlier writings. When he left Russia at the beginning of 1880, Plekhanov had already entered the severe ideological crisis that would culminate in his momentous rejection of the populist faith.[1]

The understanding of Russia's economic problems presupposed the acceptance of a system of economic analysis and a willingness and ability to apply its principles to actual economic conditions. But in the seventies the study of economic phenomena had been unthinkable for those dedicated to the radical cause. Their projection of ideals onto the countryside assumed a world where economic forces independent of the human will did not exist, and where the justice or injustice of a given set of economic circumstances depended upon the benevolence or malignancy of the prevailing human agencies. Economic analysis that amounted to more than blanket condemnation seemed to the members of the intelligentsia of the seventies a consecration of the system being analysed; it signified that the relationships being studied constituted more than the artificial creation of a predator class and that these operated according to immutable laws defying human efforts at change. They regarded Political Economy condescendingly as a scholarly apologia for the capitalist system, a callous justification of the exploitation of man by man to be studied solely for purposes of refutation. On the pretext of maximizing the wealth of all, capitalism—and

---

[1] *Ibid.* pp. 35–6. For detailed descriptions of the tortuous evolution of Plekhanov's thought in this period, see Leopold H. Haimson, *The Russian Marxists and the Origins of Bolshevism* (Cambridge, 1955), pp. 26–40; Samuel H. Baron, *Plekhanov, The Father of Russian Marxism* (Stanford, 1963), pp. 48–77.

with it Political Economy—impoverished the many for the benefit of the few. Nikolai Mikhailovskii expressed the intelligentsia's empyrean contempt for contemporary economic thought when he wrote in 1879:

Liberal economics has never brought the principle of individualism to its logical conclusion. Like Jupiter hiding in his Olympian clouds after his divine sin and fall, liberal economics concealed itself in the mist of 'the wealth of the nation', when it committed its sin of violence against the individual.[1]

The economic attitudes of the intelligentsia of the seventies were derived primarily from Chernyshevskii and Marx, particularly the former. But Chernyshevskii's notes to Mill's *Principles of Political Economy*, his most influential work on economics, were little more than an abstract proof of the economic and moral superiority of collectivist to capitalist production, and offered no help in fathoming the meaning of the complex economic changes taking place. Of the writers the *intelligenty* read, only Marx presented both a theory that appealed to them and a method of analysing and comprehending the functioning of the existing economy.

The writings of Karl Marx had always enjoyed an enormous popularity among the Russian intelligentsia. *The Poverty of Philosophy* and *The Critique of Political Economy*, received indifferently in Europe, were acclaimed in Russia. Nikolai Daniel'son's translation of *Das Kapital*, appearing in 1872, was the first rendering of the work into any foreign language. But the intelligentsia admired Marx's teachings without assimilating their meaning. They took his thought as a trenchant moral indictment of European capitalism, not applicable as a whole to Russian conditions, and then incorporated in their own doctrines whichever of his ideas conduced to their current viewpoints. Thus, when radical thinkers in the early seventies did not make clear conceptual distinctions between Russian and European reality, the capitalistic system was vaguely assumed to prevail in Russia. The peasants were viewed as equivalent to proletarians, the landlords to entrepreneurs; and Marx's scheme for a working-class revolution was assumed to have equal validity for Russia. The economic and historical premises of

[1] N. Mikhailovskii, 'Politicheskaia ekonomiia i obshchestvennaia nauka', *Otechestvennye Zapiski*, no. 246 (September 1879), p. 522.

his theory, however, received little attention.[1] In the second half of the seventies, when the intelligentsia became more aware of the distinctive character of Russian life, Marx's economic determinism exerted a considerable appeal. The nature of the social and political system of each country was seen as determined by the economic system endemic to it; therefore, Russia as an agricultural country could not be expected to follow the same path of social development as the industrial West. But the historical dynamic of Marxism was either omitted from consideration or assumed not to have relevance for the Russian scene.[2]

The two members of the intelligentsia who first attempted to apply Marxian analysis directly to actual Russian conditions were, significantly, sons of merchants. Nikolai Sergeevich Rusanov and Nikolai Frantsevich Daniel'son (known by his pseudonym, Nikolai-on) grew up close to the problems of commerce and economics and developed an unusual awareness of the economic dimension of social phenomena. Both became familiar with Marx's economic teachings early in their lives and acquired a point of view somewhat different from that of the other radical *intelligenty* of their era. Deeply attached to the peasantry and to the notion of an agrarian socialist society, they endeavoured to use Marxian concepts to illuminate the meaning of the ominous and inscrutable developments in the countryside. In 1880, both published articles analysing the recently gathered data on the basis of Marx's theories. But Rusanov and Daniel'son answered the vague apprehensions of the intelligentsia merely by providing clearer and more persuasive grounds for concern, thus widening the gulf that had appeared between thought and feeling. Their new approach ascertained the relentless growth of a money economy in Russia and opened a Pandora's box that they found themselves unable to close.

Nikolai Rusanov began to participate in revolutionary circles

---

[1] K. A. Pazhitnov, *Razvitie sotsialisticheskikh ideii v Rossii* (Petrograd, 1924), I, 193–5; M. Bakunin, *Izbrannye sochineniia* (St Petersburg–Moscow, 1922), I, 95; V. V. Flerovskii, *Izbrannye ekonomicheskie proizvedeniia* (Moscow, 1958), I, 313–14; Naumov, I, 182–8.

[2] O. Aptekman, 'Zachatki kul'turnogo narodnichestva v 70-kh godakh', in *Istoriko-revoliutsionny sbornik No. 1* (Leningrad, 1924), pp. 23–36; Iakovlev, *Revoliutsionnaia zhurnalistika*, pp. 243–55 (article of Plekhanov in no. 3 of *Zemlia i Volia*).

while still a gymnasium student in the mid 1870s. During the latter part of the decade, he came in contact with a wide variety of radical groups and committed himself fully to the revolutionary cause. But none of the theories embraced by the members of the intelligentsia seemed to be satisfactory ways of explaining the world. His interest in economics and his attraction to Marxism made him look beyond current doctrines.

Elements of insurrectionism, Jacobinism, and something that I cannot call Marxism, but which entered my soul from Marx after the reading of *Capital, The Communist Manifesto* and *The Civil War in France*—all this was planted in my mind, and there it seethed without settling, without being clarified, only deepening my theoretical doubts and preventing me from attaching myself to any tendency for the purpose of practical work.[1]

In 1878, at the age of nineteen, he was expelled from medical school and imprisoned for his involvement in radical activities. He used his free time in confinement to verse himself more thoroughly in economic theory and to clarify and formulate his own overall view of reality. With his sophistication in economics, he became increasingly dissatisfied with the techniques being employed to investigate and describe the condition of the countryside. His first published work was a critique of recent works on the rural commune by Prince A. Vasil'chikov and A. Posnikov, two leading authorities on rural problems in Russia. Rusanov systematically refuted the major points of each study. He concluded that no progress could be made in understanding the commune while its investigation remained in the hands of people 'who take it upon themselves to decide social problems without previously mastering scientific method and who use in their investigations techniques rejected by scientific methodology long ago'.[2]

Rusanov presented his own interpretation of the new materials on the countryside in an article entitled '*Sovremennye proiavleniia kapitalizma v Rossii*' ('Contemporary Manifestations of Capitalism in Russia') which appeared in *Russkoe Bogatstvo* side by side with Plekhanov's article on the rural commune. He confidently set out to prove what no other radical would dare to consider: that Russia had already embarked upon the

[1] Rusanov, *Na rodine* (*1859–1882*), p. 113.
[2] N. S. Rusanov, *Noveishaia literatura po obshchinnomu zemlevladeniiu v Rossii* (Moscow, 1879), p. 57.

capitalist path of development, and that Marxist formulas could shed light on Russian reality. He first took issue with the accepted radical interpretation of the dialectic and the Hegelian triad—with the notion that the commune was an element common to the lowest and highest stages of development and therefore could be perpetuated. The dialectic, he thought, indicated that all social relations without exception were evanescent and subject to the laws of change.[1] Then he proceeded to draw abundant proof of such change from the recently published data on the countryside (particularly Orlov's). While Plekhanov hesitated fearfully before the meaning of Orlov's material, Rusanov rushed to make its implications explicit. The growth of the 'small workshop' (*kustar'*) industry and the increasing differentiation in the village he construed as signs of an embryonic stage of capitalism. Most *kustar'* owners, he showed, though not themselves capitalists, were falling under the power of the *kulaki*, who were acting as middlemen. Many had been reduced to an outwork relationship, with the *kulak* both supplying their raw materials and marketing their finished products. The independent *kustar'* owner was beginning to disappear, auguring the concentration of ownership along the Western European pattern. 'In the near future, all these forms of acquisition of surplus value will turn into a genuine West European factory regime.'[2]

In this atmosphere of trade and exploitation, the commune and other peasant institutions atrophied and lost their original character. Peasants in large numbers left the land to join the swelling class of vagabonds.[3] A proletariat was forming, and Rusanov, as a budding Marxist, welcomed it as the bearer of socialist consciousness. In the 'laboratory' of the industrial regions of Moscow, Petersburg, Tula, and Pavlovo, 'the kernel of a future proletariat is being prepared and is filling with new layers of factory population. Thus, the class consciousness [of the workers] is beginning to arise.'[4]

Rusanov also took upon himself the task of championing what he understood to be Marxian theories of social change. He thought that Marx had taught that the political system was

[1] N. S. Rusanov, 'Sovremennye proiavleniia kapitalizma v Rossii', *Russkoe Bogatstvo* (January 1880), p. 82.

[2] *Ibid.* pp. 97–9 (February 1880), pp. 65–6, 70, 76.

[3] *Ibid.* (February 1880), pp. 50–3.

[4] *Ibid.* p. 87.

merely a superstructure, shaped by the underlying social and economic relationships and that it could be changed only by altering those relationships and not by political means. This conviction led him to do battle with the ideologists of The People's Will, who held that the economic and social structure could be transformed by toppling the autocracy. In a debate with Lev Tikhomirov in the journal *Delo*, Rusanov insisted that political change was feasible only when based upon the support of the labouring masses.

Since the masses are moved by exclusively material interests, the individual who desires to act in society's interest should go hand in hand with the masses, in the name of the economic ideals created in the labouring classes by history—in the name of the economic ideals of the people during a given epoch.[1]

But Rusanov soon found that his youthful infatuation with Marxism was leading him to conclusions that offended his deepest affinities. Despite his bold salute to the forces of the future, he had not broken away from his emotional attachment to the peasantry and his joy at the growth of a proletariat in no way affected his devotion to the commune. In the very article heralding the advent of capitalism, he reaffirmed his faith in the commune as an essentially socialistic institution and extolled its capacity to survive in the face of adverse historical circumstances; it had succeeded 'over the long period of its existence in turning its members' attachment to their form of life from the instinctive to the conscious'.[2]

Gradually the two sides of Rusanov's personality—the intellectual, striving for a convincing explanation of the world, and the emotional, striving for a comforting one—came in conflict. Given his description of the changes in the countryside, he could continue to uphold his 'Marxian' notion of social development only if he transferred his sympathies to the proletariat and resigned himself to the demise of the commune. But he still regarded the destruction of traditional peasant society as an unmitigated personal and national catastrophe, and longed for swift and decisive prophylactic action. He increasingly felt the attraction of the doctrines of The People's Will, though his social theories were closer to those of The Black Partition.

---

[1] N. S. Rusanov, 'Ekonomika i politika', *Delo*, no. 15 (March 1881), part II, p. 74.   [2] Rusanov, 'Sovremennye...' (January 1880), p. 103.

From one tendency, I was separated by my sceptical attitude toward the rosy hopes placed on the idealized peasant; from the other, by an equally sceptical attitude toward the implementation of a progressive political programme on the basis of a backward economics.[1]

In the end, the whole theoretical edifice Rusanov had so painstakingly constructed and defended crumbled. The pull of old affinities, the inviting vision of sudden triumph, the grief over executed revolutionary heroes—all raised his desire for some kind of action on behalf of his original cherished beliefs. 'I moved towards The People's Will, but along a path of great spiritual crisis in which mind played a much smaller role than feeling.'[2] Joining in the high expectations and transports of the moment, Rusanov lost the ability to relate his immediate sympathies to a consistent conception of the world and spent his intellectual energies on meaningless abstract questions of doctrine. Bereft of a philosophical basis for his aspirations, he went abroad to seek the elusive explanation of reality.[3]

Though Nikolai Daniel'son's active participation in revolutionary circles ended after he left the University of St Petersburg in the late sixties, he maintained his ties with the movement of the seventies and shared its reigning ideals and attitudes. Unlike most radicals, however, Daniel'son was closely involved with the problems of economics. He received his secondary education in a commercial school and after graduation from the university went to work in The Mutual Credit Association, where he rose in the course of the seventies to the post of credit controller. The link between his interest in economics and his radical sentiments was Marxism. From the end of the sixties, he revered Marx as his mentor and devoted himself to his service. Marx's faithful agent in Petersburg, he arranged the publication of *Das Kapital* in Russian and did the major part of the translating. In his correspondence with Marx, which lasted from 1869 till the latter's death in 1883, he remained the deferent pupil, happy to execute his master's wishes, and undisposed to question his teaching.[4]

Daniel'son early felt the need for a study of Russian economic conditions from the radical viewpoint, comparable to Marx's on Europe. He wrote to Marx in 1869:

[1] Rusanov, *Na rodine*, p. 255.   [2] *Ibid.* p. 268.   [3] *Ibid.* pp. 278–82.
[4] 'Nikolai Frantsevich Daniel'son', *Deiateli revoliutsionnogo dvizheniia v Rossii* (Moscow, 1927–34), II, pp. 335–6: Karl Marx and Friedrich Engels, *Perepiska K. Marksa i F. Engel'sa s russkimi politicheskimi deiateliami* (Leningrad, 1951), *passim*.

Up to now a work has not appeared either in Russian or Western literature which would illuminate correctly, not from the official or the bourgeois viewpoint, the fate and economic situation of the Russian peasant, factory worker and craftsman, or of the Russian working classes in general.[1]

Daniel'son did not consider undertaking such a work himself. His energies were absorbed in mastering Marx's theories and learning to understand the Western experience through his teacher's eyes. His remark was made, rather, with the tacit expectation that Marx could be induced to write on Russia. Though Marx never betrayed such an inclination, Daniel'son persisted in his hope through the seventies. He dutifully mailed him the most important of the statistical compendia, believing that the rich material in them would confirm 'some of the basic premises of *Kapital*' and would illustrate 'the genesis of surplus value in its capitalistic form, by showing its transitional stages from forced labour (*barshchina*) to sharecropping, from outwork, for loan (*otrabotka*) to rental'.[2] He also hoped that Marx would provide a theoretical framework for the new materials, so that

the data the [statisticians] have gathered become links in a chain tying the social economy into a single whole, and in this manner not only illuminate the direction of our development but show the *zemstvo* statisticians themselves what was most essential in their work, what was less essential, and perhaps, what was lacking.[3]

Wedded to a populist conception of the world, Daniel'son was at first loathe to follow his own suggestions and to formulate an interpretation of recent Russian economic development according to Marx's ideas. During 1879 and early 1880, however, he overcame his reluctance and devoted himself to this task. The work that resulted, '*Ocherki nashego poreformennogo khoziastva*' ('Studies of our Social Economy in the Reform Era'), was the first general treatment of the Russian economy from a populist viewpoint. In the 1880s it became the principal source disclosing the cause, extent, and direction of the transformations imperilling rural society. Works as different in aim as Kravchinskii's *The Russian Peasant* and Plekhanov's *Our Differences* relied heavily on its interpretative insights.

Two incidents in his correspondence with Marx were instru-

---

[1] Marx and Engels, *Perepiska...*, p. 70.

[2] N. F. Daniel'son, 'Pis'ma Karla Marksa i Fridrikha Engel'sa k Nikolai-onu', *Minuvshie gody*, no. 1 (January 1908), p. 41.   [3] *Ibid.*

mental in leading Daniel'son to embark on his own analysis of the new materials. The first was a request from Marx for data on Russian banking. This compelled Daniel'son to analyse and correlate for the first time the information that passed through his hands in the credit office.

This request forced [me] to undertake more systematic work, which had as its goal the study of all the chief aspects of Russia's social and economic life, including the source of the government's financial means, in order to show their mutual dependence and the driving force which animated and inspired it.[1]

When his attention focused on the rows of figures he had collected, Daniel'son suddenly became aware of a general pattern governing Russian economic life. All the mechanisms of the economy—trade, credit, and transportation—seemed to be engaged in the single overriding task of stripping the countryside of its product. He saw money as the sinister factotum executing the work of exploitation. Money played the lead role in the '*Ocherki*': Daniel'son showed it stalking the countryside like a greedy spirit carrying off all it could find. It left the city in September:

And truly in September it is money that is needed. The bank coffers empty. The State Bank releases more in this month than all the rest of the year combined. In other words money, money and more money, is needed, and money makes its pilgrimage to the people. It is the only month of the year when the peasant sees it near him. Let it go there. Who cares? It knows its master and will not remain in the peasant's boot for long. It will return to the pocket whence it came and will bring with it the products it went to fetch.[2]

In the winter money returned from the countryside and trade quickened in the city. By the spring it was again resting in the coffers of banks. But the countryside never ceased suffering its ravages. Everything became an object of sale; 'everything is turning into money,' Daniel'son sadly concluded.[3] Even the commune did its bidding and drove the peasants to the market for the funds to pay their taxes.[4]

The second incident persuading Daniel'son to undertake his study was a statement of Marx's to the effect that governments

[1] *Ibid.* p. 42; Marx and Engels, *Perepiska...*, p. 105; 'Nikolai Frantsevich Daniel'son', p. 336.
[2] N. F. Daniel'son (Nikolai-on), 'Ocherki nashego poreformennogo obshchest- vennogo khoziastva', *Slovo*, no. 3 (October 1880), p. 96.
[3] *Ibid.* no. 3, pp. 97–101.   [4] *Ibid.* no. 3, p. 137.

of backward countries often tried to build capitalist systems before the underlying economic conditions were ripe, thus encouraging the breakdown of the old economy and the premature onset of capitalism.[1] This freed him of the notion burdening Rusanov, that Marx viewed economic development as a self-propelling dynamic in which human will and political factors could play no role. It opened for him the possibility of analysing economic phenomena without resigning himself to their ineluctability and allowed him to join the partisans of The People's Will in assigning responsibility for Russia's economic condition to the state while continuing to view himself as a student of Marx. It enabled him to document the progress of capitalism in Russia without relinquishing his populist faith.

In the 'Ocherki' Daniel'son attributed the growth of a money economy not to the natural operation of economic forces but directly to the actions of the Russian government. The increasing flow of money had not been brought about by a rise in production, for production, he claimed, had actually fallen; rather it had resulted from the state's determination to use the products of the countryside to compete on the international market. The state overburdened the peasants with taxation and thus created the need for money that kept the proliferating financial mechanism in motion. With large quantities of foreign gold, it then proceeded to divest them of their crops. The railroads, which it supported with twenty per cent of its annual budget, completed the process by carrying the grain from the countryside to the city.[2]

The inevitable result of the unleashing of a money economy was the total destruction of the productive forces of the country. In Daniel'son's tableau, Russia was shown being driven towards certain economic exhaustion and collapse. The store of capital increased at the expense of the peasant, impoverishing him and depriving him of the means to till the land adequately. But the large sums of money were not financing the construction of a new economic base to replace the old. Capital merely accumulated in the banks until needed for its annual round. Little found its way into production of any kind.[3]

---

[1] Marx and Engels, *Perepiska...*, pp. 103–5.
[2] Daniel'son, 'Ocherki...', no. 3, pp. 102–7.
[3] *Ibid.* no. 3, pp. 123–8, 107–10. The point about peasant poverty was further developed in the 1893 edition of the *Ocherki*. By that time Daniel'son had come to

Only the bold action of the members of the intelligentsia, Daniel'son thought, could enable Russia to avert economic catastrophe and save its peasant population from ruin. Implicit in his writings of this time was the hope that the government would succumb to the revolutionaries' blows and leave the fate of Russia to educated society. He ended his article with a plea for the intelligentsia to stem the tide of capital and to ensure that the instruments of production remained in the hands of the peasants. In February 1881, a month before the assassination of the tsar, he asserted that progressive society should learn to master objective reality rather than yield to it. 'Society is not directing itself, but becoming the plaything of a series of economic conditions,' he wrote. 'It is making no effort to study them in order to bring them under its control.'[1]

The effort of The People's Will aborted. The murder of Alexander II failed to bring about the downfall of the Russian state. Instead, it hardened the autocracy's resolve and, by the end of 1881, the revolutionary forces were broken. Such exhortations as Daniel'son's, then, seemed no more than shouting in a void. A new period of reaction promised to give the elements of destruction in the countryside ample time to complete their work. Left with the grim machinery of an economic analysis that predicted the devastation of peasant life and the growth of a European-type trade and financial system, Daniel'son did not pursue his investigation. He held his silence and his next work did not appear for over a decade.

The survival of the autocracy shattered the intelligentsia's last comforting supposition about reality. The hope that the entire governmental structure would collapse when put to the test proved illusory, and the Russian state loomed as the dominant force in Russia's future development—an ever present leviathan that could not be conjured away or excluded from consciousness. Undaunted, it would continue to propagate its diseased by-products and to lay waste to everything the intelligentsia cherished. 'The process of disintegration has been prolonged', S. N. Krivenko, the chief publicist of *Otechestvennye*

see peasant poverty as an effective *brake* on Russia's capitalist development. No such notion was present in the 1880 version, which constituted only the first section of the later work.

[1] *Ibid.* no. 3, pp. 141–2; N. F. Daniel'son (Nikolai-on), 'Zamechaniia na stat'iu G. Antonovicha, "O reformakh krestianskoi i obshchestvennoi khoziastvennosti"', *Novoe Obozrenie* (February 1881), pp. 188–9.

Zapiski, wrote in the summer of 1881. 'It is spreading outward across the country and promising to last so long that it will engulf the milieu of the people...promising to recall for long the strife and the grief of the Russian land.'[1]

The processes of thought now could be expected to yield no satisfactory answer to the promptings of feeling. The image of reality that had inspired the members of the intelligentsia with the sense that they were true brethren of the Russian peasantry could receive no corroboration in their examinations of the world or in their actual experience. When their last hope evaporated after the first of March, they found themselves alone in a world governed by powerful inimical forces which they were impotent to resist. Their dreams of transforming Russia seemed to have no relevance to real conditions, and they themselves no role to play in Russia's future; like the privileged classes they despised, they were threatened with oblivion. 'The invisible hand of history will take you as well,' Krivenko warned, 'lead you to the edge of the abyss, and hurl you in, if you fail to understand the ideas of your century, the problems of your time, and adapt to their demands.'[2]

[1] S. N. Krivenko, *Sobranie sochinenii* (St Petersburg, 1911), II, p. 5.
[2] *Ibid.* II, p. 4.

6

THEORETICAL RECONCILIATION AND SPIRITUAL DISSOLUTION

Bear the pain and do not grieve,
Good, be assured, can be found in bad,
And believe that for honest thought,
Not all paths are closed.

NIKOLAI KUROCHKIN, 1882

There's an end to stupid waiting,
A limit to despair,
The time, my friends, has come!
Our minds are stifled with anguish,
Our breasts, languishing from bitter pain,
Are sick of endless cursing:
The time has come,
To go forth to our great task,
To triumph or to fall with glory!

PETR IAKUBOVICH, 1882

In the history of the Russian intelligentsia the decade of the 1880s is one of receding hopes and past glories. After the first of March 1881 neither of the two grounds for populist faith—revolutionary action or the peasantry—seemed to promise the realization of radical ideals. The brave vision of a Russia delivered from social injustice and bureaucratic oppression dimmed as the heroes of previous years began terms of imprisonment or exile, fled abroad, or perished on the scaffold. The image of a peasantry sharing the aspirations of the intelligentsia and ready to join in the transformation of society fell under the shadow of the doubts and qualifications raised by the first-hand investigation of the countryside.

The members of the intelligentsia struggled to refurbish the populist faith. They tried to recapture the sense of participation in Russia's development and to recreate the unity of thought and feeling that had imbued them with the confidence to advance themselves as the true spokesmen of the people. They clung to whichever remnants of the old outlook could still afford them comfort or inspiration and tried to banish other aspects of Russian life from their consciousness. Some, convinced of the futility of action, tried to restore their faith in rural reality; others, disabused of the idealized view of the countryside, tried to keep alive their faith in action. The theoretical and activist parts of the movement then came into conflict and a rift developed over what part of the heritage of the previous decade could or should be preserved. But in either case the attempt to revive the old optimism involved a suspension of the critical faculties, a subordination of intellect to feeling that left each *intelligent* seeking an answer, like Zlatovratskii and Uspenskii, in his own private fantasy world. The result was the disintegration of Russian populism into many populisms, each striving in its own way to relive the old exaltation.

The task confronting the theorists of the early eighties was to rescue the *narodnik* faith in the peasantry from the sombre prognostications made on the eve of the assasination of the tsar. Bleak portents had to be shown to conceal intimations of hope; thought had to be made to serve once again as the handmaiden of wish. In order to survive, *narodnik* ideology, like Zlatovratskii's self-rewarding rationalizations, had to cloud reality behind a patina of explanation. Above all, political economy, which had called into question the intelligentsia's most sacred beliefs, had to be silenced. These feats of thought were accomplished by a radical nobleman, a former country doctor, by the name of Vasilii Pavlovich Vorontsov, who wrote in *Otechestvennye Zapiski* under the initials V. V. Beginning even before the first of March, Vorontsov undertook to stave off the incursion of foreign economic thought. With an elaborate and skilfully wrought casuistry, he endeavoured to show the inapplicability of Western precepts to Russian conditions and to dispel the apprehension reigning in *narodnik* circles.

Like Daniel'son, Vorontsov was a man of the study, who hovered at the edge of the revolutionary movement but joined it only for brief moments. A member of an old noble family of Ekaterinoslav province, he was attracted to Lavrovist ideas while at medical school in Petersburg in the early seventies. After graduation, he associated with Lavrovist Chaikovtsy circles, though he never became a member.[1] He wrote propaganda leaflets for them and as their emissary went to Kiev to establish

---

[1] 'Vasilii Pavlovich Vorontsov', *Deiateli revoliutsionnogo dvizheniia v Rossii*, II, p. 231.

an allied circle.[1] In the second half of the seventies, while work-ing as a doctor, he served as an intermediary for the transfer-ence of funds to the circles of Land and Freedom.[2]

Vorontsov's single ideological statement of the seventies was an article published in Lavrov's *Vpered!* (*Forward!*) in 1876, discussing the failure of the 'going to the people' movement. In it he stressed the backwardness of the Russian peasant and the need for patient work of enlightenment on the part of the in-telligentsia. The peasants' world view was virtually immobile, he argued, in reply to Bakuninists who hoped for a spontaneous revolution in the villages. He pointed to the abortion of the Razin and Pugachev uprisings as proof of the strong monarchist sentiment of the people.[3] The intelligentsia had to effect 'the intellectual reorganization of the people'. Then, once they had created a genuine peasant intelligentsia, they could retreat from the scene: 'their ideal should be self-annihilation'.[4]

A powerful sense of the survival of the old, a disbelief in his-torical change, and in the action of forces independent of the *intelligent*'s control, these were the attitudes revealed in Voront-sov's early article. Happenings of the seventeenth and eighteenth centuries were facilely bracketed with the experiences of the previous few years. The effect of the reforms was shown to be inconsequential. 'As for the recent reforms,' he wrote, 'no matter how progressive they were, their influence on the world view of the people cannot appear after a mere decade.'[5] Vorontsov saw the people as a blank slate awaiting the intelli-gentsia. Nothing, not even the peasants' poverty, could thwart the work of enlightenment. 'The economic situation cannot serve as an insuperable obstacle to intellectual development. The critical thought of the people, once aroused, will not limit itself to the social system, but will embrace morality, philosophy and religion.'[6]

At the end of the seventies, Vorontsov still maintained his faith in the educative powers of the intelligentsia and his dis-trust of historical development. When confronted with the growing evidence of economic change, he felt impelled to

---

[1] Aptekman, *Obshchestvo 'Zemlia i Volia'*, p. 39; Kovalik (Starik), 'Dvizhenie semidesiatykh godov po bol'shomu protsessu', *Byloe*, no. 1 (November 1906), p. 33.
[2] L. Deitch, *Za polveka*, II (Berlin, 1923), p. 92.
[3] V. P. Vorontsov (V. V.), *Ot semidesiatykh godov k deviatisotym* (St Petersburg, 1907), pp. 14–20. [4] *Ibid.* pp. 21–4.
[5] *Ibid.* pp. 16–17. [6] *Ibid.* p. 26.

investigate the recent developments in the countryside and to defend his beliefs. He abandoned medicine, and for a brief period served as a statistician and economist in a railroad office. Then he left this as well to devote himself completely to the study of economics.

Vorontsov became convinced that the recently published material had alarmed the members of the intelligentsia only because they possessed no orderly scientific theory to evaluate the world in the light of their views. This was the case, he thought, because too much of the energy of the movement in its early stages had been channelled into action. The formation of the *narodnik* world view had occurred at 'a moment when great practical interests had devoured so much strength that society was left with neither time nor desire to evolve a scientific basis for its various programmes'.[1] For this reason, radical ideology had suffered from fuzziness of definition throughout the seventies; now, in the face of serious challenge, he thought, it was losing all coherence and meaning. He deplored 'the transformation of a movement into a mood'.[2]

Vorontsov took it upon himself to devise the theory that would yield answers in accordance with the *intelligent*'s longings and conclusions that would strengthen his faith in his ideals. The result was a triumph of abstract theory over the mass of factual material flooding the Petersburg intellectual world, an intellectual *tour de force* of the first magnitude that would serve as the principal defence of the *narodnik* faith for the next two decades. The initial statement of Vorontsov's ideas, appearing in late 1880 and 1881 and then republished in slightly revised form as his famous *Sud'by kapitalizma v Rossii* (*The Fates of Capitalism in Russia*), immediately revealed a method and a tone that contrasted strikingly with other works on the Russian countryside. Whereas other radical authors groped uncertainly for a theoretical framework that could explain the information perplexing them, Vorontsov formulated a well-articulated *a priori* theory, then demonstrated it with suitable proof. The hopes and doubts of waiting upon a benevolent turn of reality were gone, replaced by the absolute certainty of unquestioning faith. The fear of capitalism, Vorontsov asserted, was disorienting the intelligentsia's thought and creating a gap between

---

[1] V. P. Vorontsov (V. V.), *Nashi napravleniia* (St Petersburg, 1892), pp. 2–3.
[2] Vorontsov, *Ot semidesiatykh godov k deviatisotym*, p. 91.

ideals and conceptions of reality. It was this gap that he, fortified with his belief in the fundamental stability of rural life,
set out to erase.

The people's party would stand to gain a great deal if the dichotomy
in its world view were eliminated, if to its faith in the vitality of the
foundations of peasant life was added a conviction of the historical
impossibility of the growth of capitalist production in Russia.[1]

Vorontsov endeavoured to quiet their doubts by disposing of
the precepts of political economy that pointed to capitalism's
advent in Russia. His was to be an economics that would
invalidate Western economics in the Russian setting, a new
theoretical system that would enable the *intelligent* to disengage
himself from his dependence on European models and to foresee
a unique future for Russia. When accused of being ill versed
in economics, Vorontsov proudly admitted his ignorance,
arguing that such knowledge was of little use for the student
of Russian conditions.

The ordinary intelligent individual is not burdened by this wearying
obligation, and I am in that category. In other words, I am a layman
in economic science and have started writing only by chance, only
because our patented scholars, perhaps because of their close contact
with the theoretical discipline, have not fulfilled their obligations
to society, or, in other words, have not proved sensitive enough to
the ruling tendencies in educated society. These tendencies demand
a re-evaluation of the 'basic' conclusions of science in their application to Russia; they demand the emancipation of our thought from
the 'laws' of economic development revealed by this tottering
'science'; they demand an independent quest for the forms which
our production will assume.[2]

Two strands of analysis comprise the system which Vorontsov
used to justify his belief. The first, a commentary on the contradictions of capitalism in general, was drawn chiefly from the work
of the early-nineteenth-century French economist Sismondi.
Sismondi's teaching held that capitalism suffered a chronic
shortage of markets because it paid its workers wages insufficient
to purchase its products. Consequently, the capitalist nations of
Europe were engaging in fierce competition for markets abroad.

---

[1] V. P. Vorontsov (V. V.), *Sud'by kapitalizma v Rossii* (St Petersburg, 1882), p. 4.
[2] V. P. Vorontsov (V. V.), 'Izlishek snabzheniia rynka tovarami', *Otechestvennye Zapiski*, no. 268 (May 1883), part 2, pp. 14–15.

Vorontsov explored the implications of this situation for the backward nations serving as their outlets. If highly developed countries were having difficulty finding markets for their goods, then, Vorontsov reasoned, a backward nation must find the obstacles insurmountable.[1] Even the adoption of the latest technical advantages could not help it to compete, for they would simply curtail the need for labour and thus restrict its internal market. Its industry could absorb only a small percentage of those driven from the land and in the long run would promise still bleaker prospects for increased employment.[2] Capitalism in such a country could not 'socialize labour' (*obobshchestvovliat' trud*) and create larger and more efficient productive units. Instead, it could bring only economic *débâcle*, after which it would collapse, leaving its own remnants and the debris of the old economic system.[3]

Vorontsov's second argument contained his message of hope. At first only a subsidiary premise, in time it grew in importance, until it became his dominant theme. Certain countries, Vorontsov claimed, thanks to peculiarly favourable conditions, were especially immune to capitalist forms. If a country was extremely backward, if transportation was exceptionally inadequate, if technically trained personnel were lacking and labour costs were prohibitively high, then capitalism might be avoided completely.[4] It was Russia's fortune, Vorontsov believed, to be such a state. Its economic and social conditions had changed little over the previous centuries, and its people were ignorant, primitive, and untouched. Russia's geographical position also posed acute difficulties for the growth of capitalism. Its severe climate demanded large outlays for fuel, both for production and for the workers' subsistence, placing domestic entrepreneurs at a great disadvantage vis-à-vis foreign competitors. Finally, goods in Russia had to be hauled across long distances, lifting transportation costs far above those paid in the countries of the West.[5]

Having elaborated his theoretical premises, Vorontsov pro-

---

[1] V. P. Vorontsov (V. V.), 'K voprosu o razvitii kapitalizma v Rossii', *Otechestvennye Zapiski*, no. 252, part 2 (September 1880), pp. 2–4.

[2] *Ibid.* no. 252, part 2, pp. 4–6.

[3] *Ibid.* no. 252, part 2, pp. 6–7.

[4] *Ibid.* no. 252, part 2, p. 7.

[5] V. P. Vorontsov (V. V.). 'Iz istorii russkogo kapitalizma', *Otechestvennye Zapiski*, no. 259 (December 1881), p. 216.

ceeded to show that they were supported by the data at hand. While other observers were aghast at the evidence of the rapid strides of a money economy, Vorontsov insisted that the published materials pointed, not to the triumph of capitalism, but to its decay, and his unstinting efforts to prove this contention filled numerous closely reasoned and heavily documented articles. The crux of his argument, however, rested neither on the evidence he adduced nor on his skilful dialectics, but on his original definition of terms and posing of the question. Daniel'son and Rusanov had discerned incipient capitalist *relationships* in Russia which enabled an entrepreneur to divest the worker of part of his product. Without attempting to deny the prevalence of such relationships, Vorontsov disputed the contention that they pointed to the growth of a capitalist system. He held that production could not be considered capitalistic unless it 'socialized labour'—united workers in large enterprises, disciplined them to accept the division of labour, and thereby taught them to increase output. Daniel'son had described the concentration of capital in the hands of the financial profiteers; Vorontsov objected that none of this money was finding its way into productive channels, and therefore it could not promote the socialization of labour. Thus far, he contended, the government's policy had affected not the size of the productive unit, which remained the same or was growing smaller, but the distribution of wealth, which was favouring the unproductive speculator classes to the detriment of the peasantry.[1] For Vorontsov the concentration of production was the mark of capitalism.

It makes no difference to the worker, of course, whether he is skinned alive by the *kulak*, landlord, or manufacturer; but it makes a great difference for the fate of production, which in one case preserves its small form, and in another is transformed into large.[2]

Vorontsov's conception of capitalism, thus, was unconditionally ahistoric, admitting of no preliminary stage of development, and in this respect he still viewed the world through the eyes of an unreconstructed Lavrovist. He deemed large-scale production under an entrepreneur capitalistic, and since large enterprises were present in Russia, he concluded that *capitalist*

---

[1] V. P. Vorontsov (V. V.), 'Kapitalisticheskoe obrashchenie v Rossii', *Otechestvennye Zapiski*, no. 255 (April 1881), part 2, pp. 163–6.
[2] Vorontsov, *Sud'by kapitalizma v Rossii*, p. 5.

production had already made its appearance. But these enterprises, he contended, were experiencing great difficulties and were failing everywhere, despite massive governmental subsidies, because of the basic inhospitability of Russian conditions to large-scale production. Thus, Vorontsov squared the *narodnik*'s circle: the economic distress and disintegration which had seemed the first symptoms of capitalism became in his eyes the portents of its decline.

With great energy he documented the atrophy of capitalist production in Russia. The government's enormous subsidies, he showed, had done little to bolster large manufacturing enterprises. Belittling Russian economic expansion, he invidiously compared it to European achievements. His statistics showed that total production had increased only slightly since emancipation and that the number of workers employed had actually fallen during most of the period.[1] Few entrepreneurs were prepared to invest in new areas unless their efforts were largely underwritten by the government. Russian capitalists could barely afford their wage bill, he claimed, a fact ascertained by their constant complaints of excessive wages, though the pay the worker received was inadequate. The diffidence of the Russian entrepreneur was illustrated by the stagnant economic conditions of the large southern coalfields. The companies there had difficulty finding markets because of faulty transportation. But the only two rail lines running north belonged to a single mine-owner who would carry only his own products, and no one was venturing to compete with him. The capitalist simply waited for the government to bestow its favour. 'As soon as an enterprise rises slightly over the level of mediocrity, our capitalist obediently bows his head, proud at other times, and looks to the government entreatingly. He is too weak; without treasury subsidies, he is nothing, he goes to ruin.'[2]

Under the aegis of the government, Russia had acquired the attributes of capitalism without actually developing a full-fledged capitalist system. In agriculture, where the signs of a blossoming money economy had aroused the most concern, he found even more evidence of capitalism's demise. In accordance

[1] Vorontsov, 'K voprosu o razvitii kapitalizma v Rossii', part 2, pp. 33, 35; V. P. Vorontsov (V. V.), 'Fantaziia i deistvitel'nost' russkogo kapitalizma', *Otechestvennye Zapiski*, no. 255 (March 1881), p. 3.

[2] *Ibid.* no. 255, p. 16.

with the economic conceptions of the early seventies, he identi-fied large-scale landlord agriculture with capitalist production. The dissolution of the estates of the nobility, a development well known among the intelligentsia, then became merely another indication of the breakdown of capitalist production. Through-out Russia, he maintained, the area of land farmed by the peasantry was increasing at the expense of the gentry. The landlords were selling or renting most of their holdings to specu-lators. The latter reaped their profits without regard to the condition of the land or the future of agricultural production. They invested in no improvements and when the land ceased to yield returns, they sold it and returned to the cities. Their effect on the countryside was ruinous and was responsible for much of the peasants' misery, but, in Vorontsov's eyes, they represented the antipode of a capitalist entrepreneurial class.

The mere circumstance that agricultural entrepreneurs are men of the trader class, and predominantly Jews, a class living from quick and easy profits—this alone allows us to lament the memory of our chiefly imaginary capitalist landholding. The single consequence of their practices will be the exhaustion of the land, which we hope will not, in any way, promote the growth of capitalism. Their rule points not at all to the approach of the latter. They came, they exhausted the land, and they will leave: in that lies their mission.[1]

The speculator was the agent of the artificial carnage induced by the transplantation of European forms to Russia, and the peasant was his victim. By depriving the peasants of land and money, the state had made them his helpless prey.[2] These rapacious practices, accordingly, could be halted, Vorontsov thought, by a shift in governmental policy. While it is uncertain whether he subscribed to the programme of The People's Will, Vorontsov certainly entertained the hope that the action of society could convince—or force—the government to change its approach. 'Is it not, therefore, time to abandon our care for impersonal (*bezlichny*) production and marketing and to begin working for the elimination of the *kulak* scoundrel from the land?' he asked. Then, freed from the incubus of an alien system, peasant institutions would function freely and the intel-ligentsia could promote the development of 'social forms of labour on peasant *artel*' principles'.[3]

---

[1] Vorontsov, 'K voprosu o razvitii kapitalizma v Rossii', part 2, p. 21.
[2] *Ibid*. part 2, pp. 30.   [3] *Ibid*. part 2, pp. 26, 38.

But unlike the theorists of The People's Will, Vorontsov never credited the state with the ability to introduce far-reaching transformations in the productive base of the country and therefore never had to place all his hopes in a political revolution. Russia's economic propensities, he thought, were too deep-seated to be affected by the fluctuations of government policy, and capitalism stood no more chance of success in agriculture than in manufacturing. While industrial capitalism had proved incapable of overcoming the country's harsh climate, long distances, and backward economy, agriculture faced an even more formidable adversary in the person of the Russian peasant, who stubbornly refused to leave his land to become a free wage-labourer. The peasant's attachment to his land caused a chronic shortage of labour that afflicted the landlord. Willing to work only for high wages, the peasant would pay enormous rent for an extra strip of land. Forced to pay wages far above his capacity, the landlord finally relented, gave up trying to run his estate, and rented out most of his property. The peasant, consequently, cultivated the land and the landlord lost his desire to engage in agriculture. 'Thus the landlord has sacrificed his independence to the independence of the peasant,' he wrote, and 'the latter has proved stronger than the former.'[1] With deft ideological curtain work, Vorontsov turned the peasants' suffering into a sign of noble determination, converted the appearance of a threat to peasant traditions into their mainstay, and justified indigence as a sacrifice for the cause of future independence.

It is not easy for the peasant to defend his independence; he has endured much in defending himself, the master of his own plot, (*khoziain*), from becoming a worker. It is a rare case when the renting of land yields him anything in profit besides the proud consciousness of his independence.[2]

The peasants' tenaciousness was undermining the landlord's economic condition and driving him off his land. Taking the peasants' money in rental fees, he was unwittingly destroying his own market. He sought outlets abroad, but prices there were falling due to the recent arrival of cheap American wheat, his income declining just when the exhaustion of the soil de-

[1] V. P. Vorontsov ,'Mysli o budushchem pomeshchichykh khoziastv', *Russkoe Bogatstvo* (October 1880), pp. 60–3.
[2] *Ibid.* p. 72.

manded increased expenditures for cultivation. His property would inevitably pass into the hands of the sturdy peasants, who cared nothing for profits and desired only to remain on the land.[1]

Thus Vorontsov excluded Russia from the domain of ortho-dox and Marxist political economy and dismissed the spectre of capitalism. Russia's limitless expanses and forbidding cold, the stubbornness and resilience of the Russian peasant, repre-sented elements of stability that not even the inexorable force of capitalism could move. The signs of disintegration that had disturbed the *narodnik* were not to be taken seriously. But the mode of production that Vorontsov thought would emerge after the cessation of the government's current pro-capitalist policy and the way it was to be realized were far from clear in his writings of 1880 and the first part of 1881. He still seemed to nurture a Lavrovist inclination to accord the chief role to the members of the intelligentsia. They were to be the organizers of the 'social forms of labour on peasant *artel*' principles'. Like Engel'gardt, he believed that the intelligentsia could help turn the peasant's expertise in practical matters into an ability to conduct rational agriculture.

[The peasant], to be sure, lacks knowledge. But there are qualities in him that no science can instil, that have developed in him through his close contact and millennial struggle with nature. In this category fall his love for his work, his stubbornness in the attainment of his goals, his refined powers of observation and understanding of nature. Other classes may supply individuals capable of the same thing and incontestably doing the people a great service with their knowledge and talent. But they will find worthy pupils and com-panions *en masse* only among the peasantry.[2]

He contemplated a society in which production would be geared to consumption and not to the vagaries of the market. The peasant would cultivate his grain and raise his cattle for his own use rather than for export. In *arteli*, the members would determine the items to be grown and would produce only enough to satisfy their own needs. The market would no longer be glutted with unsaleable products and no one would be left

---

[1] V. P. Vorontsov (V. V.), 'Nashi vladel'cheskie khoziastva i kapital', *Otechest-vennye Zapiski*, no. 254 (February 1881), part 2, pp. 174–5; Vorontsov, 'Fantaziia i deistvitel'nost' russkogo kapitalizma', p. 27.

[2] Vorontsov, 'Mysli o budushchem pomeshchichykh khoziastv', p. 73.

to starve.[1] Yet nowhere in Vorontsov's works of this period was there a mention of collectivist sentiment among the people, not a single reference to the rural commune. The sturdy peasant type who resisted the landlord's capitalistic impulses and prized his independence seemed, indeed, a paragon of individualistic self-interest who would hardly be likely to surrender his dearly won independence to an *artel'*. Such an institution was, apparently, to be the creation of the intelligentsia.

Before the first of March, Vorontsov's argument was predominantly negative, aimed at discounting pessimistic interpretations of reality. He strove to preserve his belief that the peasants, untouched by factors external to their life, remained a *tabula rasa* upon which the intelligentsia could imprint its own ideals. But the quiescence of social interest within the intelligentsia after the assassination prompted a gradual evolution away from this position. With the disintegration of the active forces in society, the possibility of constructive educational work on the part of the intelligentsia began to appear increasingly remote. Vorontsov's conclusion that capitalism was unsuited to Russian conditions could inspire little confidence if nothing better was in the offing and if the peasants' destiny was merely to suffer in the midst of the ruins of the old system. The vestiges of Vorontsov's Lavrovism now came into conflict with his longing for a peasantry that embodied his ideas, and the tenor of his thought shifted to answer his need for a consoling picture of reality. He began to find that a new economic system was arising among the peasantry, without the intervention of the intelligentsia.

By the summer of 1881, Vorontsov's conception of peasant mentality had changed perceptibly. Not only was the peasant instinctively maintaining his own independence, but he had 'made up his mind to destroy all the efforts of the privileged classes to implant large-scale production' and had 'decided to tear this branch of industrial activity from the hands of the landlords'. While the intelligentsia's schemes dissolved into arid talk, the peasantry, in accord with nature, was successfully resisting the growth of new forms. 'The people have proved more perspicacious or more fortunate than the intelligentsia; their problem has coincided with the natural course of things, and so they remain the victor in the struggle for the forms of cultiva-

[1] Vorontsov, 'Fantaziia i deistvitel'nost' russkogo kapitalizma', pp. 1–2.

tion.' The people, however, were not passively obeying nature's dictates. They were 'consciously resisting the sowing of the seeds of capitalist production', and the sacrifice of their own welfare attested to their determination. Nor were they motivated solely by the selfish desire to preserve their independence; they were engaged in a struggle for a better life, *'for a higher type of socio-economic progress'*.[1]

The certainty of the impossibility of capitalism now became cause for Vorontsov to exclude all disturbing economic phenomena in the countryside from his mind and to focus his attention on whatever consoling developments he could discern. Dismissing the manifestation of a money economy as transitory by-products of an artificial and decaying system, he indulged his subjective fantasy and left economics to enter the obscure realm of peasant thought and feelings. At the close of 1881 his writings began to display marked resemblances to those of the *belletristy*, particularly to the current works of Zlatovratskii, which apparently held a strong appeal for him. Like Zlatovratskii, he began to view rural conditions as a veiled reflection of his own ideals and to perceive the germ of the future communal life in every happening in the countryside. He too became particularly attentive to the subtle expressions of the peasant's changing state of mind. He began to contend that a new class of peasant leaders was arising and propagating the communal ideal among the rural population:

the bosses (*vorotila*), those who are immersed most deeply in the whirlpool of interests of peasant communes, who at every step meet with sharp and deep contradictions between the life and customs of the peasants and the legislation about them. The peasantry actually feeds on their ideas and the ferment in their minds spreads throughout their midst. Thus one meets such ferment in out-of-the-way places, where no one at any time has heard anything about socialism.[2]

During 1882 and 1883 his picture of social conditions in the countryside grew even brighter. Like Zlatovratskii, he began to think that the disintegration of rural institutions hid profound transformations unfolding in the peasant's soul. The peasants

---

[1] V. P. Vorontsov (V. V.), 'Ekonomicheskii upadok Rossii', *Otechestvennye Zapiski*, no. 258 (September 1881), pp. 150–2.

[2] V. P. Vorontsov (V. V.), 'Udachnaia propaganda', *Delo*, no. 15 (September 1881), p. 127.

who detached their lands from familial holdings, he contended, were acquiring a new sense of personal dignity and a social feeling that would impel them to seek new and stronger communal relationships. They were learning the perils of individual enterprise and many had already recognized the advantage of combining their small plots and inadequate inventories into larger units. The works of Orlov and Zlatovratskii provided him with examples of peasants pooling their tools, harvesting their land in common, and even renting whole estates together. These were cases, he thought, of 'separate individuals... uniting of their own accord—not by dint of traditional attachment to an *artel*', but to meet the real needs of contemporary existence'.[1] They indicated that the peasant was coming to a rational understanding of where his best interest lay.

Having settled down from the first excitement, the peasant will understand that the life of an unbridled stud is impossible; if you don't submit to the old world, to custom, to free agreement, you will, just the same, fall into the hands of the *kulak* factory-owner, or be the victim of any chance occurrence. This new dependency is not so pretty that the peasant will not, in his turn, feel the desire to be free from it too, or, at least, to loosen its chains.[2]

The beginnings of the new system, Vorontsov argued, were already in evidence, and as the progressive ideal unfolded in the mind of the people, it would spread. The peasant had only to be freed from the petty concerns of his daily subsistence to devote himself completely to thought and the implementation of his ideas.

Then he will be able to look upon his trade and situation more broadly. He will consider the problem without the fear for his stomach that now conditions his understanding of everything and prevents him from experiencing anything new at all.[3]

By positing an order in which capitalism could not take root, Vorontsov was able to conclude that rational men seeking their own best interest would turn to collectivistic forms of production. This reasoning, he thought, would hold for educated

---

[1] V. P. Vorontsov (V. V.), 'Ocherki obshchinnogo zemlevladeniia v Rossii', *Otechestvennye Zapiski*, no. 260 (January 1882), pp. 211–50; no. 261 (March 1882), pp. 83–111; (April 1882), pp. 331–64; V. P. Vorontsov (V. V.), 'Semeinye razdely i krest'ianskoe khoziastvo', *Otechestvennye Zapiski*, no. 266 (February 1883), part 2, pp. 155–9.

[2] *Ibid*. no. 266, p. 160.   [3] *Ibid*. no. 266, p. 161.

individuals as well: they too would realize that capitalism was materially disadvantageous and join the struggle of the peasantry for a new communal economy. He pointed out that the wilting capitalist system could not provide openings for the thousands of skilled individuals trained by the institutions of higher learning. Though there was a grievous need for doctors, teachers, and agronomists in the countryside, capitalism could not translate this into effective demand; hence many proficient men were unable to put their abilities to good use.[1] The educated individual who acted in the interests of the people did not thereby sacrifice his own material interest, for only the downfall of capitalism and the establishment of a socialist order could assure him opportunities for the development of his own talents. The clash between exalted ideals and egoistic impulses which had gnawed at Uspenskii's soul and had prompted Engel'gardt to try to turn students into peasants was now resolved with a turn of Vorontsov's subtle pen. The mission of bettering the condition of the masses was to be performed not only by the heroic, critically thinking few: it was to be the natural obligation of all educated people. They had only to achieve a correct understanding of the nature of Russian reality.

The working intelligentsia cannot take a dilettante attitude to the struggle of socio-political parties in Russia; its personal material interest forces it to participate earnestly in this struggle...The development of the industry of the people, the increasing of labour's efficiency, based on the preservation of the tie between the worker and the instrument of production—here is the salvation of the intelligentsia and the guarantee of Russia's future cultural development. The Russian intelligentsia is compelled by the laws of history to follow consciously the goal of the well-being of the people.[2]

With singular dialectical skill, Vorontsov reconciled the opposites baffling the intelligentsia and found rays of hope in the grim terrain of reality. He identified the course of history once again with the progress of justice on earth and succeeded once more in placing the *intelligent* in phase with his epoch. Reaffirming the identity of real and rational, he again made it possible for the belief in the beneficence of the historical process,

---

[1] V. P. Vorontsov, 'Kapitalizm i rabochaia intelligentsiia', *Otechestvennye Zapiski*, no. 272 (February 1884), part 2, pp. 136–42.
[2] *Ibid.* no. 272, pp. 162–3.

distilled from Hegel and the socialist visionaries of the past, to engender optimism. Vorontsov's theory, wrote the literary critic L. Z. Slonimskii, furnished 'a significant measure of comfort for the future', and his proof of the impossibility of capitalist development in Russia promised 'to instil courage in the champions of the ideals of the people, who have been frightened by the apparent successes of capitalism'.[1]

But the optimism inspired by Vorontsov's system was remote from the ebullient faith of the seventies that had fed on hopes of sudden triumph. It was an optimism invoked to banish the spectre of defeat, to rescue cherished beliefs that had fallen into doubt. Resting on *a priori* concepts, his theories turned *narodnik* ideals into truths and silenced the impulse to question that threatened the delicate balance of the *intelligent*'s psychology. Lamenting the 'transformation of a movement into a mood', Vorontsov began the transformation of a mood into a dogma and removed it even further from its sources of inspiration. After the first of March, *narodnik* ideology became an elaborate credo that kept the distinction between truth and belief blurred. The doctrine that had challenged the *intelligent* to go forth and find his ideal in reality turned into a body of sacrosanct principles, meant to comfort rather than to arouse. The change was immediately reflected in the treatment of the countryside. The uncertainty and scepticism that had helped some authors attain a dim awareness of the implications of the material they were analysing disappeared. Writings on the peasantry ceased to inquire into existing conditions and became blunt assertions of belief, substantiated and elaborated with the appropriate data. Thus at the beginning of an article in the November 1883 number of *Otechestvennye Zapiski*, the *narodnik* sociologist S. N. Iuzhakov felt able to declare that the commune 'ignores history, does not know or come to terms with external legislative law, and is directed exclusively by the idea of higher justice'.[2]

The most striking champion of this attitude was a nobleman from Lithuania by the name of Iosef Kablits, whose various professions of faith were collected and published in 1882 under the title *Osnovy narodnichestva* (*The Foundations of the Narodnichestvo*). As a participant in the movement of the seventies,

---

[1] B. P. Koz'min, *Iz istorii revoliutsionnoi mysli v Rossii* (Moscow, 1961), p. 462.

[2] S. Iuzhakov, 'Voprosy obshchinnogo byta', *Otechestvennye Zapiski*, no. 271 (November 1883) part 2, pp. 95–6.

Kablits had become a symbol of blind and fanatical adoration of the people.[1] His devotion had never flagged, even when subjected to disappointment. Rather, in the face of doubt, Kablits, convinced of his special mission, had pronounced his ideas ever more vociferously and with ever greater certainty.

As a self-appointed theoretician of Land and Freedom, Kablits had preached his faith to audiences composed of radical youth in the late seventies. The young revolutionaries listened in wonderment as this irascible one-eyed man held forth tempestuously and at great length on the moral superiority of the peasantry and on the uselessness and ineffectuality of the intelligentsia. His principal theme, which he pronounced incessantly, was the superiority of feeling to thought, of instinct to reason. He defended this notion with an elaborate scholastic argumentation, the premises of which were drawn indiscriminately from various classics of European sociology. His argument consisted largely of endless quotations, which he thought would confer the mantle of scientific truth upon his beliefs. He cited by heart long passages of Spencer, Mill, Darwin, and Comte, confident that their arguments, even when pertaining to different problems, would uphold his position.[2]

Kablits presented the main line of his reasoning in a series of articles which appeared in the newspaper *Nedelia* (*The Week*) during 1878. From various statements of Spencer and Darwin to the effect that mind and feeling were distinct, Kablits extrapolated all manner of grandiose conclusions. Feelings, he argued, had been developing from the beginning of time, when men first lived in society, whereas man's intellect had begun to evolve only recently and, consequently, had not achieved as high a stage of development.[3] Nurtured by man's association with his brother, and centuries of equal divison of the products of labour, altruistic feeling had grown steadily stronger, and, indeed, had become indistinguishable from socialist consciousness, which Kablits believed pervaded the whole evolutionary process. The highest embodiment of altruistic feeling was the Russian peasant

---

[1] P. Lavrov, *Narodniki-propagandisty 1873–1878* (Leningrad, 1925), pp. 176–8, 201; 'Iosif Ivanovich Kablits', *Deiateli revoliutsionnogo dvizheniia v Rossii*, ii, p. 521; Deitch, *Za polveka*, ii, pp. 106–8.

[2] M. M. Chernavskii, 'Demonstratsiia 6 dekabria, 1876 g. Po vospominaniiam uchastnika', *Katorga i ssylka*, no. 28–9 (1926, p. 9 n.; Rusanov, *Na rodine*, p. 147.

[3] I. I. Kablits (Iuzov), 'Um i chuvstvo kak faktory progressa', *Nedelia*, no. 13 (February 1878), pp. 188–91.

commune, the fruit of centuries of collective life. Kablits believed that this feeling was becoming increasingly conscious and widespread. Drawing on various authorities on rural life, Kablits adduced instances of heightened communal activity to corroborate his stand.[1]

Since the feelings of the Russian peasantry had attained so high a level, the intelligentsia, as men of thought, could contribute relatively little to social progress. Kablits assigned to them the role of performing exemplary displays of the feelings they were trying to encourage in the people.[2] In revolutionary meetings this was phrased as a call to agitation. On the authority of a statement of Herbert Spencer to the effect that an attribute develops only when exercised, Kablits summoned the youth to 'exercise' the peasants' social instincts.[3] In the press, he inveighed against Uspenskii and the publicists of *Otechestvennye Zapiski*, particularly Mikhailovskii. They all hoped to uplift the people, not realizing that the people did not need uplifting, that 'the average man of the people is morally superior to the average person of the educated classes'.[4]

Kablits also conceived his own terrorist scheme, which he disclosed with great stealth and mystery to revolutionary youths. His new idea was the use of dynamite, which he holds the distinction of introducing to the Russian revolutionary movement. He planned to load four carriages with the explosive, and, with three devoted comrades, to drive them simultaneously into the walls of the Winter Palace. This, he thought, would bring down the building, annihilate the imperial family, and sunder the entire structure of the autocracy.[5] The general coolness to this idea merely increased his hostility toward the intelligentsia, and at the close of the seventies he drifted away from the active movement and secluded himself completely. He began to spend his days in the Petersburg Public Library, gathering materials for a book about Russian sectarians and amassing additional proof of the peasants' natural altruism and of the superfluity of knowledge.[6]

[1] *Ibid.* no. 13, p. 227; I. I. Kablits (Iuzov), 'Kapitalizm i mirskoe vladenie', *Nedelia*, no. 13 (April 1878), pp. 488–96.   ,

[2] Kablits, 'Um i chuvstvo kak faktory progressa', no. 13, pp. 228–30.

[3] Chernavskii, p. 9 n.; Rusanov, *Na rodine*, p. 147.

[4] Kablits (Iuzov), 'Publitsisty Otechestvennykh Zapisok', pp. 600–2.

[5] Deitch, *Za polveka*, II, pp. 106–7.

[6] *Ibid.* II, p. 108.

Kablits's pedantic exposition of the *narodnik* orthodoxy might soon have passed into oblivion had not the tribulations of the early eighties made the intelligentsia doubtful of the very premises of its faith. Then, when more sceptical and searching minds began to waver, Kablits remained implacable and came to be regarded as a beacon of the faith. Pavel Aksel'rod, then a leader of The Black Partition, turned to Kablits when his own faith began to fail him, hopng that he would write for the organization's newspaper and endow it with the confident tone that it lacked.[1]

In *Osnovy narodnichestva*, Kablits strove to shape an ideological system out of his earlier writings that would give new grounds for confidence and would dispel the atmosphere of gloom. At the very beginning, he ridiculed and condemned the prevailing pessimism. He accused the members of the intelligentsia of subjecting all reality and all social groups to the impossible test of the ideal, a frame of mind that precluded constructive social work. Only faith in the people would enable educated society to accomplish the tasks needed by the country. He urged the intelligentsia to surrender themselves to optimism, to the unflagging certainty that what they believed was right: 'This stoutness of heart (*bodrost' dukha*), the very certainty that the collectivist world view comprises more elements of progress than not, we call optimism.'[2] By obviating the preconceptions inhibiting optimism, *Osnovy narodnichestva* endeavoured to liberate the *narodnik* in his faith.

Like Vorontsov's system, Kablits's consisted of both a negative argument refuting the causes of doubt and confusion, and a positive one showing the grounds for hope. In the former, he endeavoured to dispose of the notions troubling the intelligentsia and obscuring its world view. Just as Vorontsov rejected economics to preserve his belief, Kablits jettisoned all operation of the human intellect which might subject his ideals to scrutiny. One by one, he attacked all possible intellectual approaches to social change. With profuse quotation from the luminaries of European sociology, he denied all attempts to find regularity in history—to inhibit the unfolding of the ideal with historical

---

[1] Aptekman, *Obshchestvo 'Zemlia i Volia'*, p. 399.

[2] I. Kablits (Iuzov), *Osnovy narodichestva* (St Petersburg, 1888), I, 17–19. I have used the slightly revised 1888 edition of this work, since I have been unable to obtain a copy of the 1882 edition.

laws. The individual was limited only by the people, the collective experience of the race.[1] Likewise, he minimized the importance of economic forces in shaping social development. Man was driven by spiritual interests, and the desire to solve his economic problems arose from the soul.[2] Isolated from the people, the intelligentsia had squandered its energies in the academic pursuit of such questions of historical and economic determinism as were applicable only to European conditions. It was not fit even for the task of agitation he had assigned to it in 1878. Occupied with their studies in the cities, far from the countryside, the educated had ignored the soul of the peasant and had no understanding of his needs. Consequently, their attempts to help the people amounted to no more than a forcible imposition of foreign patterns upon Russian conditions. 'The historical misfortune of the intelligentsia is its tendency to look upon the people as a stagnant unthinking mass that will remain eternally in this state if the intelligentsia does not succeed in inspiring it with its own thought and feeling.' Now Kablits refused to acknowledge the existence of a bond of sympathy between the intelligentsia and the people. 'Borrowing its ideals from Europeans, the intelligentsia regards the people with contempt.'[3]

In his positive statement of doctrine, Kablits recapitulated the mind–feeling argument, supporting it with long and detailed discussions with material drawn from sympathetic writers on the countryside. He established the social instincts of the people as the cardinal precept of the *narodnik*'s faith, affirming that communal land tenure had promoted relationships that could not be improved by civilized learning.

Communal land tenure, the dominant form in Russia, helps further the development of social feelings much more than the study of science simply because it places its members in definite relationships in which they are always ready to help each other. The young generation, reared in an order based on the commune and the *artel'*, has the opportunity to exercise its instincts much more than would be the case were individualism dominant. From this stems the socio-moral superiority of the peasantry to the intelligentsia, though the latter represents the bearer of knowledge.[4]

---

[1] *Ibid.* I, 21–58.   [2] *Ibid.* I, 278–87.
[3] *Ibid.* I, 308; see Pypin, *Istoriia russkoi etnografii*, II, 397.
[4] Kablits, I, 113.

One chapter showed how peasant legal principles excelled those of the *Svod zakonov*, the book of laws governing the empire, in both justice and humanity. The peasants displayed a greater regard for human needs and feelings than did the ruling bureaucratic apparatus. Their natural penchant for equality gave rise to a system that levied assessments in proportion to the worker's ability to pay; it made them dissatisfied with all existing institutions and led them to seek reforms of local government and guarantees of freedom of speech and religion.[1]

The longest section was devoted to a lengthy presentation of the standard arguments and materials that had been advanced over the previous few years in proof of the continued vitality of the communal tradition in Russia. Countering the 'Marxist' notion that Russia was predetermined to follow a capitalist path, Kablits vehemently asserted Russia's distinctive identity and its ability to develop native traditions and institutions. Borrowing Vorontsov's arguments about capitalism's failure to generalize labour in Russia, and about the unfavourable conditions of the international market, he concluded that capitalism was unviable in Russia and posed no threat to the communal order.[2]

In Kablits's ponderous expostulation of Neo-Bakuninism, the enamourment of the people and the *intelligent*'s self-effacement became the sole articles of the *narodnik*'s credo. Gone were the earlier exhortations to agitate, to exercise the altruistic feeling of the people. Unable to envision a miraculous transformation of intelligentsia into peasantry as had Engel'gardt, Kablits made the worlds of intelligentsia and peasantry completely separate and distinct. Peasant life was not to be exposed to the misguided intrusions of the intelligentsia; the intelligentsia, by the same token, was not to be subjected to the authority of the people. Educational institutions would continue to function, though not at the expense of the people, and the intelligentsia would continue to imbibe at the sources of European learning.[3]

The intelligentsia is in its rights to demand full autonomy in the realm of higher education and scholarship for itself, just as the tillers of the land are striving to extricate themselves from all guardianship in the realm of their agricultural interests, though the latter are linked to the interests of society in general. The tiller of the land has no right to intrude *violently* into the system of higher education, just as the

---

[1] *Ibid.* 1, 288–309.   [2] *Ibid.* 1, 359–448.   [3] *Ibid.* 1, 333–40.

intelligentsia has no right to prescribe this or the other method of crop rotation. Each is competent in his own realm.[1]

Contenting himself with the certainty that the peasant, as the agent of social progress, was right and he wrong, the *intelligent* would become a *narodnik*. Preoccupied with abstract thought, he would not dare to seek verification of his faith, or, worst of all, engage in efforts to help the people which could only wreck the object of his worship. In Kablits's unhinged mind the principles of the *narodnichestvo* reached their absurd logical extremes: the *intelligent*'s feeling of inadequacy deepened into impotence, and his love of the people became idolatry. The upsurges and disappointments of social commitment were surrendered to an unquestioning belief and acquiescence in the course of events. Like Kablits, the *intelligent* was to become a learned recluse, skulking along the streets of Petersburg, and, in the isolation of his study, entertaining the vision of a just and harmonious rural life.

In subsequent years, the ideas of Vorontsov and Kablits became the nucleus of a body of thought known as 'the re-habilitation of reality'. Writers of this bent prescribed a total change in the mentality of the members of the intelligentsia. They urged them to relinquish their posture of defiant rejection of the world and to comply with the prevailing facts of nature. They stressed the need and the possibility to work within the existing order for gradual progress. At the close of the decade, the trend culminated in Iakov Abramov's famous theory of 'small deeds', which bade the intelligentsia limit its role to carrying out modest humanitarian tasks in the service of the people. The principles underlying the 'rehabilitation of reality' are typified by a passage from *Nedelia* of 1886:

The new generation was born in a sceptical mood and the ideals of the grandfathers and fathers have proved to be powerless over it. It does not feel hatred and contempt for everyday life, does not recognize the obligation to be a hero, does not believe in the possi-bility of ideal people. All these ideals are dry logical products of individual thought, but for the new generation there remains only reality, in which it must live and which it therefore recognizes. It has accepted its fate tranquilly and submissively. It is imbued with the consciousness that everything in life flows from one source,

[1] *Ibid.* I, 339.

nature; and that everything points to a single secret of life, and brings us back to the pantheistic world view.[1]

The 'rehabilitation of reality' expressed the disillusionment of many members of the intelligentsia in the possibility of rapid, far-reaching social transformations. But it was not long before voices were raised to decry this fatalistic trust in the forces of nature and to proclaim the revolutionary struggle alive. Those unable to draw comfort from the condition of Russian reality placed their faith instead in action. Nikolai Mikhailovskii, answering Vorontsov in the pages of *Otechestvennye Zapiski* disputed the latter's optimistic forecasts and pointed out many cases of European-type development in Russia. 'From the very fact that European configurations are not impossible here, it follows that one must, rather, fight against their imposition.'[2] Lev Tikhomirov, now representing the remnants of The People's Will in emigration, took issue with Kablits's version of the *narodnichestvo* on similar grounds. Kablits's distillation of *narodnik* ideals, he claimed, deprived them of their original character and turned them into dry academic maxims. 'The *narodnichestvo*', Tikhomirov wrote in *Delo*, 'was a movement that was far more practical than theoretical, and had theoretical bases that were far more broad and universal than the dogma elaborated down to the most trivial detail by Iuzov [Kablits] in his *Foundations*...'[3] A movement required unity of belief on only the most general goals, Tikhomirov continued; the intricacies of doctrine would only provoke dissension in the group and prevent unified action.[4] To demand adherence to a monolithic system of belief would be to

fall into sectarianism, to displace the centre of gravity from the sphere of practice to the realm of one's world view, which would be completely ruinous, since in such a case any social party would be doomed beforehand to small numbers, weakness, and estrangement from living social interests.[5]

But a mystique of action rested upon the anticipation of

[1] Quoted in M. N. Pokrovskii, ed., *Istoriia Rossii v XIX veke* (St Petersburg, 1910–11), IX, 20.

[2] N. M. Mikhailovskii (Postoronnego), 'Pis'mo v redaktsiiu', *Otechestvennye Zapiski*, no. 268 (June 1883), p. 111.

[3] L. Tikhomirov, 'Shatan'e politicheskoi mysli', *Delo*, no. 17 (March 1883), part 2, p. 5.

[4] *Ibid.* no. 17, part 2, pp. 11–13.   [5] *Ibid.* p. 13.

imminent success, and there seemed to be little ground for this after the first of March. Only a few scattered revolutionary circles remained extant in the capital and they, driven to desperation by the collapse of the movement, attached their hopes to wild and implausible schemes that stood scant chance of success. One group, called the Militarists, contemplated a *coup d'état* effected by the officers of the army, like that attempted by the Decembrists. Another, the *nemisty*, concocted a fantastic plan to seize power and to put forward their own tsar, who, from the throne, would decree the social revolution. Neither received a significant following and, while many circles continued their work in the provinces, no central apparatus survived to co-ordinate and direct their efforts.[1]

Like the ideologists of reality, the exponents of action had to seek ways to blot the unpleasant truths of the moment out of their consciousness. In order to sustain their revolutionary *élan*, they had to invoke myths of their own which would keep their expectations high and obviate the bleak prospects that confronted them. Tikhomirov saw the answer in an increased reliance on the revolutionary organization: it became for him the essential key to success that would enable the revolutionaries to surmount the formidable obstacles opposing a seizure of power. As revolutionaries in Russia lost contact with each other, he bade them come together. The size of the state, the dispersion of the population, and the power structure's increasing control over the fate of each individual obliged them to unite in a counter-organization as all-encompassing and lethal as the administrative machine they were combating. To confront the centralized colossus of the tsarist government, they had to build a centralized apparatus of their own that would enable them to 'direct precisely aimed blows at the whole state system in its aggregate', and to wrest control of the sprawling expanses of the empire from the autocracy.[2]

It was the same vision of a closely knit group that kept alive the hopes of Aleksandr Mikhailov, the organizational genius of Land and Freedom and The People's Will, while he awaited his death in prison.[3] He yearned to re-establish all the broken ties of his life and to feel himself again a part of a greater human

---

[1] A. V. Iakimova-Dikovskaia *et al.* (eds.), *Narodovol'stsy posle 1-ogo marta* (Moscow, 1928), p. 22.   [2] Iakovlev (ed.), *Literatura partii Narodnoi Voli*, pp. 508–9.
[3] See chapter 1, pp. 22–3; chapter 3, p. 85.

whole. He dreamed of an extended revolutionary society, united by strong affections and linked with the members' kin, who would afford shelter to comrades on missions away from home. He called upon the revolutionaries to learn more about each other and to preserve the ties of peace and love that bound them. In his confinement, the warm association he believed prevailed among his comrades heartened him. 'I press all of you, my brothers and my sisters, to my still living and burning heart. May you be happy in your cause. May you be happy in your close union.'[1]

But these notions of organization were merely the illusions of men isolated from the scene of action. To those revolutionaries still at large in Russia such appeals seemed all but irrelevant, for intensified police surveillance made organized activity perilous, if not impossible. A centralized organization was especially vulnerable to penetration and destruction by government agents, and most local groups shrank from any connection at all with the circles in the capital, not to speak of direct subordination to central authority. The organization conceived by Tikhomirov and Mikhailov had no more real existence and little more chance of arising than the idyllic communes of Zlatovratskii and Vorontsov.[2]

Only the enduring fascination of the revolutionary act itself sustained those who participated in the movement after the first of March. The exaltation of struggle silenced their sense of doubt and instilled courage in them. The posture of rebellion became a good in itself rather than a means to an end. The chief representative of this tendency, indicatively, was not a thinker

---

[1] Mikhailov, pp. 206–11.

[2] In an illuminating article on the circles of the eighties, S. V. Utechin traces the survival of the organizational tendency in the eighties and draws a connection between it and the spread of Marxism or proto-Marxism at the same time. When I speak of organization here I refer to a national revolutionary organization and not merely the use of conspiratorial practices, which undoubtedly persisted. In the early eighties, this tendency was weak, especially when compared with the desperate appeals from abroad to establish a more far-flung organization. To be sure, the members of these circles envisioned a more elaborate organization in the future, but it is hard to see how they made an effort to this end and their statements sound like faint echoes of the émigrés' prescriptions. Nor do any of the 'organizations' of the early eighties that Mr. Utrechin cites clearly warrant the name. At this time I think it is fair to conclude that this trend was hardly more than an undercurrent, one among many, though one, to be sure, with broad and far-reaching implications. See S. V. Utechin, 'The "Preparatory" Trend in the Russian Revolutionary Movement in the 1880s', St Antony's Papers, no. 12 (Soviet Affairs, no. 3), pp. 7–22.

but a poet, an impoverished young nobleman entranced by the heroic tradition of past generations of revolutionaries, by the name of Petr Filippovich Iakubovich. Before the first of March Iakubovich's poetry expressed the young generation's awe of the deeds of the revolutionary martyrs. It expressed the youth's feeling of weakness and inadequacy before the selflessness and valour displayed in the active movement. The most popular of his early poems, '*Bitva zhizni*' ('The Battle of Life'), contrasted his own empty existence, dissipated in trivial conflicts, to the majestic tragedy of the revolutionary struggle. 'My life flies by lifelessly,' it began. The shattering vision of the real battle awakened him from his torpor.

> I see in the wide field dead warriors,
> After their great martial deed,
>
> .   .   .   .
>
> With broken heads, their faces to the sky,
> Turning blue, covered with blood,
> Quietly sleep the dead,
> Their eyes fixed open.
> Like a faint shade, like a silent ghost,
> I walk around the terrible fields,
> And I count the dead, I don't know why,
> And look at their stolid faces...
> 'All dear faces! All brothers and friends!
> All are features familiar and beloved.'[1]

Iakubovich was tormented by his inability to live up to his great revolutionary heritage. A descendant of the Decembrist Aleksandr Iakubovich, he had been unable to discover traces of the latter's heroism either in his family or in himself. His father was an ordinary petty functionary, and Iakubovich spent his childhood looking to him in vain for signs of virtue and courage. He found him, instead, an example of futility and shiftlessness: a man of laudable aspirations whose native limitations and weakness of moral fibre made everything he did turn out ugly and ludicrous. As Iakubovich grew up, he watched him blunder to his downfall.[2] The memory of this inept and wasted life haunted him, and made him conscious of his own lack of resolve —the enervating spiritual torpor that prevented him from

---

[1] P. F. Iakubovich, *Stikhotvoreniia* (Leningrad, 1960), p. 59.

[2] P. F. Iakubovich, 'Na rannei zor'ke', *Russkoe Bogatstvo* (January 1909), pp. 197–224; (March 1909), pp. 130–58.

throwing himself into the revolutionary struggle. 'In the terrifying, pitiless, fierce combat, one must curse the dream of happiness,' he wrote in a poem of late 1880.

> But in the tender and turbulent soul,
> Not born for the warrior's lot,
> There is no bound to rebellious anxieties,
> No end to mad longings.
> They don't let us surrender ourselves totally
> To the power of our splendid goal.
> The heart beats with languor and with passion,
> And the young soul does not have the power
> To curse the dream of personal happiness.[1]

The arrests and executions after the first of March bereaved Iakubovich of his heroes. The struggle that had stirred his emotions came to an end, leaving him alone with no one to worship and no lofty thoughts and daring deeds to share. He wrote in September 1881:

> Forgotten world! Over every grave,
> Swirls sadness...On this one
> There is no cross.
> On that one, the cross bends in doleful resignation,
> On that one, without an epitaph, the stone is
>   covered with cracks,
> Slumber, silence, and grey desolation,
> All around a storm rages,
> But here all is oblivion.
> Everything is saying,
> 'They are no more!'
>
> And truth? Has she gone with God's thunder?
> The names are forgotten,
> But falsehood, that falsehood
> With the shameless eyes,
> Which, having drunk blood,
> Made men like dogs,
> How can we forget her?
> Or doubt that she is alive?[2]

Without the drama of conflict and sacrifice to inspire him, Iakubovich was doomed to live with the evil and the tedium of Russian life and to fall back on his father's hypocrisy and lies

---

[1] Iakubovich, *Stikhotvoreniia*, pp. 61–2.   [2] *Ibid.* p. 64.

to justify himself. Defeat only quickened Iakubovich's desire to struggle: it impelled him to abandon his role as onlooker and embark on revolutionary action himself. In 1882, at the age of twenty-two, he joined one of the surviving circles of The People's Will and rapidly asserted himself as one of the organization's leaders. His new determination was expressed in a poem written in the summer of 1882.

> Let the dead inter the dead!
> What good are the dead to us?
> To awaken them, to summon them back to life,
> Is not within our power.
> While a drop of blood runs in our veins,
> We will not cry over their graves,
> We will go to fight, to think, to live!
> Where there is disturbance, stormy weather,
> There is where feeling hearts will find happiness.
> But illusory happiness,
> That we leave to cowards and fools.[1]

But there was no optimism in Iakubovich's call to battle, no stirring hopes. The future and what it would bring did not figure in his poetry.[2] His activism was one of despair, a last alternative to spiritual death. Struggle was the sole way of living meaningfully. 'To carry the glorious banner in just combat, for you that's what it means to live,' he wrote in November of 1882. 'To love without suffering in your soul is impossible. Life is struggle and not slavery.'[3]

In Iakubovich's poetry, revolution became an intoxicant that lifted the *intelligent* above the sordid facts of reality and sent him into another more vibrant and purposeful world. While Vorontsov and Kablits were seeking grounds to worship reality, he strove to obliterate it from his consciousness and to exult in the uplift of struggle and sacrifice. No mention of the peasants appeared in his verse, though it is clear from his later writings that he shared his generation's deep attachment to them. The stage for his action was not the countryside but the capital, where the revolutionary movement had blazed spectacularly and left potent memories of tragedy. In his haunting '*Skazochny*

---

[1] *Ibid.* p. 72.

[2] On this aspect of Iakubovich's poetry, see the penetrating article by A. S. Potresov (Starover), 'O raznochintse-skital'tse', in *Etiudy o russkoi intelligentsii*, (St Petersburg, 1906), pp. 110–47.

[3] Iakubovich, *Stikhotvoreniia*, p. 72.

gorod '('Legendary City') the revolutionary struggle appeared as a striving for effect, a rehearsal of practices that had ceased to have any meaning or any chance of success. The revolutionaries were enacting an elaborate play against the grotesque and ominous backdrop of bureaucratic St Petersburg.

> This is why I love this wretched city
> With such a morbid passion,
> This graveyard of our best people,
> Of countless brothers, sisters, and friends.
> The cradle of our Russian freedom
> In the name of which sounded the first thunder,
> Summoning the people to struggle
> For the sacred ideal.
>
> I love this pool,
> Where you can smell the heady odour of wounds,
> And you can hear the volcano bubbling forebodingly
> Beneath your feet,
> Where you avidly rush to fight,
> To live, to act,
> You strain audaciously,
> Feel drunk, and sensing
> Wings on your back, you fly,
> Into the abyss with savage courage...
> As the prisoner loves his fetters,
> So I love this great city,
> Washed in the blood of innocents.[1]

This same motif dominated Iakubovich's practical plans for revolution. In 1883 he helped to form a small, short-lived group called Young People's Will (*Molodaia Narodnaia Volia*), that attempted to oppose the old Executive Committee abroad on questions of doctrine and strategy. As its major spokesman, he became the chief antagonist of the notion of a tight, centralized organization prevailing among the *émigrés*. He insisted that local circles be allowed the greatest possible scope for independent revolutionary initiative, contending that a loose organization, coordinated by periodic conferences, could maintain the desired unity of the movement without inhibiting activity in the provinces; he feared above all any structure that might bridle the revolutionary impulse.[2] The programme of the new

---

[1] *Ibid*, p. 97.

[2] S. Valk (ed.), 'K istorii protsessa 21', *Krasny Arkhiv*, no. 5 (36) (1929,) pp. 139–40.

group, which Iakubovich undoubtedly collaborated in drafting, declared that plans for a mass organization were premature, and summoned the revolutionaries to do the 'preparatory' work of establishing ties among the people. They were to strive for 'popularity'. The means to achieve this included not only agitation and propaganda, but also exemplary displays of revolutionary courage that would excite the emotions of the masses. Here, as in Iakubovich's poetry, the revolutionary act was paramount.

Our activity in all its complexity is a living example, a living model seen by the millions and itself propagandizing and agitating them. Our struggle should be a truly revolutionary struggle, broad and strikingly direct at the mark. Both our historical significance and the fascination we exert depend totally on this.[1]

Young People's Will, like most radical circles after the first of March, directed its efforts not so much at the peasantry as at the urban proletariat, which was more accessible to its influence. Agitation among the workers had been seriously pursued by both The People's Will and The Black Partition, each group viewing them as potential emissaries of revolution to be sent into the countryside. But Young People's Will did not follow such reasoning, though its members continued to regard the workers' main tasks as auxiliary to the revolution of the whole people.[2] The role the workers were to play—when one penetrates the verbiage used to dignify it in the eyes of the *émigrés*—turned out to be identical to that of the revolutionaries themselves; they were to act not in behalf of immediate social transformations or betterment of their lot, but in order to keep the revolutionary spirit alive and to spread the example of their heroism. In a letter written shortly before his arrest in 1884, Iakubovich asserted that their principal task should not be to increase the size of the organization through propaganda and agitation, but to stage spectacular revolutionary outbursts that would arouse sympathy and admiration across the empire. The workers were to join the intelligentsia in a stirring performance of revolutionary virtues; they were to give themselves on a public altar for the sake of the inspiring effect their gesture would make. The revolutionary movement was to be re-awakened in a fury of self-annihilation.

[1] Iakovlev (ed.), *Literatura partii Narodnoi Voli*, pp. 670–1.   [2] *Ibid.* pp. 666–75.

What is important is not living individuals, not material strength, but principles, ideas. These of course will be incomparably more vital, vibrant, powerful and widespread, if they are proclaimed not by the mouths of separate verbalizing individuals but by the thunder of heroic facts, stunning the mind and fantasy with the brilliance of sacrifice, the brilliance of struggle, and the power of our faith in the justice of our cause.[1]

[1] Valk, 'K istorii protsessa 21', p. 163.

7

CONCLUSION

The Great Reforms of the 1860s irreparably undermined the established values of Russian life. The transformations in the existing social and political system disclosed imperfections and injustice throughout the old political and social order, and revealed its guiding precepts to be no more than deceit and cant. When the ancient claims to legitimacy could no longer justify unthinking adherence to traditional ways, the young and educated began to search for new values and new roles for themselves. Dreaming of a swift and total renovation of Russian reality, they sought their guides to life in the principles of philosophy and science. They came together in the cities and formed what came to be known as the Russian intelligentsia.

But having dissociated themselves from the past, the members of the intelligentsia felt a need for new attachments to replace those they had known in their early lives. They yearned to participate in a new group that embodied values they could respect and that presented a model of a better way of life. They sought this group in the peasantry, and as their efforts to transform reality became more grandiose, they saw their and the peasant's fate linked ever more closely. With the disappointment of the 'going to the people', their self-esteem weakened, and their need for the peasant mounted and turned into a dependent longing. Their sympathy for the peasant became an enamourment with rural life, and they began to live vicariously in the virtuous world they believed existed in the countryside. They preserved their radical identity by assuming the role of organizers, whose superior skill and consciousness could unite and channel the forces of the people.

At the end of the seventies and the beginning of the eighties, the intelligentsia's image of the world and its optimistic conceptions of social change were dealt severe blows. The organized forces of revolution collapsed before the colossus of the tsarist state. Persecuted by the police, isolated from active support on the part of both peasantry and society, they resorted to a tactic of desperation that was bound to bring failure and their own destruction. At the same time radical views of the peasantry were also subjected to stress. Those who investigated the countryside felt little rapport with the peasants they met and found slight reflection of their social ideals in village life.

The general illusion that had sustained the intelligentsia through the seventies and eighties then began to break down. The doctrines of the group lost their power to answer the psychological needs of the individual members, who now began to seek in themselves the strength to keep alive their conception of reality. The single social myth dissolved into many individual myths, into fantasies designed to contain the individual's doubts and anxieties. Each *intelligent* invoked an elaborate complex of psychological defences to shield his eyes from the disturbing sights of reality, and in his growing isolation, his image of the world began to take on the features of delusion. Thus the breakdown of the *narodnichestvo* of the seventies was both a social and psychological phenomenon: the disintegration of the unity of the group was accompanied by a loss of coherence in the vision of its members, who called upon all their psychological resources to fortify their image of the peasantry. We have seen this process at work in the minds of the three most influential investigators of the countryside of the 1870s. Engel'-gardt gave free rein to his scientific imagination and conceived of the possibility of combining the virtues of peasant and *intelligent* in a higher human type that was both educated and capable of working the land. Uspenskii struggled unsuccessfully to exempt the peasants from the merciless invasions of his conscience by creating fantasy images of them. Zlatovratskii projected his childhood dreams on the countryside, then accorded a higher reality to them than to the disturbing reality he saw before him. In each case hope was derived from a private gratification, a last alternative to despair, that isolated the individual from the ideas and feelings inspiring the intelligentsia as a whole.

A comparable process was under way in the realm of populist economic theory. The ideologists of the beginning of the seventies, preoccupied with problems of revolutionary action, had neglected the analysis of actual conditions. As a result, at the close of the decade populism offered little concrete intellectual content, and few means to withstand the rising onslaught of facts. At the beginning of the eighties several populist authors tried to apply the conceptual apparatus of Western political economy to the recently discovered data, hoping to arrive at a more objective and scientific evaluation of reality. Their ventures, however, invariably revealed truths intolerable to their audience and to themselves and impelled them to retreat in defence of their own life ideals. *Narodnik* ideology then began to lose its aggressive, self-confident tone, and became defensive, expressing doubt and fear, rather than the expansive spirit of change. Vorontsov's economic theories explained objective reality away with an elaborate rationalization and allowed the populist to return to his subjective dreams. The turgid evasions of Iosif Kablits reveal such an attempt to retreat into a private fantasy world. At the same time the active populist movement lost its basis in theory, and turned into futile gestures of isolated individuals, like the personal revolutionary romanticism of Iakubovich.

The generation of radical youth reaching maturity in the early eighties inherited a legacy of failure and tragedy. Its members, faced with evidence of breakdown and disappointment, had little cause for hope. Before their eyes, radical ideology had become a dogma, and the revolutionary struggle a masquerade of past glories. Thought became divorced from both action and reality, providing them with no means of comprehending the world. Moved by the old urge for change, the youth lacked an approach to Russian life that would enable them to act, and many struggled to find new systems that could replace the old. The hero of Iakov Abramov's story '*Gamlety—para na grosh*' ('Hamlets—two for a *grosh*') flew from doctrine to doctrine, finding none of them satisfactory.

The trouble was that I could not settle on any of the current systems. As soon as I was infatuated with one, and I felt myself its full-fledged adherent, I encountered, without fail, a fact which did not fit its framework, and which wrecked it. I clearly saw that the system was the product of carrion. I discarded it and pined until I was carried away by a new system.[1]

Aleksandr Ertel', a young writer who came to Petersburg at the beginning of the eighties, felt the same inability to cope with the confusion of ideas around him and to define his own attitudes. He could not decide whether to choose Zlatovratskii

[1] Ia. Abramov, 'Gamlety—para na grosh', *Ustoi*, no. 1 (December 1882), p. 72.

or Uspenskii as his literary model.[1] He too yearned for an all-encompassing system. He wrote to his wife in 1883:

Never has such a war between old ideas and new bewilderment been waged in me. Something in me demands a system of these ideas, a construct of infallible convictions, harmoniously and solidly erected in one whole, but meanwhile reason, with a malicious irony, ridicules the attempt at such a construct and with corrosive analysis destroys every brick that has been borne to the edifice.[2]

The stalwarts of the old faith could convey little confidence to these youths and allay few of the latter's doubts. 'If a person is devoid of the possibility of entering the sphere of alien sensations, no programme will help him,' Zlatovratskii wrote to Ertel'.[3] The people, he explained, was a nebulous and indefinable quantity which could be understood by intuition but not apprehended in phrases. Least of all could one expect to understand the people through learned intellectual discourse. 'I am dazed by all these different categories and theories,' Zlatovratskii wrote. Yet the youth continued to entreat him to reveal the secret of his faith.

For three days in a row a whole group of 'bright young things' visited me and, nearly breaking their arms, and groaning from their hearts, asked various questions. 'What is your programme?', stuttering, shrieking, agitated, they asked. Should they go on living tomorrow? Should they enjoy the bliss of a beloved's love or should they put bullets in their heads? Where, in what, is the meaning of their life?...Then everything became clear to me. I understood myself, the person I was talking to, and the *so-called narodnichestvo*.[4]

Unsure of the tenets of their faith, yet unable to reject them, the youth began to turn upon themselves and to indulge in the grim catharsis of self-hatred. They conceived of the evil outside as a reflection of the evil within them and blamed themselves for the ravages of civilization and for the survival of social structure. Many, like Engel'gardt's students, tried to purge their moral failings by retreating from the world and practising Tolstoy's teachings of self-purification, simplification, and gentleness. Others found comfort in the mystical religious teaching of Vladimir Soloviev. The older generation beheld

---

[1] Rusanov, *Na rodine*, p. 256.
[2] Ertel', A. I., *Pis'ma A. I. Ertelia* (St Petersburg, 1909), p. 47.
[3] Bush, *Ocherki literaturnogo narodnichestva 70-80 gg.*, p. 17.
[4] *Ibid.* p. 11.

these tendencies with chagrined disbelief. To them the development of progressive thought seemed to have been reversed. In the 1860s the youth had attended lectures on physiology, in the 1870s on political economy, wrote one literary critic, and now they had become enthralled by disquisitions on Christianity.

The reason is that the soul of Russian youth has become weary and sad and thirsts for a word of generalization like manna from heaven. The ideals of the sixties proved narrow, the ideals of the seventies, for some reason, practically groundless, and now the youth, with the bitter and painful experience of two generations resting on their souls, stand at the crossroads in painful meditation and await a new word, seek new ways. For the youth, for all our future development, a critical moment having profound significance has arrived.[1]

A new answer was not long in coming. In the months after the assassination of the tsar, a handful of devotees of the *narodnik* orthodoxy abroad, led by Aksel'rod and Plekhanov, embraced the major tenets of Marxism and made the urban proletariat the bearer of their ideals. But during the eighties their viewpoint met with little sympathy among the intelligentsia. Though their literature immediately attracted the attention of radical circles, it won few adherents within Russia, and these displayed a commitment that was at best unsure.[2] Despite the revolutionaries' growing preoccupation with the urban workers during the eighties, few deserted the peasantry as the basis of their hopes.

Through the eighties the members of the intelligentsia continued to cherish their bond with the peasantry. They clung to it as the single source of stability and virtue, and their only guarantee of a just heritage in the midst of the tumult and uncertainty of the reform era. To embrace Marxism meant to betray their *alter ego*, to countenance and even to foster the destruction of the only counterpart of their own moral purity in Russian life: it was to welcome the rude forces of economic transformation and to accept the poverty and insecurity of modern society as part of the logic of history. Like Abramov's hero, they viewed Marxism as a doctrine 'full of cruelty, not spontaneous and zoological, but conscious and directed against the whole world', one that strove to raise the masses to

---

[1] Koz'min, *Iz istorii...*, p. 475.
[2] For a discussion of these groups, see Utechin.

consciousness by turning them into 'a group of idiots—semi-animals'.[1] Locked in the closed circle of their belief, they took solace where they could find it. The movement was broken; its dreams had gone up in smoke, but across Russia believers continued to propagate their ideas and to seek out others with whom they could share their faith. Gathering in small circles, like the one that so amazed the young Gorkii, they joined in lonesome communions with the *narod*.

[1] Abramov, 'Gamlety—para na grosh', pp. 77–8.

BIBLIOGRAPHY

Listed below are the sources and works that I have found useful or relevant in the treatment of my subject. I have by no means attempted an inclusive listing of the massive literature on Russian Populism, or indeed even of the vast material, most of it uninteresting, on the individual writers I have considered.

PRIMARY WORKS

Unpublished primary sources

Engel'gardt Archive, Pushkinskii Dom, Leningrad, No. 577.
Zlatovratskii Archive, Pushkinskii Dom, Leningrad, No. 111.

Writings of chief figures

Abramov, Ia. 'Gamlety—para na grosh', *Ustoi*, no. 1 (December 1882), pp. 53–79.
—— 'Nekotorye osobennosti nashikh posemel'nykh otnoshenii', *Otechestvennye Zapiski*, no. 271 (November 1883), part II, pp. 1–42.
—— 'V stepi', *Ustoi*, no. 1 (January 1882), pp. 133–62; (March 1882), pp. 96–126; (May 1882), pp. 94–118.
Bakunin, M. *Izbrannye sochineniia*. Petrograd–Moscow, 1922. vol. I.
Chaslavskii, V. 'Voprosy russkogo agrarnogo ustroistva', *Otechestvennye Zapiski*, no. 239 (August 1878), pp. 281–312; no. 242 (January 1879), pp. 219–32.
Chernyshevskii, N. G. *Polnoe sobranie sochinenii*. 16 vols. Moscow, 1939–53.
Daniel'son, N. F. (Nikolai-on). 'Ocherki nashego poreformennogo obshchestvennogo khoziaistva', *Slovo*, no. 3 (October 1880), pp. 77–142.
—— 'Pis'ma Karla Marksa i Fridrikha Engel'sa k Nikolai-onu', *Minuvshie Gody*, no. 1 (January 1908), pp. 38–76.
—— 'Zamechaniia na stat'iu G. Antonovicha, "O reformakh krest'-ianskoi i obshchestvennoi khoziaistvennosti"', *Novoe Obozrenie*, no. 1 (February 1881), pp. 177–89.
Dobroliubov, N. A. *Polnoe sobranie sochinenii*. 6 vols. Moscow, 1934–9.
Eliseev, G. Z. 'Kogda blagodenstvoval russkii muzhik i kogda nachalis' ego bedstviia', *Otechestvennye Zapiski*, no. 182 (January 1869), part II, pp. 1–41.
—— 'Krest'ianskaia reforma', *Otechestvennye Zapiski*, no. 212 (January 1874), pp. 141–86; (February 1874), pp. 443–84.
—— 'Krest'ianskii vopros', *Otechestvennye Zapiski*, no. 177 (March 1868), pp. 151–86.

Eliseev. *Pis'ma G. Z. Eliseeva k M. E. Saltykovu-Shchedrinu.* Moscow, 1935.

—— 'Proizvoditel'nye sily Rossii', *Otechestvennye Zapiski*, no. 176 (February 1868), pp. 409–96.

Engel'gardt, A. N. 'Iz istorii moego khoziaistva', *Otechestvennye Zapiski*, no. 224 (January 1876), pp. 85–118; no. 225 (March 1876), pp. 139–68; no. 237 (March 1878), pp. 285–322.

—— *Iz derevni: 12 pisem.* St Petersburg, 1897.

—— *Iz derevni: 12 pisem.* Moscow, 1956.

—— 'Liebig v russkom perevode', *Sankt-Peterburgskie Vedomosti*, no. 272 (6 December 1863), pp. 1105–6.

—— *O khoziaistve v severnoi Rossii i primenenii v nem fosforitov.* St Petersburg, 1888.

—— 'Voprosy russkogo sel'skogo khoziaistva', *Otechestvennye Zapiski*, no. 200 (February 1872), part II, pp. 149–76.

Ertel', A. I. *Pis'ma A. I. Ertelia.* Moscow, 1909.

Flerovskii, V. V. *Izbrannye ekonomicheskie proizvedeniia.* 2 vols. Moscow, 1958.

Iakubovich, P. F. *Stikhotvoreniia.* Leningrad, 1960.

Ianson, Y. *Opyt statisticheskogo izsledovaniia o krestianskikh nadelakh i platezhakh.* St Petersburg, 1881.

Imperatorskoe Geograficheskoe Obshchestvo (compiled). 'Opyt programmy izsledovaniia pozemel'noi obshchiny', *Otechestvennye Zapiski*, no. 239 (August 1878), part II, pp. 331–52.

Imperatorskoe Geograficheskoe Obshchestvo i Imperatorskoe Vol'no-Ekonomicheskoe Obshchestvo (compiled). *Sbornik materialov dlia izucheniia sel'skoi pozemel'noi obshchiny.* St Petersburg, 1880.

Iuzhakov, S. 'Voprosy obshchinnogo byta', *Otechestvennye Zapiski*, no. 271 (November 1883), part II, pp. 94–119.

Kablits, I. (Iuzov). 'Kapitalizm i mirskoe vladenie', *Nedelia*, no. 13 (April 1878), pp. 488–96.

—— 'Liberal o serom muzhike', *Nedelia*, no. 13 (March 1878), pp. 283–7.

—— *Osnovy narodnichestva.* vol. I, St Petersburg, 1888; vol. II, St Petersburg, 1893.

—— 'Publitsisty Otechestvennykh Zapisok', *Nedelia*, no. 13 (May 1878) pp. 596–602.

—— 'Um i chuvstvo kak faktory progressa', *Nedelia*, no. 13 (February 1878), pp. 187–92, 225–30.

Klements, D. A. (Toporin). 'Iz russkoi zhurnal'noi letopisi', *Slovo*, no. 1 (March 1878), part II, pp. 89–124; (April 1878), part II, pp. 121–44.

Kotelianskii, L. 'Ocherki podvornoi Rossii', *Otechestvennye Zapiski*, no. 236 (February 1878), part II, pp. 125–63; no. 239 (August 1878), pp. 13–44; no. 240 (September 1878), pp. 40–73.

Kravchinskii, S. *Smert' za smert'* (*Ubiistvo Mezentsova*). St Petersburg, 1920.

Krivenko, S. N. *Sobranie sochinenii.* 2 vols. St Petersburg, 1911.

Lavrov, P. *Istoricheskie pis'ma.* St Petersburg, 1905.

—— *Po povodu samarskogo goloda.* London, 1874.

Lichkov, L. 'Pervye opyty po izsledovaniiu pozemel'noi obshchiny', *Delo*, no. 15 (January 1881), part II, pp. 46–86.

Mikhailovskii, N. K. 'Iz pisem N. K. Mikhailovskogo', *Russkoe Bogatstvo* (January 1914), pp. 370–98.

—— *Polnoe sobranie sochinenii.* 10 vols. St Petersburg, 1907–13.

Mordovtsev, D. L. 'Deistvitel'nye prichiny samarskogo goloda', *Otechestvennye Zapiski*, no. 211 (April 1874), pp. 365–90.

—— 'Moskovskaia guberniia v trudakh ee zemskikh statistikov', *Otechestvennye Zapiski*, no. 250 (May 1880), part II, pp. 1–35.

Naumov, N. N. *Sobranie sochinenii*, 2 vols. St Petersburg, 1897.

Orlov, V. I. *Sbornik statisticheskikh svedenii po Moskovskoi gubernii: Formy krest'ianskogo zemlevladeniia v Moskovskoi gubernii.* Moscow, 1879.

Pisarev, D. I. *Sochineniia.* 4 vols. Moscow, 1955–6.

Plekhanov, G. 'Ob chem spor', *Nedelia*, no. 13 (December 1878), pp. 1739–45.

—— 'Pozemel'naia obshchina', *Russkoe Bogatstvo* (January 1880), pp. 35–55; (February 1880), pp. 17–36.

—— *Sochineniia.* St Petersburg, 1920.

Pomialovskii, N. G. *Polnoe sobranie sochinenii.* 2 vols. Moscow–Leningrad, 1935.

Posnikov, A. *Obshchinnoe zemlevladenie.* Odessa, 1878.

Protopopov, M. 'Khoziaistvennaia delovitost'', *Delo*, no. 16 (September 1882), part II, pp. 1–19.

Reshetnikov, F. M. *Sochineniia.* 2 vols. Moscow, 1874.

Rusanov, N. S. 'Ekonomicheskii printsip v sotsiologii', *Delo*, no. 15 (October 1881), pp. 85–115; (December 1881), pp. 183–217.

—— 'Ekonomika i politika', *Delo*, no. 15 (March 1881), part II, pp. 41–74.

—— *Noveishaia literatura po obshchinnomu zemlevladeniiu v Rossii.* Moscow, 1879.

—— 'Preemstvennost' ekonomicheskikh aksiom', *Delo.* no. 15 (January 1881), pp. 240–66.

—— 'Protiv ekonomicheskogo optimizma', *Delo*, no. 14 (December 1880), part II, pp. 59–82.

—— 'Sovremennye proiavleniia kapitalizma v Rossii', *Russkoe Bogatstvo* (January 1880), pp. 79–110; (February 1880), pp. 49–88.

'Sbornik materialov sel'skoi pozemel'noi obshchiny' (anonymous review), *Otechestvennye Zapiski*, no. 254 (January 1881), part II, pp. 89–93.

Shchedrin, N. (Saltykov, M. E.). *Polnoe sobranie sochinenii.* 20 vols. Moscow–Leningrad, 1933–41.

Skabichevskii, A. 'Zhizn' v literature i literatura v zhizni', *Ustoi*, no. 1 (January 1882), pp. 76–94; (February 1882), pp. 41–71.

Tikhomirov, L. 'K voprosu ob ekonomike i politike', *Delo*, no. 15 (May 1881), part II, pp. 2–38.

—— 'Nerazreshennye voprosy', *Delo*, no. 15 (January 1881), part II, pp. 1–31.

—— 'Shatan'e politicheskoi mysli', *Delo*, no. 17 (March 1883), part II, pp. 1–28.

Tkachev, P. (Nikitin). 'Muzhik v salonakh sovremennoi belletristiki', *Delo*, no. 13 (March 1879), part II, pp. 1–28; (June 1879), part II, pp. 1–32; (July 1879), part II, pp. 1–23; (August 1879), part II, pp. 1–31; (September 1879), pp. 1–33.

Uspenskii, G. I. *Polnoe sobranie sochinenii.* 14 vols. Moscow, 1940–54.

Vasil'chikov, A. *Zemlevladenie i zemledelie v Rossii i drugikh evropeiskikh gosudarstvakh.* 2 vols. St Petersburg, 1876.

Vorontsov, V. P. (V. V.). 'Ekonomicheskii upadok Rossii', *Otechestvennye Zapiski*, no. 257 (August 1881), part II, pp. 113–38; no. 258 (September 1881), pp. 103–54.

—— 'Fantaziia i deistvitel'nost' russkogo kapitalizma', *Otechestvennye Zapiski*, no. 255 (March 1881), part II, pp. 1–29.

—— 'Iz istorii russkogo kapitalizma', *Otechestvennye Zapiski*, no. 259 (December 1881), pp. 205–42.

—— 'Izlishek snabzheniia rynka tovarami', *Otechestvennye Zapiski*, no. 268 (May 1883), part II, 1–39.

—— 'Kapitalisticheskoe obrashchenie v Rossii', *Otechestvennye Zapiski*, no. 255 (April 1881), part II, pp. 155–73.

—— 'Kapitalizm i rabochaia intelligentsiia', *Otechestvennye Zapiski*, no. 272 (February 1884), part II, pp. 133–63.

—— 'K voprosu o razvitii kapitalizma v Rossii', *Otechestvennye Zapiski*, no. 252 (September 1880), part II, pp. 1–38.

—— 'Mysli o budushchem pomeshchichikh khoziaistv', *Russkoe Bogatstvo* (October 1880), pp. 43–82.

—— 'Nashe krest'ianskoe khoziaistvo i agronomiia', *Otechestvennye Zapiski*, no. 263 (August 1882), part II, pp. 143–69; no. 264 (September 1882), part II, pp. 1–35.

—— *Nashi napravleniia.* St Petersburg, 1892.

—— 'Nashi vladel'cheskie khoziaistva i kapital', *Otechestvennye Zapiski*, no. 254 (February 1881), part II, pp. 159–87.

—— 'Obmen i zemledelie', *Vestnik Evropy*, no. 18 (October 1883), pp. 484–504; (November 1883), pp. 146–83.

—— 'Ocherki obshchinnogo zemlevladeniia v Rossii', *Otechestvennye Zapiski*, no. 260 (January 1882), pp. 211–50; no. 261 (March 1882), pp. 83–111; (April 1882), pp. 331–64.

Vorontsov, 'Odin iz nashikh optimistov', *Slovo*, no. 4 (March 1881), part II, pp. 76–104.

—— *Ot semidesiatykh godov k deviatisotym*. St Petersburg, 1907.

—— 'Razdelenie truda zemledel'cheskogo i promyshlennogo v Rossii', *Vestnik Evropy*, no. 19 (July 1884), pp. 319–56.

—— 'Semeinye razdely i krest'ianskoe khoziaistvo', *Otechestvennye Zapiski*, no. 266 (January 1883), part II, pp 1–23; (February 1883), part II, pp. 137–61.

—— 'Sravnenie khoziaistva krest'ian tambovskogo i nassauskogo', *Ustoi*, no. 1 (July 1882), pp. 1–32.

—— *Sud'by kapitalizma v Rossii*. St Petersburg, 1882.

—— 'Udachnaia propaganda', *Delo*, no. 15 (September 1881), part II, pp. 120–33.

Vvedenskii, A. 'Gleb Uspenskii i N. Zlatovratskii', *Slovo*, no. 3 (July 1880), part II, pp. 50–91.

Zlatovratskii, N. N. 'Bab'e tsarstvo', *Russkoe Bogatstvo* (December 1879), pp. 17–26.

—— 'Chuprinskii mir', *Otechestvennye Zapiski*, no. 167 (August 1866), pp. 475–98.

—— 'Derevenskii Abraam', *Otechestvennye Zapiski*, no. 241 (December 1878), pp. 5–26.

—— 'Derevenskie budni', *Otechestvennye Zapiski*, no. 243 (March 1879), pp. 229–76; (April 1879), pp. 481–508; no. 244 (June 1879), pp. 507–44; no. 245 (July 1879), pp. 269–302; no. 246 (October 1879), pp. 439–76; no. 247 (December 1879), pp. 527–67.

—— *Derevenskie budni*. St Petersburg, 1882.

—— 'Derevenskii Lir', *Russkoe Bogatstvo* (January 1880), pp. 151–202.

—— 'Dve pravdy'. *Otechestvennye Zapiski*, no. 267 (March 1883), p. 210.

—— 'Kaban', *Otechestvennye Zapiski*, no. 252 (August 1880), pp. 303–32.

—— 'Na rodine', *Otechestvennye Zapiski*, no. 259 (November 1881), pp. 243–64; (December 1881), pp. 509–54.

—— (Oranski, N.). 'Narodny vopros v nashem obshchestve i literature', *Russkoe Bogatstvo* (March 1880), part II, pp. 25–48; (May 1880), part II, pp. 1–19; (June 1880), part II, pp. 1–20.

—— 'Ocherki derevenskogo nastroeniia,' *Otechestvennye Zapiski*, no. 254 (February 1881), part II, pp. 221–42; no. 255 (March 1881), part II, pp. 103–23; (April 1881), part II, pp. 194–217; no. 256 (May 1881), part II, pp. 80–108.

—— 'Ocherki narodnogo nastroeniia', *Russkaia Mysl'*, no. 5 (January 1884), pp. 82–103.

—— 'Otkrytoe pis'mo A. N. Pypinu po povodu ego stat'i', *Russkie Vedomosti*, no. 22 (December 1884, no. 48), p. 3.

—— 'Padezh skota', *Iskra*, no. 12 (March 1868), pp. 118–22.

—— 'Pis'ma', *Literaturnoe Nasledstvo*, nos. 13–14 (Moscow, 1934).

—— 'Pis'ma', *Literaturnoe Nasledstvo*, nos. 51–2 (Moscow, 1949).

—— 'Pis'ma Zlatovratskogo F. D. Nefedovu', *Stary Vladimirets*, no. 274 (17 December 1911), p. 2; no. 275 (18 December 1911), p. 276; no. 276 (20 December 1911), p. 2.

Zlatovratskii, 'Prosvetiteli', *Iskra*, no. 12 (May 1868), pp. 328–30, 337–40.

—— *Sobranie sochinenii*. 3 vols. Moscow, 1897.

—— 'Strannye liudi', *Slovo*, no. 1 (June 1878), pp. 1–25.

—— 'Strogii (Ocherk iz Ustoev)', *Russkoe Bogatstvo* (April 1880), pp. 147–61.

—— 'Ustoi (Istoriia odnoi derevni)', *Otechestvennye Zapiski*, no. 261 (March 1882), pp. 193–224; no. 262 (May 1882), pp. 161–82; no. 263 (August 1882), pp. 501–36; no. 264 (September 1882), pp. 173–216; no. 265 (November 1882), pp. 155–99.

—— 'Ustoi (Istoriia odnogo poselka)', *Otechestvennye Zapiski*, no. 238 (May 1878), pp. 117–65; no. 240 (October 1878), pp. 275–324; no. 241 (December 1878), pp. 455–84.

—— 'Ustoi (Roman novogo cheloveka derevni)', *Otechestvennye Zapiski*, no. 252 (October 1880), pp. 329–94; no. 253 (November 1880), pp. 5–40.

—— *Vospominaniia*. Moscow, 1956.

—— 'V rodnykh mestakh', *Nedelia*, no. 18 (September 1883), pp. 1194–1201.

—— 'Zolotaia rota i eia predvoditel'', *Remeslennaia Gazeta*, no. 1 (1876), pp. 10–11; no. 2, pp. 34–5; no. 4, pp. 70–2; no. 6, pp. 102–5.

Documents, memoirs and secondary works by contemporaries

Aksel'rod, P. B. *Perezhitoe i peredumannoe*. Berlin, 1923.

Aptekman, O. B. *Gleb Ivanovich Uspenskii*. Moscow, 1922.

—— *Obshchestvo 'Zemlia i Volia'*. Petrograd, 1924.

—— 'Zachatki kul'turnogo narodnichestva v 70-kh godakh (Kruzhok studentov Zemledel'cheskogo Instituta)', *Istoriko-revoliutsionny sbornik No. 1*. Leningrad, 1924.

Barannikov, A. I. *Narodovolets A. I. Barannikov v ego pis'makh*. Moscow, 1935.

Boborykin, P. D. *Za polveka*. Moscow–Leningrad, 1929.

Bogodaevskaia-Iasevich, Z. I. 'Yubilei narodnika-belletrista', *Istoricheskii Vestnik*, no. 71 (January 1898), pp. 277–91.

Burtsev, B. *Za sto let*. London, 1897.

Bykov, P. V. *Siluety dalekogo proshlogo*. Moscow–Leningrad, 1930.

Chernavskii, M. M. 'Demonstratsiia 6 dekabria 1876 g. Po vospominaniiam uchastnika', *Katorga i ssylka*, nos. 28–9 (1926), pp. 7–20

Cherny Peredel. Moscow–Leningrad, 1923.

Chronique du mouvement socialiste en Russie 1878–1887. St Petersburg, 1890.

Debogorii-Mokrievich, V. *Ot buntarstva k terrorizmu.* Moscow, 1930.

Deitch, L. (ed.). *Delo 1go marta 1881 goda.* St Petersburg, 1906.

—— 'Odin iz poslednikh semidesiatnikov', *Golos Minuvshego*, no. 2 (June 1914), pp. 86–109.

—— *S. M. Kravchinskii.* Petrograd, 1919.

—— *Za polveka.* 2 vols. Berlin, 1923.

Deniker, I. E. 'Vospominaniia', *Katorga i ssylka*, no. 4 (11) (1924), pp. 20–43.

Dmitrieva, D. I. *Tak bylo.* Moscow–Leningrad, 1930.

Dubov. 'Leto sredi sel'skikh rabot', *Otechestvennye Zapiski*, no. 239 (July 1878), pp. 5–54.

Engel'gardt, N. A. 'Aleksandr Nikolaevich Engel'gardt i Batishchev-skoe delo', in A. N. Engelgardt, *Iz derevni: 12 pisem* (St Petersburg, 1897), pp. 1–62.

—— 'Batishchevskoe Delo', *Knizhki nedeli*, no. 18 (March 1895), pp. 60–72; (April 1895), pp. 5–24; (May 1895), pp. 138–50; (June 1895), pp. 71–86; (July 1895), pp. 149–64.

—— 'Bukovskii intelligentny poselok', *Novoe Slovo*, no. 1 (March 1895), part II, pp. 17–35; (April 1895), part II, pp. 11–29.

—— 'Davnye epizody', *Istoricheskii Vestnik*, no. 119 (February 1910), pp. 529–55; no. 122 (October 1910), pp. 123–44; no. 124 (April 1911), pp. 42–68; (May 1911), pp. 527–59; (June 1911), pp. 844–71; no. 125 (July 1911), pp. 99–124.

Faresov, A. I. *Semidesiatniki.* St Petersburg, 1905.

Figner, V. I. 'Portrety narodovol'tsev', *Byloe*, no. 32–33 (April–May 1918), pp. 70–82.

—— 'S gorst'iu zolota sredi nishchikh', *Russkoe Bogatstvo* (March 1912), pp. 89–114.

—— 'Sofia Perovskaia', *Byloe*, nos. 32–33 (April–May 1918), pp. 3–11.

—— *Zapechatlenny trud.* 2 vols. Moscow, 1921.

Frolenko, M. F. 'Komentarii k stat'e N. A. Morozova, "Voznik-novenie Narodnoi Voli"', *Byloe*, no. 12 (December 1906) pp. 22–33.

—— 'Lipetskii i voronezhskii s'ezdy', *Byloe*, no. 13 (1907), pp. 67–87.

Glinka-Volzhskii, A. S. *Gleb Uspenskii v zhizni.* Moscow–Leningrad, 1935. (The memoir literature on Uspenskii is vast, but for the most part adulatory and therefore useless. This volume supplies a valuable selection of material.)

Gosudarstvenny literaturny muzei. *Gleb Uspenskii.* Moscow, 1939. (Contains additional useful memoir literature and a lengthy bibliography by Glinka-Volzhskii of memoirs about Uspenskii.)

Hourwich, Isaac A. (Gurvich). *The Economics of the Russian Village.* New York, 1892.

Iakovlev, V. Ia. (B. Bazilevskii). *Literatura partii Narodnoi Voli.* Paris, 1905.

—— *Revoliutsionnaia zhurnalistika semidesiatykh godov.* Paris, 1905.

Iakubovich, P. F. 'Iz istorii protsessa 21 (pis'ma i pokazaniia P. F. Iakubovicha)', *Krasny Archiv*, no. 26 (1929), pp. 122–79; no. 37 (1929), pp. 102–37; no. 38 (1930), pp. 70–108.

—— (L. Mel'shin). 'Na rannei zor'ke', *Russkoe Bogatstvo* (January 1909), pp. 197–224; (February 1909), pp. 188–216; (March 1909), pp. 130–58.

Iasinskii, I. *Roman moei zhizni.* Moscow–Leningrad, 1921.

Itenberg, B. S., Volk, S. S. (*et al.* (ed.). *Revoliutsionnoe narodnichestvo 70-kh godov XIX veka: sbornik dokumentov.* 2 vols. Moscow–Leningrad, 1964–5.

Iur'ev, M. M. 'Pamiati Petra Grigor'evicha Loseva', *Izvestiia Leningradskogo Lesnogo Instituta*, Vypusk xxxv (Leningrad, 1927). (On Engel'gardt.)

Ivanchin-Pisarev, A. I. *Khozhdenie v narod.* Moscow–Leningrad, 1929.

Ivanov, S. 'Iz vospominanii ob 1881 gode', *Byloe*, no. 46 (1906), pp. 228–42.

'K biografam A. I. Zheliabova i S. L. Perovskoi', *Byloe*, no. 8 (1906), pp. 108–29.

Korba-Pribyleva, A. P. 'Ispol'nitel'ny komitet 1879–1881 gg.', *Katorga i ssylka*, no. 3 (24) (1926), pp. 27–31.

Kovalevskaia, S. V. *Vospominaniia detstva i avtobiograficheskie ocherki.* Moscow, 1945.

Koz'min, B. P. (ed.). 'K istorii Zemli i Voli 70-kh godov (Programma tambovskogo poseleniia zemlevol'tsev)', *Krasny Arkhiv*, no. 19 (1926), pp. 166–77.

Kravchinskii, S. M. (Stepniak). 'Iz perepiski S. M. Kravchinskogo', *Krasny Arkhiv*, no. 19 (1926), pp. 195–202.

—— *Podpol'naia Rossiia.* St Petersburg, 1905.

Kviatovskii, A. A. 'Avtobiograficheskoe zaiavlenie A. A. Kviatovskogo', *Krasny Arkhiv*, no. 14 (1926), pp. 159–73.

Korolenko, V. *Istoriia moego sovremennika.* 3 vols. Moscow, 1930–1.

—— 'Nikolai Konstantinovich Mikhailovskii', *Russkoe Bogatstvo* (January 1914), pp. 203–12.

—— *Otoshedshie.* St Petersburg, 1908.

—— *Vospominaniia o pisateliakh.* Moscow, 1934.

Kovalik (Starik). 'Dvizhenie semidesiatykh godov po bol'shomu protsessu', *Byloe*, no. 1 (November 1906), pp. 30–72.

Krivenko, S. N. *Na rasput'i.* Moscow, 1901.

Lavrov, P. L. *Narodniki-propagandisty 1873–1878.* Leningrad, 1925.

Literatura partii 'Narodnaia Volia'. Moscow, 1930.

Marx, Karl, and Engels, Friedrich. *Perepiska K. Marksa i F. Engel'sa s russkimi politicheskimi deiateliami*. Leningrad, 1951.

Mertvago, A. P. *Ne po tornomy puti*. St Petersburg, 1900.

Metelitsyna, P. 'God v batrachkakh', *Otechestvennye Zapiski*, no. 252 (September 1880), pp. 71–112.

Mikhailov, A. D. *Narodovolets Aleksandr Dmitrievich Mikhailov*. Leningrad, 1925.

Mikhailovskii, N. K. 'Gleb Uspenskii kak pisatel' i chelovek', in *Literaturno-kriticheskie stat'i* (Moscow, 1957), pp. 318–432.

—— 'Literatura i zhizn'', *Russkoe Bogatstvo* (November 1897), part II, pp. 15–39 (On Zlatovratskii.)

—— *Literaturnye vospominaniia i sovremennaia smuta*. St Petersburg, 1900.

Morozov, N. A. *Povesti moei zhizni*. 2 vols. Moscow, 1961.

—— 'Vozniknovenie Narodnoi Voli', *Byloe*, no. 12 (1906), pp. 1–21.

'Novye materialy o Glebe Uspenskom', *Krasny Arkhiv*, no. 106 (1941), pp. 147–56.

Panteleev, L. F. *Iz vospominanii proshlogo*. Moscow–Leningrad, 1934.

Plekhanov, G. 'Predislovie', in A. Thun, *Istoriia revoliutsionnykh dvizhenii v Rossii* (Geneva, 1903), pp. 3–64.

—— *Za dvadtsat' let*. St Petersburg, 1906. (On Naumov and Uspenskii.)

Plekhanova, P. M. 'Nashi zhizni do emigratsii', *Gruppa osvobozhdenie truda Sbornik VI* (Moscow–Leningrad, 1928), pp. 65–119.

—— 'Perifeiny kruzhok Zemli i Voli', *Gruppa osvobozhdenie truda Sbornik IV* (Moscow–Leningrad, 1926), pp. 81–116).

'Pokazaniia pervomartsev', *Byloe*, no. 32–33 (April–May 1918), pp. 230–310.

Polonskoi, M. N. 'K istorii partii Narodnoi Voli. Pokazaniia M. N. Polonskoi', *Byloe*, no. 6 (18) (1907), pp. 1–10.

Popov, M. P. *German Aleksandrovich Lopatin*. Moscow, 1926.

—— 'Iz moego revoliutsionnogo proslogo', *Byloe*, no. 1 (May 1905), pp. 268–305.

—— *Zapiski zemlevol'tsa*. Moscow, 1933.

Protopopov, M. A. *Literaturno-kriticheskie kharakteristiki*. St Petersburg, 1896.

Pypin, A. N. *Istoriia russkoi etnografii*. 2 vols. St Petersburg, 1891.

—— 'Narodnichestvo', *Vestnik Evropy*, no. 19 (January 1884), pp. 152–82; (February 1884) pp. 702–51.

Rusanov, N. S. 'Arkhiv N. K. Mikhailovskogo', *Russkoe Bogatstvo*, no. 39 (January 1914), pp. 129–64.

—— 'Ideinye osnovy Narodnoi Voli', *Byloe*, no. 21 (September 1907), pp. 37–76.

—— *Na rodine 1859–1882*. Moscow, 1931.

—— 'N. K. Mikhailovskii i obshchestvennaia zhizn' Rossii', *Golos Minuvshego*, no. 2 (February 1914), pp. 5–27.

—— 'Politika N. K. Mikhailovskogo', *Byloe*, no. 3 (July 1907), pp. 124–50.

—— *Sotsialisty zapada i Rossii.* St Petersburg, 1908.

Rysakov, N. I. 'Iz pokazaniia N. I. Rysakova', *Krasny Arkhiv*, no. 19 (1926), pp. 178–94.

Sharapov, S. A. N. *Engel'gardt i ego znachenie dlia russkoi kul'tury i nauki.* St Petersburg, 1893.

Skabichevskii, A. *Belletristy-narodniki.* St Petersburg, 1888.

—— *Istoriia noveishei russkoi literatury.* St Petersburg, 1897.

—— *Literaturnye vospominaniia.* Moscow–Leningrad, 1928.

—— 'Pod gnetom reaktsii', *Russkaia Mysl'*, no. 27 (January 1906), part II, pp. 74–91.

—— *Sochineniia*, 2 vols. St Petersburg, 1903.

Sukhomlin, V. I. 'Iz epokhi upadki partii Narodnoi Voli', *Katorga i ssylka*, no. 3 (24), (1926), pp. 75–90; no. 4 (25) (1926), pp. 29–46; no. 6 (27) (1926), pp. 65–87.

Teleshov, N. N. *Zapiski pisatelia.* Moscow, 1952.

Thun, A. *Istoriia revoliutsionnykh dvizhenii v Rossii.* Geneva, 1903. (With Plekhanov's *introduction.*) (Petrograd, 1917, edition has notes and commentary by the populist L. Shishko.)

Tikhomirov, L. *Vospominaniia L'va Tikhomirova.* Moscow–Leningrad, 1927.

Tiutchev, N. S. 'Razgrom "Zemli i Voli" v 1878 g. Delo Mezenstova', *Byloe*, no. 30 (February 1918), pp. 157–79.

Valk, S. N. (ed.). *Arkhiv Zemli i Voli i Narodnoi Voli.* Moscow, 1930.

—— 'Iz narodovol'cheskikh avtobiograficheskikh dokumentov', *Krasny Arkhiv*, no. 20 (1927), pp. 205–31.

Vasiukov, S. I. 'Bylye dni i gody', *Istoricheskii Vestnik*, no. 112 (April 1908), pp. 138–62; no. 113 (July 1908), pp. 93–115; (August 1908), pp. 468–86.

Vitorova-Val'ter, S. A. 'Iz zhizni revoliutsionnoi molodezhi 2oi poloviny 70-kh godov', *Katorga i ssylka*, no. 4 (11) (1924), pp. 64–78.

Vorontsov, V. P. (V. V.). 'Nekrolog V. I. Orlov', *Vestnik Evropy*, no. 20 (November 1885), pp. 451–7.

SECONDARY WORKS

Books

Andrei Ivanovich Zheliabov i Sof'ia L'vovna Perovskaia. Rostov, nd..

Asheshov, N. *Sof'ia Perovskaia.* Petrograd, 1920.

Balabanov, M. *Istoriia revoliutsionnogo dvizheniia v Rossii.* Kharkov, 1925.

Bel'chikov, N. *Narodnichestvo v literature i kritike.* Moscow, 1934.

Billington, J. *Mikhailovskii and Russian Populism*. Oxford, 1958.

Bogdanovich, T. A. *Liubov liudei shestidesiatykh godov*. Leningrad, 1929.

Bush, V. V. *Gleb Uspenskii (V masterskoi khudozhnika slova)*. Saratov, 1925.

—— *Literaturnaia deiatel'nost' Gleba Uspenskogo*. Moscow, 1927.

—— *Ocherki literaturnogo narodnichestva 70–80 gg*. Leningrad–Moscow, 1931.

Cheshchikhin-Vetrinskii, V. *Gleb Ivanovich Uspenskii*. Moscow, 1929.

Evgen'ev-Maksimov, V. *Ocherki po istorii sotsialisticheskoi zhurnalistiki v Rossii XIX veka*. Moscow–Leningrad, 1927.

Footman, David. *Red Prelude*. New Haven, 1945.

Gleb Uspenskii: Ocherki i issledovaniia. Moscow, 1938.

Gurevich, I. (Dan). *Proiskhozdenie bol'shevizma*. New York, 1946.

Iakimova-Dikovskaia, A. V. *et al*. (ed.). *Narodovol'tsy posle pervogo marta*. Moscow, 1928.

Iakovlev, V. Ia. (V. Bogucharskii). *Aktivnoe narodnichestvo semidesiatykh godov*. Moscow, 1912.

—— *Iz istorii politicheskoi bor'by v 70-kh i 80-kh XIX veka. Partiia Narodnoi Voli, ego proiskhozhdenie, sud'ba i gibel'*. Moscow, 1912.

Istoriia russkoi literatury: 70-kh i 80-kh godov XIX veka. Moscow–Leningrad, 1956.

Itenberg, B. S. Dvizhenie revoliutsionnogo narodnichestva. Moscow, 1965.

Ivanov-Razumnik. *Istoriia russkoi obshchestvennoi mysli*. 2 vols. Petrograd, 1918.

Kolosov, E. E. (D. Kuz'min). *Narodovol'cheskaia zhurnalistika*. Moscow, 1930.

Kleinbort, L. M. *Grigorii Zakharovich Eliseev*. Petrograd, 1923.

—— *N. I. Ziber*. Petrograd, 1923.

Koz'min, B. P. *Iz istorii revoliutsionnoi mysli v Rossii*. Moscow, 1961.

—— *Ot 'deviatnadtsatogo fevralia' k 'pervomu marta'*. Moscow, 1933.

—— *Russkaia zhurnalistika 70-kh i 80-kh godov XIX veka*. Moscow, 1948.

Lampert E. *Sons Against Fathers*. Oxford, 1965.

Levin, Sh. 'Obshchestvennoe dvizhenie 70-kh godov', in *Ocherki po istorii Leningrada*. 2 vols. Moscow–Leningrad, 1957. Vol. II.

—— *Obshchestvennoe dvizhenie v Rossii v 60-kh i 70-kh godakh XIX veka*. Moscow, 1958.

Literaturnoe Nasledstvo, nos. 13–14. Moscow, 1934.

—— Nos. 51–52. Moscow, 1949.

Lothe, Jean. *Gleb Ivanovic Uspenskij et le populisme russe*. Leiden, 1963.

Nechuiatov, P. *Aleksandr Nikolaevich Engel'gardt*. Smolensk, 1957.

Nevskii, V. I. *Ot 'Zemli i Voli' k gruppe 'Osvobozhdenie truda'*. Moscow, 1930.

Obshchestvennoe dvizhenie v poreformennoi Rossii. Moscow, 1965.

Ovsianiko-Kulikovskii, D. N. *Istoriia russkoi intelligentsii.* 3 vols. St Petersburg, 1914.

—— (ed.). *Istoriia russkoi literatury.* 5 vols. St Petersburg, 1910.

Pashitnov, K. A. *Razvitie sotsialisticheskikh idei v Rossii.* Petrograd, 1924.

Potresov, A. N. *Etiudy o russkoi intelligentsii.* St Petersburg, 1906.

Prutskov, N. I. *Tvorcheskii put' Gleba Uspenskogo.* Moscow–Leningrad, 1958.

Robinson, Geroid Tanquary. *Rural Russia under the Old Regime.* New York, 1961.

Serebriakov, E. *Ocherk po istorii Zemli i Voli.* St Petersburg, 1906.

Sokolov, N. *Masterstvo G. I. Uspenskogo,* Leningrad, 1958.

Tkachenko, P. S. *Revoliutsionnaia narodnicheskaia organizatsiia Zemlia i Volia.* Moscow, 1961.

Venturi, Franco. *Roots of Revolution.* London, 1960.

Volk, S. S. *Narodnaia volia.* Moscow–Leningrad, 1966.

Zaslavskii, D. I. *Demokraticheskii zhurnal Otechestvennye Zapiski.* Moscow, 1956.

Articles

Avakumovic, Ivan. 'A Statistical Approach to the Revolutionary Movement in Russia', *American Slavic and East European Review,* vol. 18, no. 2 (April 1959), pp. 182–6.

Becker, Christopher, '*Raznochintsy*: the Development of the Word and of the Concept', *American Slavic and East European Review,* vol. xviii, no. 1 (February 1959), pp. 63–74.

'Blizkii znakomets G. I. Uspenskogo', *Russkaia Literatura* (1963, no. 3), pp. 153–6.

Bush, V. 'Gleb Uspenskii o Karle Markse', *Na literaturnom postu,* nos 21–2 (1929), pp. 70–4.

Cheiner, Jules. 'Nicolas Zlatovratski', *Maintenant,* no. 7 (1947), pp. 211–17.

Chernov, V. 'Dva poliusa dukhovnogo skital'chestva (Lev Tolstoi i Gleb Uspenskii)', *Novy Zhurnal,* no. 2 (May 1943), pp. 261–74.

Emel'ianov, N. P. 'Zhurnal "Otechestvennye Zapiski" v gody revoliutsionnoi situatsii 1879–1881 gg.', *Vestnik Leningradskogo Universiteta: seria istoriia iazyka i literatury,* Vypusk 1, no. 2 (1957), pp. 133–51.

Ershov, A. 'K istorii russkoi zhurnalistiki: Otechestvennye Zapiski, 1818–1884', *Obrazovanie,* no. 14 (April 1905), pp. 67–101, (May 1905), pp. 9–37.

Ginev, V. I. 'Revoliutsionnaia deiatel'nost' narodnikov 70-kh godov sredi krest'ian i rabochikh Srednego Povol'zhia', *Istoricheskie Zapiski,* no. 74 (1963), pp. 220–44.

Glinka-Volzhskii, A. S. 'Itinerariia Gleba Uspenskogo', Gosudar-stvenny literaturny muzei, *Gleb Uspenskii* (Moscow, 1939), pp. 225–40.

—— 'Krest'ianskie ocherki Gleba Uspenskogo', *Literaturnaia ucheba*, no. 5 (May 1939), pp. 51–74.

Kolosov, E. 'M. A. Bakunin i N. K. Mikhailovskii v starom narod-nichestve', *Golos Minuvshego*, no. 1 (May 1913), pp. 61–89; (June 1913), pp. 69–105.

—— 'N. K. Mikhailovskii i russkaia revoliutsiia', *Sotsialist-revo-liutsioner*, no. 3 (January 1910), pp. 69–94.

Koz'min, B. '"Narodniki" i "narodnichestvo"', *Voprosy literatury*, no. 1 (September 1957), pp. 116–35.

—— 'Ocherki "Iz derevenskogo dnevnika" v tvorchestve Gl. Uspenskogo', in G. I. Uspenskii, *Polnoe sobranie sochinenii*, v (Moscow, 1940), 388–412.

—— 'Otzyvy kritiki i otkliki chitatelei', in G. I. Uspenskii, *Polnoe sobranie sochinenii*, v (Moscow, 1940), 425–68.

—— 'Spravka ob ekonomicheskom sostoianii Novgorodskoi i Samarskoi gub. v 70-kh godakh', in G. I. Uspenskii, *Polnoe sobranie sochinenii*, v (Moscow, 1940), 413–24.

Lifshits, G. M., Liashchenko, K. G. 'Kak sozdavalas' programma vtoroi "Zemli i Voli"', *Voprosy istorii*, XL, no. 9 (September 1965), pp. 36–50.

Malia, Martin. 'Herzen and the Peasant Commune', in E. Simmons (ed.), *Continuity and Change in Russian and Soviet Thought* (Cambridge, 1955), pp. 197–217.

—— 'What is the Intelligentsia?', *Daedalus*, vol. 89, no. 3 (summer 1960), pp. 441–58.

Markova, O. 'Otkliki na Kapital v Rossii 1870-kh godov', *Letopisi Marksizma*, no. 1, XI (1930), 115–22.

Mordovchenko, N. I. 'M. E. Saltykov-Shchedrin—redaktor G. I. Uspenskogo', *Gleb Uspenskii, materialy i issledovaniia* (Moscow, 1938), pp. 395–427.

Pipes, Richard. 'Narodnichestvo: A Semantic Inquiry', *Slavic Review*, vol. XXIII, no. 3 (September 1964), pp. 441–58.

Reuel', A. 'Polemika vokrug "Kapitala" Karla Marksa v Rossii 1870-kh godov', *Letopisi Marksizma*, no. 1, XI (1930), 67–114.

Sakulin, P. N. 'Narodnichestvo N. N. Zlatovratskogo', *Golos Minuv-shego*, no. 1 (January 1913), pp. 117–33.

Slobozhanin, M. 'Cherty iz zhizni S. N. Krivenko', *Minuvshie Gody*, no. 1 (January 1908), pp. 29–78; (March 1908), pp. 213–39; (May–June 1908), pp. 278–96.

Solov'ev, E. 'Semidesiatye gody', *Zhizn'*, no. 3 (January 1899), pp. 101–28; (October 1899), pp. 256–86.

Tvardovskaia, V. A. 'Krizis "Zemli i Voli" v kontse 70-kh godov', *Istoriia S.S.S.R.* (1959, no. 4), pp. 60–74.

—— 'Problema gosudarstva v ideologii narodnichestva', *Istoricheskie Zapiski*, no. 74 (1963), pp. 148–86.

—— 'Organizatsionnye osnovy "Narodnoi Voli"', *Istoricheskie Zapiski*, no. 67 (1960), pp. 103–44.

Utechin, S. V. 'The "Preparatory" Trend in the Russian Revolutionary Movement in the 1880s', *St Antony's Papers*, no. 12 (Soviet Affairs, no. 3) (1962), pp. 7–22.

Volk, S. 'Iunosheskie tetradi P. F. Iakubovicha', *Russkaia Literatura* (1964), no. 3, pp. 204–10.

Journals and newspapers

Delo, 1878–84.
Nedelia, 1877–8.
Otechestvennye Zapiski, 1875–84.
Russkoe Bogatstvo, 1879–82.
Slovo, 1878–81.
Ustoi, 1882.

Reference works

Deiateli revoliutsionnogo dvizheniia v Rossii. 4 vols. Moscow, 1927–34.
Entsiklopedicheskii slovar' Brokgauza-Efrona. 85 vols. St Petersburg, 1890–1907.
Entsiklopedicheskii slovar' Granat. 58 vols. Moscow, 1910–48.
Russkii biograficheskii slovar'. 25 vols. Moscow–St Petersburg, 1896–1918.

INDEX